Transition

The First Ten Years

*Analysis and Lessons for Eastern Europe
and the Former Soviet Union*

Transition

The First Ten Years

Analysis and Lessons for Eastern Europe and the Former Soviet Union

THE WORLD BANK
Washington, D.C.

Contents

Tables

Foreword

This study looks at lessons to be drawn from the ten-year experience of the transition countries in Eastern Europe and the former Soviet Union in the period 1991 to 2000. The World Bank's *World Development Report 1996: From Plan to Market* focused on the transition process during the first half of this period. It recognized that while initial conditions are critical, decisive and sustained reforms are important for recovery of growth and should be accompanied by social policies designed to protect the most vulnerable groups until growth takes hold. It highlighted the need to create institutions in support of markets, and it emphasized that investing in people is a key to growth.

Today we have more evidence and data on the transition experience. The variability in growth performance across countries has intensified. Poverty and income inequality in some countries have increased to levels not foreseen earlier. In many countries, reform efforts that started in the early 1990s have been interrupted and in some cases even stalled. As a result, output recovery in some of the transition countries was sharply reversed during the second half of the 1990s.

Many of the prescriptions of the 1996 *World Development Report* continue to be valid today. At the most general level, the present study confirms that while initial conditions were critical for explaining the output decline at the start of transition, the intensity of reform policies explains the variability in the recovery of output thereafter. Beyond this, important new lessons highlight some key tradeoffs facing countries in transition that can be translated into priorities for policy.

First, this study highlights the key role of the entry and growth of new firms, particularly small- and medium-size enterprises, in generating economic growth and in creating employment. The growth of new firms depends in part on direct policies to encourage entry—what this report calls the *encouragement* strategy. Does this mean that policymakers can focus on encouraging the new sector while postponing the pain of liquidating and restructuring the old sector to a later time when a cushion has been put in place? Not so. The report shows that to succeed the encouragement strategy needs to be accompanied by a strategy of *discipline*; that is, policies that impose hard budget constraints on the old-large enterprises that remain from pretransition days. Soft budget constraints that allow these enterprises to not pay their taxes, social security contributions, and bank debts undermine the level playing field between different kinds of enterprises and have also been at the root of explosive fiscal and banking crises.

The combined encouragement-and-discipline strategy that this study proposes is crucial to re-allocate assets to more productive uses and to provide economic space for new emerging firms. This perspective of encouragement and discipline allows the report to shed light on issues such as privatization and fiscal policy, which have been major elements of economic reform in transition countries. Privatization is important to the extent that it facilitates hard budget constraints on old enterprises and creates incentives for production and innovation rather than asset stripping and rent seeking in new enterprises.

A second lesson concerns the need to develop or strengthen legal and regulatory institutions to oversee the management and governance of enterprises, both those in the new private sector and those remaining under state ownership. In countries where direct sales of assets to strategic investors—a preferred method of privatization—was unavailable, policymakers were confronted with the often difficult choice between privatization to ineffective owners in a context of weak corporate governance on the one hand and continued state ownership until strategic investors could be found on the other. However, continued state ownership does not lead to efficient stewardship of enterprise assets unless there is a political commitment to transparent privatization outcomes and a minimum institutional capacity to prevent asset stripping by managers during the intervening period. In either event, rules to protect minority shareholders; rules against insider deals and conflicts of interest; adequate accounting, auditing, and disclosure standards; and takeover, insolvency, and collateral legislation, together with development of enforcement capacity, are key to preventing asset stripping that reduces the true long-term value and competitiveness of a firm.

A third lesson involves the recognition that winners from the early stages of reforms such as liberalization and privatization may oppose subsequent reform steps when these reduce their initially substantial, but potentially temporary benefits or rents. These winners will tend to resist reforms such as further trade liberalization; entry of new competitors, including foreign direct investment; and legislation protecting minority shareholders and creditors to the extent they reduce such rents. Furthermore, if the rents are large as a fraction of total gross domestic product, which is usually the case in natural resource- and energy-rich countries, these early winners may capture the state and force the economy into a trap of a low-level reform equilibrium. Understanding how such reform traps arise and how to break out of them is an important area of inquiry addressed by this study. To the extent underlying political economy considerations permit a reform-minded team room to maneuver, fiscal policy can play an important role here, by redirecting support away from ailing enterprises and toward worker training and severance payments; by divesting social assets such as housing, child care, and health facilities from enterprises to governments; and by maintaining the high levels of human capital with which countries entered transition.

The experience of transition from centrally planned to a market economy is an historically unprecedented process, and one that is by no means finished in many countries in Eastern Europe and the former Soviet Union. We hope that this study will encourage further discussion among policymakers and think tanks in the transition countries and will assist their dialogue with external donors and advisers on how to better support the transition process.

Johannes F. Linn
Vice President
Europe and Central Asia Region

Acknowledgments

This report was prepared by a team led by Pradeep Mitra and Marcelo Selowsky that comprised Joel Hellman, Ricardo Martin, Christof Ruehl, and Asad Alam. Important contributions to specific sections were made both from within the World Bank and by external partners. Contributors from the World Bank include Harry Broadman, Alan Gelb, Christine Jones, Ira Lieberman, John Nellis, Samuel Otoo, Ana Revenga, Roberto Rocha, Randi Ryterman, Sergei Shatalov, Mark Sundberg, and Marina Wes. External contributors include Barry Eichengreen of the University of California at Berkeley, Simon Johnson of the Massachusetts Institute of Technology, and Christian Mumssen and Thomas Richardson, both at the International Monetary Fund. Bruce Ross-Larson was the principal editor. The selected bibliography was prepared by Graeme Robertson, Columbia University.

The team is also indebted to many country economists in the World Bank's Poverty Reduction and Economic Management Unit in the Europe and Central Asia region for background notes and analyses of specific transition economies: Sebnem Akkaya, Ritu Anand, Robert J. Anderson, Carlos Cavalcanti, Mark Davis, Ilker Domac, Mansour Farsad, Lev Freinkman, Reza Ghasimi, Ardo Hansson, Erika Jorgensen, Brian Pinto, Rosanna Polastri, Carlos Silva-Jauregui, Andriy Storozhuk, Jos Verbeek, Dusan Vujovic, and Leila Zlaoui.

An earlier version of the report was first discussed at a seminar at the World Bank chaired by Johannes Linn. Peer reviewers were Nicholas Stern, Alan Gelb, and Marek Dabrowski. The team thanks all of them for their comments and suggestions. The team also thanks the Bertelsmann Foundation for sponsoring a seminar for policymakers in transition economies in May 2000 in Kronberg, Germany that originally helped to motivate and sharpen many of the issues addressed in this report. Participants included Vahram Avanessian, Marek Belka, Lajos Bokros, Aleksandar Bozhkov, Oraz A. Jandosov, Vladimir A. Mau, Ivan Miklos, Viktor Pinzenik, Ion Sturza, and Marat Sultanov. Earlier versions of the report were presented at seminars at the Institute for Economies in Transition in Moscow, at the United Nations Commission for Europe in Geneva, at the Center for Economic Research and Graduate Education of Charles University and the Economic Institute of Sciences of the Czech Republic in Prague, and at a conference on "Trade, Integration, and Transition" held in Bela Balassa's memory in Budapest in October 2001, where it benefited from the comments of János Kornai and Andras Nagy.

Book design, production, and dissemination were coordinated by the World Bank Publications team.

Overview

A dozen years have elapsed since the world witnessed the euphoria greeting the fall of the Berlin wall. Ten years ago last summer, Boris Yeltsin claimed his place in history by climbing atop a tank in the streets of Moscow in defiance of the last defenders of an imploding Soviet Union. Thus did the march from plan to market capture the world's imagination. In those heady days, famously dubbed a time of "extraordinary politics" by a leading reformer from the region, everything seemed possible (Balcerowicz 1995).

At the beginning of the new millennium, a profound divide lies between Central and Southeastern Europe and the Baltics (CSB) and the Commonwealth of Independent States (CIS).[1] In the CSB, officially measured gross domestic product (GDP) bounced back from a transition recession, recovered to its 1990 level by 1998, and exceeded that level by 6 percent in 2000. However, in the CIS GDP in 2000 stood at only 63 percent of its 1990 level. While GDP in Poland, the most populous country in the CSB, increased by more than 40 percent between 1990 and 1999, it shrank by 40 percent during the same period in the Russian Federation, the most populous country in the CIS.[2, 3]

In 1998 one in five people in the region survived on less than US$2.15 a day, a standard poverty line.[4] A decade before fewer than one in 25 lived in such absolute poverty. While absolute income deprivation at those levels is virtually nonexistent in many Central European countries, its incidence is as high as 68 percent in Tajikistan, 50 percent in the Kyrgyz Republic, and 40 percent in Armenia. Inequality, which has just barely increased in Central Europe since the onset of transition, has increased so much in CIS countries such as Armenia, the Kyrgyz Republic, and Russia that they have come to rival the most unequal countries in the world (box 1).

A similar divide runs across the political landscape as well. Competitive democracies—underpinned by widespread political rights to participate in multiparty elections and an extensive range of civil liberties—have taken root in nearly all of Central Europe and the Baltics. In contrast, limitations on rights to participate in elections and constraints on civil liberties during at least some period of the transition have concentrated political power in many countries in the CIS and in Southeastern Europe. Nevertheless, this concentration has been associated with diminished state capacity to provide public goods needed for the market economy as a result of corruption, weak public sector management, and in some cases war

Box 1.

Increased Inequality

The countries of Europe and Central Asia started the transition with some of the lowest levels of inequality in the world. Since then, however, inequality has increased steadily in all transition economies and dramatically in some of them (see figure A). Countries such as Armenia, the Kyrgyz Republic, Moldova, and Russia are now among the most unequal in the world, with Gini coefficients (a standard measure of inequality) nearly twice their pretransition levels.

It is tempting to attribute increasing inequality to reforms and liberalization. But this is only part of the story. While inequality has increased almost everywhere, the more advanced reformers show much more equal, rather than more unequal, outcomes, compared with less advanced reformers. This difference cannot be solely explained by different conditions across the countries at the start of transition.

Rather, a recent World Bank study (2000b) shows that positive developments largely explain the rise in inequality in the CSB: rising returns to education, decompressing wages, and emerging returns to risktaking and entrepreneurship. These forces are welcome despite the increase in inequality, because they signal that the market is now rewarding skills and effort, as in more mature market economies. In the CSB, moreover, strong social transfers and redistribution mechanisms have dampened the rise in education premiums and wage dispersion, in line with the demands these societies have placed on their governments for such measures.

The experience of the CIS is very different. Rising education premiums and wage dispersion explain very little of the rise in inequality. In Armenia, Georgia, the Kyrgyz Republic, Moldova, and Russia income differences linked to educational achievement explain less than 5 percent of inequality, compared with 20 percent in Slovenia and 15 percent in Hungary and Poland. The causes of the huge rise in inequality lie:

FIGURE A.

Changes in Income Inequality in Selected Transition Economies

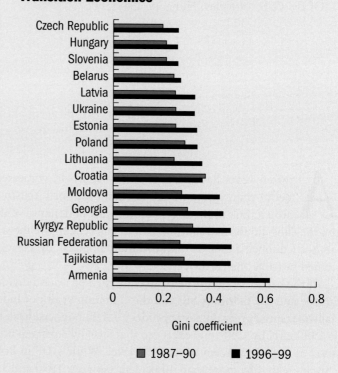

Source: World Bank (2000b).

- In the prevalence of widespread corruption and rent seeking. There is a strong correlation between higher corruption and higher inequality (and higher poverty) in the region. The poor are disproportionately affected by corruption (World Bank 2000c).
- In the capture of the state by narrow vested interests, which have modified policy to their advantage, often at a high social cost. These interests have been able to limit competition and concentrate their economic power through such mechanisms as special licenses and monopolies. They have undermined state institutions and blocked reforms that would serve the public good.
- In the resulting collapse of formal wages and income opportunities. Wages at old jobs have collapsed or are not paid, while new formal job opportunities are stifled by the lack of competitive markets and by the pervasiveness of corruption. People, except for a privileged few, are largely stuck in their low-paying (and sometimes nonpaying) jobs. To make ends meet they supplement their incomes with diverse forms of self-employment, much of it subsistence agriculture in small household plots. Throughout the CIS, earnings from such small plots account for 40–70 percent of total household earnings. Access to connections and informal networks and an ability to pay are key to finding a job and getting ahead. This has led to highly unequal outcomes.

and civil strife. Outside Central Europe and the Baltics the optimism pervading the beginning of transition has been tempered by the harsh economic realities of its first decade.

However, the starkness of this binary picture needs to be softened; growth outcomes have varied significantly even within the two broad groups of countries. Furthermore, all countries went through the transitional recession, which caused real GDP to dip from its 1990 levels by nearly 15 percent in the CSB and by more than 40 percent in the CIS.

Of the CSB countries, Hungary, Latvia, Poland, Slovenia, and to some extent Estonia and Lithuania have enjoyed several years of uninterrupted growth. By contrast, growth in Bulgaria and Romania was sharply interrupted by serious macroeconomic crises brought on by insufficient structural reform in the mid-1990s, and GDP in 2000 stood at four-fifths its 1990 level. The Czech Republic had a similar but less severe experience; GDP declined during 1997-99 because of a macroeconomic crisis with structural origins. In fact, the Czech Republic was the only country in Central Europe that had not reached its 1990 GDP level by 2000.

In the CIS such early reformers as Armenia, Georgia, and the Kyrgyz Republic, whose GDP fell steeply, and such nonreformers as Belarus and Uzbekistan, where the decline in GDP was smaller, have been growing in the past five years. But Russia, barring a short-lived upturn in 1997, did not begin to grow until 1999, while Ukraine did not return to growth until 2000.

The wide variation in transition across the region raises questions:

- Why has the growth of some transition economies been better than that of others? To what extent can these differences be ascribed to economic policy choices rather than circumstances at the start of transition or external economic shocks?
- Do the policy lessons from the countries that enjoyed several years of rapid growth continue to be relevant for the CIS and Southeastern Europe, which have made less progress with the transition? Do transition

economies have some common characteristics that make those lessons applicable today?
- If the advantages of economic reform are so obvious, why do countries mired in a no man's land between centrally planned and market economies not adopt them? How might political support for reform be built in those countries?
- In what key respects should policy advice to transition economies be modified to reflect experience from the first decade and the new conditions prevailing today?

This report seeks answers to these questions.

The Quest for Growth: Promoting Discipline and Encouragement

The focus on economic growth needs to be put into a broader perspective. For much of the CIS and Southeastern Europe the restoration of sustained growth is a key priority. Without it these countries will not generate income-earning opportunities for households. Nor will they have the resources needed to provide basic public goods such as legal and judicial systems, secure property rights, and basic infrastructure; maintain essential investments in education and health; or set up social safety nets targeted to the most vulnerable. In this respect transition economies are no different from other economies.

Continued growth is also important for the leading reformers in Central Europe and the Baltics. While all the Central European countries except the Czech Republic had surpassed their 1990 GDP by 2000, per capita incomes in the three wealthiest countries aspiring to European Union accession were still only 68 percent of the European Union average for Slovenia, 59 percent for the Czech Republic, and 49 percent for Hungary. However, an exclusive focus on growth, while providing basic public goods and protecting the most vulnerable, is not enough for them. They need to consolidate the gains of the first decade of transition and address "second generation" reform issues. They have to secure control over quasi-fiscal and contingent liabilities. They have to undertake reforms in labor and financial markets to allow the benefits of growth to be more widely shared. They also have to restructure social expenditures to make them fiscally more affordable without impairing the effectiveness of the social safety net. Several of these reforms overlap with those required to join the European Union.[5]

This report is primarily about economic growth. But the focus is not meant to be exclusive. Two companion reports on poverty and inequality and on anticorruption deal with issues particularly important in the transition (World Bank 2000b, c).

The common heritage of socialism implied that all countries in the region began their transition with a production system adapted not to a competitive environment but to the exigencies of a command economy. External liberalization at the beginning of transition generated significant productivity differences across sectors and enterprises in a production system based on cheap energy and subsidized transport. For example, energy intensity, measured as the amount of energy used per unit of GDP, was 0.95 tons of oil equivalent per US$1,000 of GDP in the Soviet Union in 1985, compared with 0.50 tons of oil per US$1,000 of GDP in OECD countries (IMF and others 1991). In April 1992, after Russia had adjusted the price of oil several times, its domestic price was still only 3 percent of the world price (Tarr 1994). Many sectors and enterprises were not viable after price liberalization.

Two challenges had to be confronted:

- First, the imposition of market discipline on inherited enterprises so that they would face the incentive to restructure and, in so doing, become more productive and able to compete at the new prices. Failure to do so should lead to closure.
- Second, encouragement of the creation of new enterprises willing and able to compete in the marketplace without seeking special favors from the state.

Economic growth reflects the interplay between old enterprises in need of state support, which reduce growth by absorbing more resources than they produce, and restructured and new enterprises, which increase growth. The fall in growth is initially dominated by the drag of old enterprises, which leads to a period of decline. With time, if the business environment favors production and innovation rather than rent seeking, restructured and new enterprises gain the critical mass to overcome the negative effects of old enterprises, leading to recovery and economywide growth.

The initial conditions of geography, history, and price and output distortions at the start of transition and the external economic shocks arising from the breakup of the Soviet Union, war, and civil strife were of course important. However, analysis done for this report shows that initial conditions were significant factors during the initial period of output decline (1990-94), rather than throughout the full ten years of transition, even after accounting for differences across countries in policy reform and the impact of external economic shocks. That analysis also demonstrates that policy reforms have been significant factors in differences among countries in the speed of economic recovery, once due account is taken of differences among countries in initial conditions and the impact of external economic shocks. Furthermore, market-oriented policy reform not only speeded up economic recovery and promoted growth in the medium term, but it also mitigated the effects of the transitional recession in the short term. How effective policies have been in disciplining the old sector and encouraging the new therefore holds the key to understanding why growth has been better in some transition economies than in others.

Discipline forces old enterprises to release assets and labor, which are then potentially available to restructured and new enterprises. It does this by hardening budget constraints, introducing competition in product markets, providing exit mechanisms, and monitoring managerial behavior to generate incentives for production and innovation (rather than for asset stripping and theft).[6] Discipline also pushes old enterprises to divest themselves of such social assets as housing, health clinics, and kindergartens to local governments, shifting the locus of social protection away from enterprises to governments. The social safety net then needs to be strengthened to ensure that labor shed by contracting enterprises and other losers from reform do not fall into poverty, while not eroding these workers' incentives to find employment in new enterprises.

Encouragement entails policies to create an attractive and competitive investment climate in which restructured and new enterprises have incentives to absorb labor and assets rendered inexpensive by the downsizing and to invest in expansion. These policies include reducing excessively high marginal tax rates, simplifying regulatory procedures, establishing secure property rights, and providing basic infrastructure, while maintaining a level playing field among old, restructured, and new enterprises. At the same time the policy environment must provide incentives for wealth creation rather than rent seeking and asset stripping by new enterprises. This mode of adjustment broadly corresponds to the experience to date of economies in Central Europe and the Baltics.

The Flipside: Protection and Discouragement

The disposition of assets among old, restructured, and new enterprises also provides a useful perspective on the experience of many of the CIS countries and, to some extent, Southeastern Europe. These countries have tended to protect rather than discipline old enterprises through subsidies granted through the budget, energy consumption, and the banking sectors. Where institutions of public and corporate governance are not strong enough, asset stripping, theft, and other violations of property and shareholder rights become widespread. Entry of new enterprises is discouraged—or, at best, only selectively encouraged—because of opposition from entrenched interests that would lose from further liberalization of entry. Furthermore, because of a poor investment climate where tax rates are high, licensing and registration procedures are open to abuse, and the legal and judicial system is weak, corruption becomes a serious obstacle to the growth of new enterprises.

Support for the old sector is ultimately financed through taxes on households, new enterprises, and enterprises that have restructured successfully to survive the market test. The social safety net is unable to prevent people from moving into subsistence and low-productivity activities to ensure their survival. Such a protect-and-discourage strategy creates an environment where resource transfers tend to flow in a direction opposite to that in a discipline-and-encourage environment. Transfers from efficient to inefficient enterprises and sectors undermine the credibility of government policy, with detrimental consequences for the economy.

The logic of discipline and encouragement is intended to apply broadly to the production of goods. But it may also be applied, with some modification, to the banking system, an important part of the investment climate required to attract new enterprises. Hard budget constraints on state banks and a credible threat of exit for failed banks are essential to discipline banks and enterprises alike. However, encouragement does not always imply free entry of new banks. Free entry could help make the banking sector competitive, but potential entrants must satisfy prudential norms, such as those for minimum capital requirements and capital adequacy. It is also important that expansion of the banking system not outpace the capacity for effective supervision and growth in the number of creditworthy borrowers.

Shading the Classification

The juxtaposition of discipline-and-encouragement and protection-and-discouragement highlights two contrasting modes of adjustment. In reality, country outcomes span a range of intermediate possibilities, depending on whether liberalization was implemented, hard budget constraints imposed, and an enabling business environment promoted and in what order and how vigorously.

• The discipline of hard budget constraints and institutions of corporate governance to monitor managerial behavior and encouragement through liberalization and a climate hospitable to domestic and foreign investment are perhaps seen most clearly in Estonia, Hungary, and Poland.

- Even in the broad category of discipline and encouragement, however, softer budget constraints and hence less discipline prevailed for a long time in the Czech Republic, Lithuania, and the Slovak Republic.
- Bulgaria, the Kyrgyz Republic, Moldova, Romania, Russia, and Ukraine liberalized their economies, but for a long time failed to maintain discipline through hard budget constraints. They were also unable to contain tunneling, the expropriation of assets and income belonging to minority shareholders, and theft through either rule of law or administrative control. Though many of these countries did encourage new entry early in the transition, the capture of the state by a narrow set of vested enterprises—old enterprises and well-connected early entrants—discouraged further entry and created a poor investment climate, resulting in a pattern of protection and selective encouragement.
- Belarus, Turkmenistan, and Uzbekistan, which have undertaken some liberalization, but have not imposed hard budget constraints, strongly discourage new entry. Policies such as access to foreign exchange and credit on special terms soften budget constraints for state enterprises. But continuing reliance on centralized political power and mechanisms of administrative control inherited from the command economy did limit extensive asset stripping and other forms of theft at the enterprise level. That led to a situation incorporating some elements of discipline in an otherwise strongly protective stance, together with discouragement of entry.

New Enterprises Spur Economic Growth

The growth-enhancing effects of new enterprises and the growth-restraining effects of the old broadly suggest that new enterprises in transition economies are more productive than old enterprises. This is supported by data from 10 transition economies covering both the

leading and lagging reformers in the region, drawn from the World Bank's database on small and medium-size enterprises (SMEs). It is also supported by a comparison between old and new enterprises in the Business Environment and Enterprise Performance Survey, conducted jointly by the European Bank for Reconstruction and Development and the World Bank in 1999 (see box 3.1). The survey finds that new enterprises outperform old enterprises in sales, exports, investment, and employment (chapter 3). Thus a transfer of resources from old enterprises to new can be a source of growth. Whether that potential is realized depends on the discipline imposed on old enterprises to shed resources and the encouragement extended to new enterprises to absorb them.

The interaction between old and new enterprises is key to economic growth. The share of total employment and value added accounted for by small enterprises (defined as employing fewer than 50 workers) as a proxy for new enterprises divides transition economies into two groups.[7] In the Czech Republic, Hungary, Lithuania, and Poland, new enterprises grew very rapidly. They now account for 50 percent or more of employment, the average for the European Union, and for between 55 and 65 percent of value added. But in Kazakhstan, Russia, and Ukraine, which have seen modest or no growth in new enterprises, the share of employment has stayed at or below 20 percent and the share of value added has stayed between 20 and 30 percent.

Hungary and Poland saw a sharp and early decline in employment and a rapid demise of the old sector, which initially made resources available cheaply to the new sector. Such discipline is important but insufficient; encouragement is also needed. Growth takes off only when the new sector evolves from a passive receptacle for absorbing resources into an active competitor, rapidly increasing its share of employment and attracting the most qualified workers. The evidence suggests that new enterprises must reach a threshold of around 40 percent in their contribution to employment before they can become an engine of growth. In Russia and Ukraine, where the contribution of the new sector to employment is well below the threshold, a large proportion of the labor force remains mired in old, unrestructured enterprises not generating increases in productivity. The new sector has not emerged as a source of growth.

New enterprises are more productive than old ones, but productivity differences diminish with transition. The difference is greater in Kazakhstan, Russia, and Ukraine than in the Czech Republic, Hungary, Latvia, Lithuania, and Poland. Why? It is because closure and restructuring can raise the productivity of factors in the old sector and because fast growth of enterprises and employment can reduce the productivity of factors in the new sectors. Thus a comparison of labor productivity shows a difference in favor of new enterprises of more than 100 percent in Ukraine, where the contribution of the new sector to total employment is 17 percent. That difference narrows to just more than 40 percent in Hungary, where the contribution of the new sector to total employment is 55 percent.[8]

Creating a policy environment that disciplines low-productivity old enterprises into releasing resources and encourages high-productivity new enterprises to absorb those resources and to undertake new investment, without tilting the playing field in favor of any particular type of enterprise and while strengthening the social safety net to protect the most vulnerable, is central to economic growth in transition economies. This is the main lesson from the successful reformers in Central Europe and the Baltics.

When Is Transition Over?

Do transition economies at different levels of gross national income per capita (ranging in purchasing power parity terms from US$2,100 in Moldova in 1999 to US$16,050 in Slovenia in 2000 [World Bank 2001]) have anything in common that would make lessons from economies in the region leading in reform applicable to those lagging in reform? The wide dispersion in the productivity of labor and capital across types of enterprises at the onset of transition and the erosion of those differences between old and new sectors during reform provide a natural definition of the end of transition.

Enterprises in a typical transition economy can be distinguished by history: are they new,

restructured, or old? They can also be distinguished by economic performance: are they productive? Furthermore, history and performance are related. New enterprises are expected to be more productive than restructured enterprises, which are expected to be more productive than old enterprises. As markets develop and resources are allowed to flow to their most valued uses, the role of history progressively weakens, and differences in productivity arising from membership in any of the categories tends to disappear, consistent with the evidence on the behavior of differences in productivity.

This is not to suggest that differences in productivity across enterprises will disappear altogether. These differences always exist as a result of technical innovation and new export market penetration, among other factors. However, the variation in productivity could not be systematically attributed to the enterprises' historically determined categories: old, restructured, and new. When that distinguishing characteristic is lost in a country, the transition can be taken to be over. At that point, the economic issues and problems policymakers must deal with are no longer specific to transition. At what level of per capita income will this occur? The answer depends on the success of disciplining the old sector and encouraging the new one. It also depends on the success of the business environment in attracting investment.

Do Central Europe and the Baltics Point the Way Forward?

The striking diversity in challenges and circumstances among countries that have not proceeded far in the transition—in particular, countries in the CIS and Southeastern Europe—raises the question of whether 10 years after the dissolution of the Soviet Union these countries can learn from the successful reforms in Central Europe and the Baltics.

Countries in the CIS and Southeastern Europe continue to face significant productivity differences across old, restructured, and new enterprises characteristic of the transition and are therefore a long way from the end of transition. Hence, the framework of discipline and encouragement and its associated policy and institutional implications remain relevant for understanding what needs to be done to restore growth and protect the most vulnerable in these economies (the policy and institutional reforms associated with discipline and encouragement are summarized in annex 1).

However, the political context for pursuing reform policies has changed greatly in a decade. At the beginning of transition, implementing reforms focused on overcoming the resistance of the *nomenklatura*, whose political and economic privileges fueled support for the prevailing economic system, and on building support for reform among the newly mobilized public. But in the past decade power over economic resources has shifted, often in a highly concentrated pattern, from state bureaucrats to the private sector, even in much of the CIS and in Southeastern Europe. That has made it easier for narrow special interests to capture the state and block further reforms that may undermine short-term rents.

Other problems, specific to individual countries or subgroups of countries, have little to do with the transition but demand urgent resolution. Securing peace and inaugurating the painstaking task of nation building in the South Caucasus and the Balkans, wracked by war and civil strife, are priorities. So is controlling the spread of tuberculosis and HIV/AIDS, which threaten millions of lives. But these challenges are outside the scope of this report.

Can We Have It Both Ways: Encouragement without Discipline?

The implementation of policies associated with both discipline and encouragement presents a challenge. Is it possible to downsize the old sector slowly while encouraging the new sector and thus to avoid the pain of liquidation and restructuring until a cushion has been put in place? Encouragement without discipline will not work if old enterprises absorb resources that would otherwise flow to new enterprises. For example:

- Protection of state-owned enterprises and farm collectives through the banking sector in Bulgaria and Romania led to a sharp increase in

nonperforming loans as a share of total banking sector loans in the 1990s (in Romania, 34 percent in 1998). These loans prevented the expansion of bank credit to new, small, and politically less-connected enterprises. They also triggered banking and macroeconomic crises that called for stabilization and a tightening of credit, hurting new enterprises.

- Protection of the old industrial sector in Belarus and Uzbekistan through specially favorable foreign exchange regimes, directed credit, and high trade protection has meant that whatever credit and foreign exchange remain are available only to new smaller enterprises at prices several times higher than what would have been paid in unified markets. In Uzbekistan small enterprises have to pay three times more for foreign exchange to finance their imports than do large state enterprises.

- Protection through tax and utility arrears in countries such as Georgia, the Kyrgyz Republic, Moldova, Russia, Romania, and Ukraine meant that new and more energy-efficient enterprises were charged more to compensate for revenue losses from nonpayment by old, less energy-efficient enterprises to utilities in the energy sector. Tax exemptions for large enterprises and agricultural collectives in Ukraine, negotiated offsets to pay taxes in Russia, and tax avoidance in exchange for bribes by large enterprises in Georgia typically worked to the disadvantage of new and smaller enterprises, which ended up paying higher prices and bribes as a proportion of their annual revenue.

The lack of a vibrant emerging private sector, because of a policy of discouragement, limits the outside options available to those in old enterprises. These limited private sector job options increase the social cost of restructuring the old enterprises, resulting in the need for additional protection for the old sector. The complementary relationship between discipline and encouragement also sheds light on why a relaxation in discipline—brought about, for example, by special treatment for powerful lobbies—is associated with selective rather than complete encouragement. It also helps explain why policy reform must cover both discipline and encouragement, thus proceeding along an ambitiously broad front, and therefore why there are no magic bullets in transition.

Learning from China?

The success of encouraging entry of new enterprises in China (where GDP per capita grew 8 percent per year from 1978 to 1995, lifting 200 million people out of absolute poverty) without imposing significant discipline on state enterprises raises a question of the applicability of China's reform to the transition economies of Eastern Europe and the former Soviet Union. Through different channels China modulated the tradeoff between encouraging new enterprises and not imposing hard budget constraints on existing state enterprises. The country reaped spectacular gains from liberalizing repressed sectors such as agriculture, which had surplus labor, and rural industries and from a massive inflow of foreign direct investment.

Part of these gains, helped by a high savings rate, could be transferred through the banking system to finance loss-making state enterprises, which were far less important in China than in most countries in Eastern Europe and the former Soviet Union. For example, only 19 percent of the Chinese labor force worked in the state sector and were thus entitled to a range of social benefits, compared with 90 percent in Russia. Furthermore, tight political control over asset stripping, arbitraging between controlled and market prices for private gain and corruption, together with some state capacity to manage public assets allowed China to move its loss-making state enterprises more slowly to market conditions at the same time that explosive growth of new enterprises took place. If a substantial inflow of resources, for example, from liberalizing a previously repressed sector or from foreign direct investment, and state capacity to manage the process allow a country to follow such a phased transition, it is less likely to experience a period of contraction in output.

These conditions were largely absent in most transition economies covered by this report. But the costs of soft budget constraints on China's state enterprises remain to be fully recognized. The share of nonperforming loans in the banking system, which served as a conduit for assistance to state enterprises, is between 30 and 40 percent of annual GDP. Addressing this problem is likely to pose a major fiscal challenge. In sum, the transition economies of Eastern Europe and the former Soviet Union did not have the resources for a phased transition for state enterprises, but they would be well advised to draw from China's experience the importance of encouraging new enterprises as a basis for wealth creation and economic growth.

Institutions Are Important, but So Are Policies

Early on, Fischer and Gelb (1991) flagged the role of institutional reforms in the transition. Given that it is now argued that a key deficiency of the transition has been insufficient attention to building a market-friendly institutional framework, reflecting on the experience of East Germany's unification with West Germany in 1990 is instructive. It illustrates, among other things, how inappropriate policy choices can undermine performance even in the most favorable of institutional environments. East Germany was able to adopt all the institutions of West Germany without delay. It also received massive financial transfers, which averaged between 40 and 60 percent of East Germany's GDP over the period 1991 to 1997, and which continue at levels exceeding 4 percent of West Germany's GDP per year. Furthermore, German reunification conferred on East Germany automatic membership in the European Union.

Despite these considerable advantages, East Germany suffered an initial decline in GDP that was deeper than its transition economy neighbors' declines, and it has experienced one of the slowest GDP growth rates in Europe, disappointing expectations that it would catch up rapidly with West Germany. This occurred, first, because the one-to-one conversion rate between West German and East German marks led to a substantial overvaluation of the East German currency and, second, because attempts to bring East German wages in line with West German wages, in the face of much lower labor productivity in the East, undermined East Germany's competitiveness. As a result, a much larger part of the inherited capital stock was rendered unproductive than would have been the case had more appropriate macroeconomic policies been chosen. Thus, while institutional change is important, so too is policy reform, and it is essential that they proceed hand in hand.

The Political Economy of Discipline and Encouragement

Many transition economies outside Central Europe and the Baltics are stuck in a no man's land between plan and market. If the advantages of economic reforms are so obvious, why doesn't every country adopt them? Can economic policy choices be systematically related to particular institutional characteristics of political systems in transition?

The political economy of reform within the framework of discipline and encouragement can be expressed graphically by tracing the paths of winners and losers from the transition. Figure 1 depicts the gains and losses in income accruing to three different constituencies at different doses of reform in a typical transition economy.

- *State sector workers,* employed in state enterprises and lacking the skills to become new entrants in the competitive market, face a sharp drop in income as discipline calls for downsizing the sector, with little hope of any substantial recovery with the intensification of reform.
- *Potential new entrants,* workers in state enterprises and new entrepreneurs with skills to become new entrants in the competitive market, have a classic J-curve pattern of income. They face significant adjustment costs at low levels of reform as they exit the state sector. In addition, they realize gains only when enough progress has been made with policy and institutional reforms to promote and support new entry into the competitive market.
- *Oligarchs and insiders* begin the transition with substantial de facto control rights over state assets and close ties with the political elite inherited from the previous command

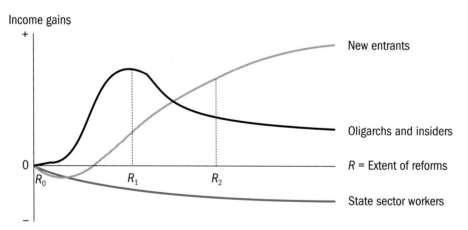

FIGURE 1.

Winners and Losers from Reform

Note: R_0 = no reforms; R_1 = point at which income gains of oligarchs and insiders are maximized; R_2 = level of reforms that allows the winners of reforms beyond R_1 (new entrants) to compensate for or exercise enough political pressure to neutralize the resistance of oligarchs, insiders, and state sector workers.

Source: Authors.

system. However, because of limited skills to compete in the market economy, they face an inverted U-curve of income gains. They are the immediate beneficiaries of liberalization and privatization, as de facto control rights over state assets can be converted into de jure control and cash flow rights. They reap concentrated gains in the early stages of reform from the opportunities for arbitrage, rent seeking, and tunneling that arise if liberalization and privatization are not combined with discipline and encouragement. But these gains dissipate as further reforms lead to increasing competition and market entry.

Given these patterns of gains and losses, each constituency prefers a different combination of reforms. State sector workers prefer the status quo R_0 and reject all reforms. Oligarchs and insiders prefer a partial reform and sustain the reform process through R_1, the point where their gains are maximized and beyond which further implementation of policies of discipline and encouragement threaten to undermine gains from rent seeking and tunneling. For potential new entrants, the reform process offers sacrifices at the beginning for the promise of gains when the reforms are further advanced.

Where the risk of oligarchs and insiders blocking anything more than partial reform is high, potential new entrants and state workers will either reject reform or support only partial reform, because the latter, by limiting the downsizing of the state sector and maintaining the flow of subsidies, imposes lower adjustment costs. Yet it is precisely such partial reforms—liberalization without discipline and with selective encouragement—that make capture of the state by oligarchs and insiders a self-fulfilling prophecy. This has led to a so-called partial reform paradox in many transition economies in which governments lack credibility and are highly susceptible to state capture. This leads potential new entrants at the outset of transition to discount substantially the potential gains from any proposed radical reforms and instead support partial reforms that offer lower costs early in the reform process, even though they are more likely

to lead to barriers to entry. Public support for radical reforms therefore depends on perceptions of government credibility in its commitment to follow through with such reforms.

The risk of "getting stuck" at a low level of reform (R_1) characterized by liberalization without discipline and limited encouragement of new entry is high. As both insiders and state sector workers face declining incomes after R_1, these groups have a strong incentive to join forces to oppose further economic reforms. It is only when reforms reach a critical threshold (R_2) that the added gains to new entrants are enough to allow these winners to either compensate the losses of the other groups or to generate enough political pressure to neutralize opposition to continued reform.

By recognizing that different combinations of reforms produce different configurations of winners and losers, the framework of discipline and encouragement suggests two political challenges in promoting economic reform:

• Securing the support of potential new entrants for comprehensive reforms until wider efficiency gains from discipline and encouragement are realized.
• Preventing the early winners from liberalization and privatization from undermining further reforms that would impose discipline and encourage new entry and competition and thus reduce their rents.

To meet these challenges, governments must appear credible to potential new entrants in its commitments to follow through with the long and difficult process of economic reform. Governments must also be able to constrain oligarchs and insiders from using their initial advantages in the reform process to derail further reforms that would create a more competitive market economy.

Credibility and constraint are rooted in political institutions shaped by the cultural and historical legacies that guided the exit from communism. In many countries in the CIS and Southeastern Europe, where the state has been captured by narrow private interests, the collapse of communism was rooted in a contest among competing elites rather than in any broad social movement. The new political arrangements in these "concentrated political regimes" were designed by incumbent leaders, often as a way to consolidate their power. They lacked the credibility to build and sustain broad popular support for a comprehensive reform program.

As a result, these countries embarked on transition without a broad social consensus on the goals of reform and without a way of organizing the public behind these goals. Instead, incumbent politicians sought alliances with powerful incumbent enterprises. In addition, the politicians continued partial liberalization and privatization in the context of soft budgets and barriers to entry that created tremendous opportunities for rent seeking by old and new enterprises, especially in economies rich in natural resources. Countervailing pressures from competing groups were weak and the disaffection and apathy of the "losers" minimized the direct costs to politicians of poor policy choices. As a result, countries with concentrated political regimes have tended to languish in an equilibrium trap of partial economic reforms. Political and economic power has been used to preserve market distortions that benefit narrow vested interests at considerable social cost.

This partial reform equilibrium can be contrasted with the situation in the "competitive democracies" prevailing in Central Europe and the Baltics. In the aftermath of popular revolutions against communist rule, political institutions in most of these countries emerged from roundtable negotiations among broadly representative popular fronts and a wide range of other organized interests. This, together with the close ties of these countries to Western and Northern Europe and the pull of potential European Union accession, contributed to a wider social consensus on the main directions of reform and broad public support for comprehensive reform programs in the early stages of transition.

New governments in competitive democracies tended to focus first on promoting new constituencies of "winners" by removing entry barriers, quickly tackling severe macroeconomic instability (with its high costs to the public), and using social protection to support the "losers" from the dislocations of reform. A legacy of

strong public administration allowed for greater security of property and contract rights and better public infrastructure, important preconditions for promoting new entry. As reform progressed to promote entry and improve the enabling environment, constituencies with a stake in advancing reform grew stronger, and the emergence of powerful insiders and oligarchs diminished. This combination allowed these countries to implement and sustain comprehensive reforms.

Political developments and economic reforms are closely interrelated. Political systems affect the incentives of politicians to make certain economic policy choices; reform choices shape the configuration of social groups and the distribution of power, which affects the structure and functioning of the political system. For example, economic reforms that facilitate new entry also strengthen the constituency of SMEs, which build support for increasing political competition.

Nevertheless, given the sharp break with communism and the disintegration of the Soviet Union, choices about the structure of political systems in the transition economies were generally made before decisions about the nature and pace of economic reform. Moreover, in all but a couple of countries—Croatia and the Slovak Republic—the nature of the political regime has not changed much since the start of transition. This suggests that while the pace and direction of economic reforms may have reinforced initial choices about the structure of the political system, they do not appear to have decisively shifted the course of political transition. As a result, a stronger case can be made for identifying the direction of causation from political choices to economic choices, thus providing part of the explanation for why some countries have been unable to move beyond partial reform.

Shifting Policy Priorities to Account for Experience and New Conditions

Much economic policymaking is endogenous from the broader perspective of political economy. Designing effective reform strategies must therefore take into account the political incentives and constraints that block progress in transition. But although initial conditions and political institutions influence reform paths, these factors cannot wholly predetermine outcomes in a process as complex and multifaceted as transition. Experience from across the world demonstrates that talented political leaders can maneuver countries out of so-called reform traps. Critical elections or external shocks can break long-term stalemates on reform. New leaders can mobilize alternative coalitions and spark collective action that tips the balance of power between the potential winners and losers from further economic reforms. Clever winners can devise win-win strategies that co-opt their opponents to build support for reform.

In what ways should policy advice during these extraordinary opportunities for reform reflect the experience of the past decade and today's conditions? Three broad areas can be identified.

From Privatization and Restructuring to Promoting Entry

Policy needs to shift its emphasis from privatization and restructuring of assets to creating wealth through new enterprises. The early emphasis on rapid privatization entailed removing ownership of enterprises from the state, creating a constituency for private ownership to help guarantee the irreversibility of reform, and stopping abuses such as asset stripping by enterprise managers and other forms of "spontaneous privatization." Although much remains to be done, particularly in privatizing medium-sized and large enterprises, these past concerns weigh less heavily on policymakers today. To this must be added the suggestion from the empirical literature that privatization has promoted restructuring in the CSB, but not in the CIS (see Djankov and Murrell 2000 and chapter 7 in this volume).

New enterprises are important to promoting growth. In both the leading and lagging reformers, new enterprises enjoy a productivity advantage over old enterprises. So transferring resources from old enterprises to new ones is a source of growth. Although causality cannot be inferred from the evidence, countries that have returned to sustained growth have relied on a vibrant new sector to absorb labor and other resources released by the downsizing of the old

sector and to provide a major share of employment (50 percent) and value added (55–65 percent) in the economy. By contrast, in countries where restoring sustained growth has proved more elusive, new enterprises account for a low share of employment (10–20 percent) and value added (10–20 percent).

That is why encouraging an investment climate attractive for new entrants and meeting the policy and institutional challenges of encouragement should be the highest priorities for policymakers in transition economies. Remember, though, that encouragement cannot go very far without discipline. Therefore, the emphasis on encouragement is more effective the more it is accompanied by hard budget constraints, exit mechanisms, product market competition, and stronger institutions for monitoring managerial behavior.

From Depoliticizing Enterprises to Monitoring Managers

The lack of restructuring in privatized enterprises in the CIS, together with tunneling and theft, renew interest in the question of what institutions are needed to encourage managers to become effective stewards of enterprise assets. Although developing these institutions of corporate governance has been on the reform agenda since the start of transition, the difficulty of doing so in countries without recent market experience was probably underestimated.

International experience suggests that without effective legal protection, suppliers of finance do not enter into contracts with enterprises to ensure that they get a return on their investment—the essence of the corporate governance problem—even if such arrangements are in the interest of both parties. Concentrated ownership, by providing enhanced monitoring of managers by shareholders, can overcome some of the corporate governance problems that plague transition economies lacking such legal protection. But the type of concentrated ownership matters as well. Enterprises controlled by strategic investors, particularly if they are foreign, have performed much better than those controlled by holding companies or other financial institutions.

The selection of strategic investors matters too. Enterprises sold through transparent tenders or auctions have generally attracted better owners, outperforming enterprises sold directly to politically connected parties, frequently at highly subsidized prices. Without such safeguards, concentrated ownership does not avoid the risk of expropriation of assets and income belonging to minority shareholders.

In countries where the preferred method of privatization—direct sales through transparent tenders or auctions to strategic investors—was unavailable, the relevant comparison in assessing privatization is not between the actual method chosen and the ideal method, but between the actual method and continued state ownership until strategic investors were found. Countries where mass privatization using vouchers originally dispersed ownership and where secondary trading has not led to transparent consolidation of shares witnessed expropriation of assets and income of minority shareholders by those that were able to gain control over the enterprise in the first stages of the privatization program. But the success of continued state ownership is not assured unless there is a political commitment to transparent privatization outcomes and a minimum institutional capacity to prevent asset stripping by enterprise managers in the interim period. Indeed, navigating between continued state ownership with eroding control rights on the one hand and a transfer to ineffective new private owners with an inadequate institutional framework on the other hand was one of the most difficult challenges confronting policymakers in charge of privatization. Irrespective of the alternative chosen, governments need to enshrine investor protection in the legal system and supplement it with a system of regulation for financial intermediaries, such as investment funds and brokers (Johnson and Shleifer 2001).

Developing laws and institutions to protect investors and monitor managerial behavior and thus facilitate the development of bank and nonbank financial intermediation in countries with no recent market experience is far more difficult when opposed by early winners from transition. Further reforms would dissipate the rents accruing to the early winners. In Russia, for example, powerful insiders with a stake in weak corporate governance have frequently hampered the work and enforcement efforts of the Securities and Exchange Commission. In environments of high state capture, privatization has not created enough demand for the enforcement of property rights. Indeed, quite the opposite is true. While privatization is positively associated with public governance (the latter summarizing the state's capacity to provide key public goods) in low-capture environments, the association is negative in high-capture environments (EBRD 1999).

Several of these issues were not foreseen at the beginning of the transition. One was the apparent stability of such partial reform equilibriums. Another was the unexpectedly perverse relationship between privatization and the quality of governance in such environments. That increased the challenge of enhancing creditors' and shareholders' rights; promoting internationally recognized accounting and auditing standards; and enforcing takeover, insolvency, and collateral legislation in the face of opposition from a narrow set of entrenched private interests.

The need to strengthen corporate governance, despite opposition from oligarchs and insiders, is an important lesson from the first decade of transition. This is, however, a time-consuming process, during which policymakers still need to make choices about the appropriate stewardship of state assets, including privatization. The following broad principles should guide a program of privatization:

• Privatization should be part of an overall strategy of discipline and encouragement.
• Small enterprises still owned by the state should be sold directly to new owners through an open and competitive auction and without restrictions on who may bid for the shares.
• In general, medium-size and large enterprises should be privatized to strategic outside investors, who, with a concentrated controlling stake, will best use enterprise assets. Although several transaction methods may be used, including negotiated sales, the evidence suggests

this can be brought about most effectively through competitive case-by-case methods, which are more deliberative than voucher schemes or rapid, small auctions. They use independent financial advisors who both prepare the enterprise for sale and act as sales agents on behalf of the state. Rapid privatization to insiders or through mass privatization should be avoided. In countries such as Belarus, Turkmenistan, and Uzbekistan, each of which has a substantially unfinished agenda of privatization of medium-sized and large enterprises, but where the state retains the capacity to provide public goods, the state should use its administrative capacity to control the disposition of public assets as transparently as possible, while developing institutions of corporate governance. Transparency would be enhanced, for example, if decisions regarding public assets were to be reviewed by independent boards of directors and accompanied by public disclosure.

- Privatization should be accompanied by increasing competition in the market for the products sold by the enterprise in question and vigorously enforced by the competition policy authority. This can help discipline managers when corporate governance is weak.
- Divestiture of enterprises in sectors characterized by a natural monopoly or oligopoly (becoming rarer with advances in technology) must proceed with caution, if at all. Establishing an efficient regulatory regime is a prerequisite to protect the public interest, lest divestiture transform an inefficient public monopoly into a poorly regulated or unregulated private monopoly.
- The state's property and cash flow rights should be clarified and strengthened in enterprises in which the state continues to hold a stake.

Mobilizing the Winners from Further Reform

Breaking the political economy equilibrium underlying partial reforms is the most important and difficult challenge in advancing transition in many countries of the region, particularly in the CIS. Where the state is already susceptible to influence by powerful vested interests in the new private sector, granting extraordinary decree-making powers to the executive branch to dissipate rents and level the playing field has not won against strong opposition from insiders and oligarchs.

What is needed instead is to mobilize through greater political inclusion and coordination all constituencies that lose from partial reform and that stand to gain from further progress toward a more competitive market economy. For example, given the wide and generally regressive impact of high inflation, political parties in several transition economies mobilized enough electoral support for macroeconomic stabilization to overcome the opposition of powerful commercial banks and other actors that gained from economic volatility. Similarly, banking crises in Bulgaria, the Czech Republic, and Hungary sparked electoral appeals to disgruntled savers that helped break the stalemate over such issues as banking privatization and regulatory reform.

Business associations could serve as vehicles of collective action by SMEs, new enterprises, and "second-tier" enterprises that suffer from an unlevel playing field, discretionary taxation and regulation, and anticompetitive barriers. In countries with concentrated political regimes, such associations are weaker than those in the competitive democracies of Central Europe, which have more voice. So political parties have yet to seek strategic alliances with such actors as an alternative base of support and funding.

Overcoming the coordination dilemmas of mobilizing the highly dispersed winners of further reform is not easy. A major challenge for the reformist team that comes to power during a period of extraordinary politics in countries with concentrated political regimes is to make clear the links between rents from partial reform and the direct costs to society. Tax arrears, tax and duty exemptions for high-profile conglomerates, and nonpayments need to be linked in the public mind to delayed public sector wages and pensions and the poor provision of social services. The complex web of nontransparent subsidies to powerful businesses needs to be uncovered, revealing that such subsidies tend to benefit incumbent managers rather than workers.

To advance reforms, governments should focus on smoothing the curves of the winners and losers at the initial stages of reform (see figure 1). This means lowering the adjustment costs for potential new entrants and reducing the high concentration of gains to oligarchs and insiders. One way to do this is by strengthening the provision of basic public goods, such as secure property rights and a legal and judicial system. Another way is by reducing excessively high marginal tax rates and broadening the tax base that promotes entry of enterprises from the unofficial to the official economy. This can break the vicious cycle of informalization, lower tax revenue, and further intensification of tax rates on a shrinking base. Developing a rule-based tax administration to enforce efficient taxation of the new private sector is also important.

To align the incentives of local governments to identify with small business and increase entry, taxes on small enterprises should be allocated to local government. Simplifying entry and licensing arrangements for new enterprises is critical. These measures, by encouraging the emergence of new enterprises, offer a stable outside option to state workers, creating opportunities for them to become potential entrants into the burgeoning sector of new enterprises and lessening their opposition to reform.

As entry occurs gradually at the margin, these actors become an effective constituency demanding reforms to remove weaknesses in the investment climate over the long run. Furthermore, a gradual reallocation of public expenditures from nontransparent and discretionary subsidies to worker training, severance payments, and grants for improving services in communities affected by downsizing can create further momentum for reform. More broadly, strengthening the social safety net and divesting such social assets as housing, child care, and health facilities shifts the burden of social protection from enterprises to governments, thus facilitating the restructuring that will foster a return to growth. Fiscal policy therefore has the potential to smooth the curves described in figure 1 and redistribute a part of the reform dividend to those who would otherwise bear its costs. It is thus a key element in supporting comprehensive reform.

Conclusions

Analysis of the first ten years of transition in Eastern Europe and the former Soviet Union highlights the following lessons, which could be applied in future to economies that have made limited progress with reform.

- While the initial conditions that prevailed at the beginning of transition were critical for explaining the output decline that occurred initially in all countries, market-oriented policy reforms have played a significant role in promoting subsequent economic growth. Creating an environment that disciplines old enterprises into releasing assets and labor and encourages new enterprises to absorb those resources and undertake new investment, without tilting the playing field in favor of any particular type of enterprise, is central to economic growth.

- Policymakers cannot postpone the pain of liquidating and restructuring the old sector until the cushion provided by new enterprises is in place. The success of the encouragement strategy requires simultaneous application of discipline, because a lack of discipline undermines the level playing field between different kinds of enterprises. Furthermore, the practice of allowing old and large enterprises to avoid paying taxes and social security contributions and to avoid repaying bank debts has been at the root of macroeconomic crises.

- Developing legal and regulatory institutions to oversee enterprise management, though time-consuming, is important. In the meanwhile, where direct sales of state assets to strategic investors—a preferred method of privatization—is not feasible, policymakers face a difficult choice between (i) privatization to ineffective owners in a context of weak corporate governance, with the risk of expropriation of assets and income of minority shareholders by those who gained control over the enterprise, and (ii) continued state ownership in the face of inadequate political commitment to transparent privatization outcomes and limited institutional capacity to prevent asset stripping by incumbent enterprise managers.

- Breaking out of low-level equilibrium traps in which the immediate beneficiaries of liberalization and privatization have captured the state and oppose measures of encouragement such as competition and free entry that would reduce their rents requires mobilizing small, medium-sized, and new enterprises and second-tier businesses that suffer as a result of the uneven playing field and stand to gain from further reform. Fiscal policy has an important role to play here, by redirecting support away from ailing enterprises and toward worker training and severance payments, and by divesting social assets such as housing, child care, and health facilities from enterprises to governments.

Annex 1.   Discipline and Encouragement: The Reform Agenda

What policy and institutional reforms are needed to create an environment favorable to discipline and encouragement? While no individual policy can be assigned to a single outcome in an interrelated system, it helps to think of policy packages as those primarily directed at disciplining the old sector and those primarily directed at encouraging the new sector without tilting the playing field in favor of any particular type of enterprise.

Discipline

In an environment of price and trade liberalization, discipline requires imposing hard budget constraints on enterprises, providing exit mechanisms for insolvent enterprises, monitoring and influencing managerial behavior to reward efficient stewardship of assets and to discourage tunneling and theft, increasing product market competition, transferring social assets from enterprises to local governments, and using the social safety net as a cushion for displaced workers and other losers from reform.

Imposing hard budget constraints requires:

- Eliminating tax exemptions, fiscal and financial subsidies, budget and tax offsets, and directed credits.

- Controlling fiscal risks arising from implicit and contingent liabilities on account of state-owned enterprises, banks and pension systems, guarantees for projects and balance sheets of special purpose agencies, and the fiscal stance of subnational governments.
- Implementing bankruptcy laws to facilitate exit through a formal process and to create incentives for closure through informal mechanisms.
- Reforming the budget process so the state can meet its expenditure obligations in cash and on time, with a view to eliminating arrears and noncash payments.

Monitoring and influencing managerial behavior requires:

- In reforming economies, where the bulk of assets are in private hands, improving institutions of corporate governance by strengthening legal protection for minority shareholders and creditors, bringing in management by concentrated owners or strategic investors, promoting internationally recognized accounting and auditing standards, and working, as capital markets grow, to develop a market in corporate control.
- In nonreforming economies, where assets remain largely in the public sector and where the state retains the capacity to provide public goods, the state should use its administrative capacity to control asset disposition as transparently as possible, while developing institutions of corporate governance.

Promoting competition in product markets is an important ingredient of discipline, especially because of competition's effect on the behavior of enterprise managers. In the CIS, for example, competition can compensate to some extent for weak monitoring of managers by shareholders and creditors. This requires:

- Opening markets and promoting free entry, including trade liberalization
- Enforcing competition laws through a government agency vested with the requisite authority.

Transferring responsibility for social assets such as housing, utilities, clinics, and kindergartens from enterprises to local governments will allow enterprise restructuring to proceed in countries that have relied heavily on enterprises as instruments of social policy. This requires:

- Clarifying the roles and responsibilities of subnational governments
- Giving those governments resources to fulfill their assigned responsibilities
- Reforming communal services (including central heating and gas) and moving tariffs to cost-recovery levels
- Replacing across-the-board housing and utility subsidies with targeted social assistance to the poorest households, sometimes combined with lifeline tariffs.

Social insurance programs that cover pensions and unemployment insurance and social assistance programs make it more feasible to discipline old enterprises into shedding labor and to help create a constituency for discipline. Reform of social insurance programs requires:

- Moving pension reform in Central Europe and the Baltics to multipillar systems, with a minimum poverty-based benefit. Because structural unemployment is falling in these countries, they can implement unemployment insurance programs.
- Reforming pay-as-you-go systems in Bulgaria, Romania, Russia, and Ukraine to put them on a firmer fiscal footing, with a minimum poverty-based benefit. Unemployment insurance might involve a flat benefit or severance payment.
- Moving to a flat benefit structure in the resource-constrained, low-income countries of the CIS, to protect the poorest elderly.

The reform of social assistance programs requires:

- Moving to a means-tested cash benefit assistance program in Central Europe and the Baltics
- Moving to categorical cash benefits, either universal or targeted by category, in Bulgaria, Romania, Russia, and Ukraine and using means-tested benefits only where local institutions are strong

- Improving targeting of limited cash benefits in the low-income CIS countries through geographical targeting, community-based identification, or self-targeting through some form of public works scheme.

Encouragement

In addition to liberalizing prices and trade, improving the investment climate for domestic and foreign investors is key to encouraging new enterprises. This requires establishing secure property and contract rights and providing basic infrastructure, reducing excessive marginal tax rates, simplifying regulatory and licensing procedures, and developing a competitive and efficient banking system.

Ensuring the adoption of laws best suited to securing property rights and contracts requires emphasis on two areas:

- The process for drafting laws: enterprises should have input in their design and be informed beforehand of changes in rules that will affect their operations
- The effectiveness of the judiciary: its fairness (bias, honesty, and consistency) and the likelihood of enforcement.

Tax reform should:

- Raise the turnover threshold for becoming a value-added taxpayer high enough to exclude small enterprises, which should instead be subject to a small-enterprise tax regime. This regime should be simple enough to lighten the administrative and reporting burden on taxpayers and reduce interactions between the taxpayer and the tax authority.
- Allocate small business taxes and property taxes to subnational governments to help them identify with new emerging enterprises, which are typically a source of job creation, rather than with large, bankrupt enterprises to save jobs that should be cut.

Streamlining the business licensing and registration requirements that govern entry of new enterprises is a high priority. Addressing these issues requires:

- Simplifying and making transparent entry and licensing procedures
- Reducing the scope for arbitrary decision-making and abuse of power.

Insecure property rights are more of a constraint on investment for new enterprises than the availability of bank finance, particularly in the CIS, which is less far along in the transition (Johnson, McMillan, and Woodruff 2000). But as the transition proceeds and legal and judicial reforms strengthen property rights, financial deepening and development will be essential to support the growth of a private sector led by new enterprises.

Developing a competitive banking sector requires a strategy to deal with the exit of failed banks, the entry of new banks, and bank privatization and restructuring. Strengthening the regulatory authority for bank supervision is extremely important for performing these activities effectively. This will require:

- The resolution of failed banks, which dominate the banking system in transition economies and have large interbank exposures and loans to loss-making enterprises, therefore poses special problems. Liquidation and restructuring options should be assessed carefully in the event of systemic risks to the financial sector and the need to impose hard budget constraints on banks and enterprises.
- The fostering of a competitive and efficient banking system requires encouraging the entry of new banks that satisfy prudential criteria for minimum capital requirements and capital adequacy. Because supervisory responsibility resides mainly with the home country regulatory authority, entry by foreign banks and acquisition of stakes in existing banks by foreign banks is a quick way of importing managerial and governance expertise and improving bank regulation in a transition economy. In any event, the expansion of the banking system should occur only in line with the growing capacity for bank regulation and growth in the number of creditworthy borrowers.
- The privatization of banks to strategic investors whenever possible. If foreign, they

can help upgrade managerial and supervisory standards. The alternative—privatizing banks to concentrated owners—should occur only if there is a clear separation between shareholders and borrowers. The pace of privatization should not outrun the development of adequate supervision authority.

Notes

1. The CSB comprises Albania, Bosnia and Herzegovina, Bulgaria, Croatia, the Czech Republic, Estonia, Hungary, Latvia, Lithuania, the former Yugoslav Republic of Macedonia, Poland, Romania, the Slovak Republic, and Slovenia. The Federal Republic of Yugoslavia is not included in the aggregates for the CSB countries because no data are available before 1998. The CIS comprises Armenia, Azerbaijan, Belarus, Georgia, Kazakhstan, the Kyrgyz Republic, Moldova, the Russian Federation, Tajikistan, Turkmenistan, Ukraine, and Uzbekistan.

2. The terms "Russia" and "Russian Federation" are used interchangeably and refer to the same country.

3. Conceptual and measurement problems plague the GDP data (see box 1.1). However, these problems do not modify the qualitative thrust of the statements presented here.

4. These estimates are based on 1993 purchasing power parity rates (World Bank 2000a).

5. The agenda of accession to the European Union looms large for countries in Central and Eastern Europe. The World Bank has been engaged in a major project that examines country-specific and subregional issues arising from European Union accession. The principal outputs of the project are listed in the bibliographic guide; therefore, that subject will not be covered in this report.

6. Kornai (1986) introduced the term soft budget constraint (the opposite of a hard budget constraint) to characterize the environment faced by state enterprises in Hungary in the 1980s.

7. The analysis is based on the assumption that data for small enterprises can be used to approximate new enterprises. The approximation is not accurate inasmuch as the set of small enterprises includes small old enterprises. Annex 4.1 presents an upper bound for the error committed by this assumption in the CSB countries. While the estimate for the upper bound is substantial in 1995, it shrinks significantly under reasonable assumptions about the mortality rate of enterprises by 1998, the year for most of the data in this report. The terms "new enterprises" and "small enterprises" are henceforth used interchangeably.

8. Annex 4.2 describes the circumstances under which comparisons based on labor productivity (for which data are available) correspond to comparisons based on total factor productivity, which is the relevant concept for this report.

Part 1

The First Decade in Transition

1

How Did Transition Economies Perform?

The countries of the Europe and Central Asia region, in the first 10 years of transition, displayed some common trends and some significant variations. These variations were most evident between the Central and Southeastern Europe and the Baltics (CSB) and those countries in the Commonwealth of Independent States (CIS)—and within these two groups.

Output Fell Sharply

The trend in real gross domestic product (GDP) for the CSB matches, at least qualitatively, what was expected at the onset of the transition (figure 1.1). There was a sharp initial fall, followed by a fast recovery and then sustained growth at levels determined by factor accumulation and increases in productivity (figure 1.2). Even for these countries, though, the initial fall was larger than anticipated.[1]

The output decline was far deeper and longer in the newly independent countries of the CIS, particularly with the incipient recovery in 1997 derailed by the fiscal-financial crisis in the Russian Federation the next year.

Only now is there evidence of growth being restored in this group of countries. The magnitude and duration of the transition recession was, for all countries, comparable to that for developed countries during the Great Depression, and for most of them it was much worse (table 1.1). The CIS had an average of 6.5 years of declining output, resulting in the loss of half the initial level of measured output. Even at the end of the decade, the CIS had recovered only 63 percent of its starting GDP values (but see also Aslund 2001).

Poland had the shortest and mildest recession: a 6 percent drop in production over two years. The three Baltic countries had the longest (5–6 years) and deepest (35–51 percent) recessions among the CSB. In this, they are much closer to the average of the CIS than to other CSB countries. In the CIS Armenia, Georgia, and Moldova saw the steepest declines—Georgia, an astonishing 80 percent fall in output, largely a result of the long internal turmoil—while Belarus and Uzbekistan had mild declines.

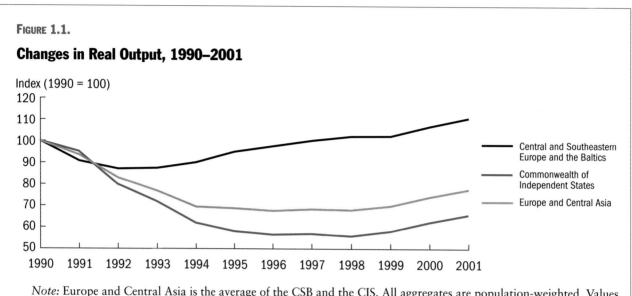

FIGURE 1.1.

Changes in Real Output, 1990–2001

Index (1990 = 100)

Note: Europe and Central Asia is the average of the CSB and the CIS. All aggregates are population-weighted. Values for 2001 are projected.

Source: World Bank country office data.

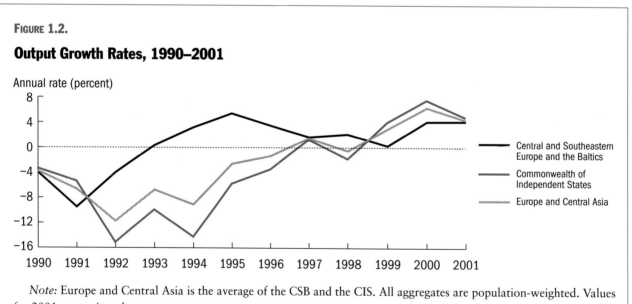

FIGURE 1.2.

Output Growth Rates, 1990–2001

Annual rate (percent)

Note: Europe and Central Asia is the average of the CSB and the CIS. All aggregates are population-weighted. Values for 2001 are projected.

Source: World Bank country office data.

The transition recession is now over—Ukraine, the only country with 10 consecutive years of output decline, registered growth in 2000. However, the recovery has not been smooth in all countries. Three CSB countries (Bulgaria, the Czech Republic, and Romania) had at least two years of output decline after their initial recovery. Four others had one-year recessions: Albania in 1997, as the collapse of a pyramid scheme led to a financial crisis and civil disturbances, and Croatia, Estonia, and Lithuania in 1999, largely because of the Russia crisis in August 1998.

Transition—The First Ten Years:
Analysis and Lessons for Eastern Europe and the Former Soviet Union

Errata

1. The last column of Table 1.1, page 5, misstates Real GDP 2000 for four countries. The correct data for those four countries are as follows:

Countries	Consecutive years of output decline	Cumulative output decline (percent)	Real GDP, 2000 (1990 = 100)
Poland	2	6	144
Romania	3	21	82
Slovak Republic	4	23	105
Slovenia	3	14	120

2. The horizontal scale in Figure 8.1, page 85, should go from 0 to 10, not 0 to 100 (that is, the numbers should read: 0 2 4 6 8 10).

TABLE 1.1.

The Transition Recession

Countries	Consecutive years of output decline	Cumulative output decline (percent)	Real GDP, 2000 (1990 = 100)
CSB[a]	*3.8*	*22.6*	*106.5*
Albania	3	33	110
Bulgaria	4	16	81
Croatia	4	36	87
Czech Republic	3	12	99
Estonia	5	35	85
Hungary	4	15	109
Latvia	6	51	61
Lithuania	5	44	67
Poland	2	6	112
Romania	3	21	144
Slovak Republic	4	23	82
Slovenia	3	14	105
CIS[a]	*6.5*	*50.5*	*62.7*
Armenia	4	63	67
Azerbaijan	6	60	55
Belarus	6	35	88
Georgia	5	78	29
Kazakhstan	6	41	90
Kyrgyz Republic	6	50	66
Moldova	7	63	35
Russian Federation	7	40	64
Tajikistan	7	50	48
Turkmenistan	8	48	76
Ukraine	10	59	43
Uzbekistan	6	18	95
Output decline during the Great Depression, 1930–34			
France	3	11	n.a.
Germany	3	16	n.a.
United Kingdom	2	6	n.a.
United States	4	27	n.a.

n.a. Not applicable.

a. Simple average, except for the index of 1990 GDP, which shows population-weighted averages.

Source: World Bank country office data; Maddison (1982).

Industry Shrank—Services Grew

Both the CSB and CIS started the transition with a much larger industrial sector and a much smaller service sector than market economies with comparable per capita incomes. During the transition, the industrial sector shrank, falling to about a third of the economy, and the share of services grew to about half (table 1.2). Perhaps less expected, the increase in services in the CIS took place at the expense of industry and agriculture, which both declined by about 9 percent of GDP. These sectoral shifts and the decline in total output mean that output in agriculture and manufacturing is now 40–45 percent of its pretransition level.

Private Enterprises Overtook the State Sector

The most basic transformation was moving resources from the state to the private sector. In 1999 the private sector in most countries in the region produced more than half of GDP (table 1.3). The share was much larger, more than

TABLE 1.2.

Composition of Output, 1990–91 and 1997–98

	Percentage of GDP		
Regions and periods	*Agriculture*	*Industry*	*Services*
CSB			
1990–91	13.7	45.1	41.2
1997–98	13.9	33.0	53.1
CIS			
1990–91	27.5	39.7	32.8
1997–98	18.7	31.2	50.1

Source: World Bank country office data.

TABLE 1.3.

Private Sector Growth, 1990s

	Percentage of GDP		
Countries	*1990*	*1994*	*1999*
CSB	*11*	*50*	*68*
Czech Republic	12	65	80
Estonia	10	55	75
Hungary	18	55	80
Romania	17	40	60
CIS	*10*	*20*	*50*
Armenia	12	40	60
Belarus	5	15	20
Russian Federation	5	50	70

Source: EBRD (2000).

70 percent, for such advanced reformers as the Czech Republic, Estonia, and Hungary. In view of the rapid growth of GDP in the CSB in recent years and the slow privatization of large state enterprises, the increase in share testifies to a dramatic increase in new private sector activity. (The role of new enterprises in promoting economic growth is discussed in part 2.)

Exports Rose—Moving Toward Industrial Countries

Countries more advanced in their recovery have been more successful in increasing their exports and reorienting them to the industrial countries. However, even in countries whose output did not grow between 1993 and 1998, such as Moldova, Russia, and Ukraine, real exports increased (table 1.4).

Important in the recovery of output was direct investment from abroad. These flows are important not only as a source of capital and new technology to modernize industries and extract natural resources, but also as a signal of confidence in the transition to a market economy. During 1996–99 more than US$70 billion in direct investment came to the region, most of it to the CSB (table 1.5). In the CIS foreign direct investment was largely confined to the energy-rich countries, with Azerbaijan, Kazakhstan, and Russia receiving 75 percent of the total. Russia's share was even lower than several of the CIS countries' shares, despite the considerably greater size of its economy and resource endowment.

Poverty Increased Sharply

The foregoing discussion suggests that the initial fall in output may overestimate the decline in living standards during the transition (box 1.1). However, the period was still one of extreme hardship for many people (World Bank 2000b). Although extreme poverty is still lower in the transition economies than in other developing countries, it increased sharply during the decade (table 1.6).[2] In 1998 one of every 20 people in the transition economies had per capita incomes below US$1 a day, up from fewer than one in 60 a decade before. Moreover, the increase

TABLE 1.4.

Export Growth and Destination, 1990s

(percent)

Countries	Real export growth 1993–98	Share of exports to industrial countries 1992–93	Share of exports to industrial countries 1998–99
CSB	8.8	35.8	67.5
Albania	22.0	62.9	94.1
Bulgaria	4.3	55.1	59.0
Czech Republic	10.4	29.9	69.3
Estonia	10.8	25.9	71.3
Hungary	11.1	67.4	81.5
Macedonia, FYR	7.3	22.2	65.5
Poland	12.9	71.6	75.5
Romania	8.7	44.3	71.0
Slovak Republic	6.9	15.9	59.2
Slovenia	5.7	33.7	70.7
CIS	3.2	28.0	29.0
Armenia	−8.6	9.4	34.9
Azerbaijan[a]	14.0	4.2	20.0
Belarus	−3.2	15.3	11.0
Georgia[a]	10.3	2.3	25.9
Kazakhstan	3.4	43.8	29.6
Kyrgyz Republic	−2.4	24.7	44.0
Moldova	4.8	6.2	31.3
Russian Federation	4.7	59.3	49.4
Ukraine	5.8	18.1	23.3

a. 1995–98.

Source: World Bank and International Monetary Fund databases.

TABLE 1.5.

Main Recipients of Foreign Direct Investment, 1992–99

Countries	1992–95 US$ millions	1992–95 Percentage of GDP	1996–99 US$ millions	1996–99 Percentage of GDP
CSB	21,091	0.5	50,558	3.3
Czech Republic	4,821	2.9	10,104	4.6
Estonia	647	3.9	1,050	5.2
Hungary	9,399	5.7	6,979	3.8
Poland	2,540	0.6	17,096	2.9
CIS	8,272	1.0	22,001	2.5
Azerbaijan	237	4.2	3,222	20.9
Kazakhstan	2,357	2.7	4,971	6.4
Russian Federation	3,965	0.3	8,412	0.7
Turkmenistan	427	3.5	334	3.0

Note: Shares of GDP are period averages of medians for the group.

Source: World Bank staff estimates and country statistical office data.

Box 1.1.

Limits of GDP Statistics for Transition Economies

Estimating GDP and using it as an indicator of living standards have some well-recognized problems. These range from data collection and aggregation issues to the omission of nonmarketed goods (pollution and family services) and depletions of exhaustible resources. Official GDP also has special limits as a welfare indicator for transition economies, particularly when comparing output performance to the pretransition period. These limits fall into three groups: index number problems, omission of informal activities, and effects of the changes on the composition of output.

Real GDP is an aggregate index constructed by weighting the outputs of individual products according to their respective prices. To be precise, the aggregation is done using value added (that is, the output price minus the cost of intermediate inputs) rather than prices. When relative prices change greatly—from transition economies opening to external trade, liberalizing domestic prices, and suffering the initial hyper-inflation—the estimated weights based on these prices can differ greatly between periods, making the calculated change in "real" output very sensitive to the base period for the aggregation. Moreover, the standard relations among different indexes do not hold when the initial prices are not good indicators of either the opportunity cost of production (say, because of artificially low energy prices) or the value to consumers (say, because of generalized shortages, rationing, and queuing). The net effect of these factors is not clear, but they do reduce confidence that the initial changes in output are accurate measures of changes in welfare. Eliminating queuing, for example, with the same amount of real output clearly improves welfare. However, the increase in the relative price of consumer goods (say, for housing and utilities) means that the same overall "real output" could be associated with lower real aggregate consumption and welfare.

The collapse of central planning meant that its statistical system became inadequate to measure real economic activity, particularly that coming from the private sector. This, compounded by the need to go from net material product to GDP, which includes services, meant that official output statistics did not capture the rapid growth of the informal sector. Subsequently, tax evasion and pressure from regulations and public sector bureaucracy provided incentives to operate business in the informal economy. Estimates of the size of the informal sector, using various methods, suggest that its share of GDP varies enormously across the region, from 6 to 60 percent of GDP.

In addition, during the transition there were sharp changes in the composition of output, reducing the proportion of goods from which consumers derived little (current or future) value, such as military output, low-productivity capital goods, and poor quality consumer goods. These qualitative factors place additional limits to the usefulness of aggregate output as a measure of changes in the population's standard of living.

TABLE 1.6.

Average Poverty Rates, 1990 and 1998

(percent)

Regions	Population living on less than US$1 a day	
	1990	1998
Eastern Europe and Central Asia	1.5	5.1
East Asia and Pacific	28.2	15.3
Latin America and the Caribbean	16.8	15.6
Middle East and North Africa	2.4	1.9
South Asia	43.8	40.0
Sub-Saharan Africa	47.0	46.4
Total	20.0	17.1

Source: World Bank data.

in poverty was much larger and more persistent than many expected at the start of the process. Even in the most successful countries—such as Poland, where poverty came down steadily from its peak in 1994—poverty rates were still higher in 1998 than in 1991 (World Bank 2000b).

Poverty increased not just because of the fall in output, but because of greater inequality in the distribution of income. Inequality increased in all transition economies, with great variation across the region (table 1.7). In some cases, the increase was modest—as in Hungary, where the Gini coefficient for per capita income rose from 0.21 in 1987 to only 0.25 a decade later. Even in the Czech Republic and Slovenia, where inequality rose more, the distribution of income remains fairly egalitarian. Yet in the CIS and elsewhere, the increases in inequality have been unprecedented. In Armenia, Russia, Tajikistan, and Ukraine, the level of inequality as measured by Gini coefficients has nearly doubled.

Notes

1. For example, one of the most authoritative early reports on the state of the socialist economies, *A Study of the Soviet Economy* (IMF and others 1991), anticipated an early recession that would end by mid-decade at the latest (or earlier, under a "radical reforms" scenario). The report projected an annual average growth rate for the 1990s of 1.1 percent (3.3 percent under the radical reform scenario), which only two countries, Poland and Slovenia, were able to achieve.

2. International comparisons of poverty rates are fraught with problems of estimation and interpretation. In transition economies in Europe and Central Asia, harsh winters, deteriorating housing stocks, utilities designed for pretransition conditions, subsidized energy prices, and similar conditions mean that families with US$2 a day are likely to have a lower standard of living than families with the same income in other regions. Furthermore, incomes do not always match people's assessment of their economic welfare, which tends to depend also on their deprivation relative to other people and their previous condition.

TABLE 1.7.

Changes in Inequality during the Transition, Various Years

Countries	Gini coefficient of income per capita		
	1987–90	*1993–94*	*1996–98*
CSB	*0.23*	*0.29*	*0.33*
Bulgaria	0.23	0.38	0.41
Croatia	0.36	—	0.35
Czech Republic	0.19	0.23	0.25
Estonia	0.24	0.35	0.37
Hungary	0.21	0.23	0.25
Latvia	0.24	0.31	0.32
Lithuania	0.23	0.37	0.34
Poland	0.28	0.28	0.33
Romania	0.23	0.29	0.30
Slovenia	0.22	0.25	0.30
CIS[a]	*0.28*	*0.36*	*0.46*
Armenia	0.27	—	0.61
Belarus	0.23	0.28	0.26
Georgia	0.29	—	0.43
Kazakhstan	0.30	0.33	0.35
Kyrgyz Republic	0.31	0.55	0.47
Moldova	0.27	—	0.42
Russian Federation	0.26	0.48	0.47
Tajikistan	0.28	—	0.47
Turkmenistan	0.28	0.36	0.45
Ukraine	0.24	—	0.47

— Not available.

a. Median of countries with data.

Source: World Bank (2000b).

2

Explaining Variation in Output Performance

The search for explanations of economic outcomes—causes, differences in magnitude, variations in speed and sustainability—has spawned a large literature. The explanations focus on the characteristics of countries at the beginning of transition, the shocks emanating from the breakdown of the central planning system, the dissolution of the Soviet Union, wars and civil strife, and the policies to facilitate the transition. The political economy of post-socialist transition has also been examined to explain why economies may be trapped in situations of partial reform—in a no man's land between plan and market, where the early gainers from reform vigorously oppose further progress toward a market economy.

Did Initial Conditions Affect Performance?

Several characteristics of the countries at the start of transition may have affected economic performance over the past decade: geography (such as endowment of natural resources and the proximity to Western markets), years spent under central planning, and the nature of economic development under socialism (such as the extent of overindustrialization, military output, and repressed inflation).

In testing for the influence of initial conditions on the economic performance of transition economies, this report used the indicators developed by de Melo, Denizer, and Gelb (1996) aggregated into three categories: structure, distortions, and institutions.[1]

Structure encompasses such variables as the share of industry, the degree of urbanization, the share of trade with the socialist block, the richness of the natural resource endowment, and the initial income. These can be described as follows:

- *Share of industry in GDP*. This share was high across the region because trade, financial services, and business and consumer services were repressed in the centrally planned economies.
- *Degree of urbanization*. This indicator is related to the level of development as higher-income countries are generally more urbanized. The proportion of people in urban areas in 1990 ranged

from around 70 percent (Estonia, Latvia, Russia) to around 30 percent (Albania, Kyrgyz Republic, Tajikistan).

- *Trade dependence.* High trade dependence on other communist countries (measured by the ratio of Council of Mutual Economic Assistance exports and imports to GDP) reflected the level of industrialization under central planning, which favored large plants and regional interdependence.[2] Inter-republic flows were especially large for the smaller republics of the Soviet Union, which had little trade outside the area.
- *Natural resource endowment.* Several countries in the region—Azerbaijan, Kazakhstan, Russia, and Turkmenistan—have rich but underdeveloped deposits of oil and gas. This gave them the potential for rapid growth, but required large investments to make production and transportation possible. Some energy exporters have tended to delay reforms—with deleterious effects on growth.
- *Income.* Incomes (in 1989 dollars adjusted for purchasing power parity) were generally higher in Central Europe and the European part of the Soviet Union, ranging from US$1,400 per capita in Albania to US$9,200 in Slovenia.

Distortions in the economy refer to such factors as repressed inflation, black market exchange rates, trade shocks arising from the dissolution of the Soviet Union, the extent of prior economic reform within the centrally planned system, and the degree of economic stagnation prior to the transition.

- *Repressed inflation.* Most transition economies had repressed inflation, measured here as the difference between the increase in real wages and real GDP from 1987 to 1990. This index was high for the Soviet Union, propelled by the federal government's gradual weakening of control over wages and regional budgets associated with the partial liberalization of the Gorbachev reforms.
- *Black market exchange rates.* This variable is defined as the difference between the black market exchange rate and the official exchange rate, indicating the rationing of foreign

exchange as well as a subsidy to imports and tax on exports. For the Soviet Union, the black market exchange rate reached as high as 1,800 percent in 1990.

- *Terms of trade loss for the CIS.* Trade flows within the Council of Mutual Economic Assistance took place at administrative prices that were not directly linked for the most part to world prices. This meant large changes in the terms of trade after trade was liberalized. The indicator measures the terms-of-trade loss as a share of GDP, as calculated by David Tarr (1994). Small energy importers, such as Moldova and the Baltic states, suffered the largest proportional losses (more than 10 percent of GDP). Countries that were net energy exporters generally had gains.
- *Reform history.* Some countries (Hungary, Poland, Federal Republic of Yugoslavia, and to a lesser extent, Bulgaria) introduced some elements of market-based reforms before the collapse of the Soviet Union. The indicator capturing reform history is the World Bank's Index of Liberalization in 1989 (de Melo, Denizer, and Gelb 1996).
- *Pretransition growth rate.* Looking at the average growth in 1985–89, the more mature countries stagnated in the late 1980s, while the poorest countries on average had higher growth.

Institutions encompass such variables as years under central planning, location in relation to Western markets, and experience with nationhood.

- *Market memory.* Some countries could draw on their market experience before the Soviet period in the design of an institutional-legal framework supporting markets at the start of the transition.
- *Location.* Countries in Central Europe, particularly those bordering on the West, had more extensive trade links with market economies and enterprises and institutions were more exposed to competitive pressures. Individuals had more freedom of travel, allowing more exposure to Western markets.
- *New states.* Countries with little experience as independent nation states may have had

more difficulty creating efficient political institutions and achieving political consensus.

External Economic Shocks Delayed Recovery

The onset of transition was accompanied by severe shocks. The collapse of the institutional and technological links of the Soviet centrally planned system disrupted the supply of inputs for production and the delivery of outputs, posing new challenges for enterprises. The loss of budget transfers from the center and the elimination of subsidized energy imports were severe blows, particularly to some of the newly independent states of the CIS. The broader external economic environment was also less favorable in the 1990s, and the transition thus coincided with lower growth rates in other developing countries.[3]

The various financial crises of the 1990s—Mexico, East Asia, and particularly Russia—also contributed to delaying or interrupting the recovery of output (box 2.1). War and civil strife—in Armenia, Azerbaijan, and Tajikistan in 1992–94, in Georgia and Moldova in 1992, and in Croatia and FYR Macedonia in 1991–94—took a major toll on lives, infrastructure, and the state, undermining the political consensus on reforms needed for successful transition. (The political economy of reform in war-torn countries is examined in part 3 of this volume.)

Policies—Do They Matter?

The shift from planned to market economies is a social and economic transformation of unprecedented scale. History offers no time-tested

---

Box 2.1.

The Regional Impact of the Global Financial Crisis and Recovery

The global financial crisis, and particularly its spread to Russia in mid-1998, had a big effect on the other transition economies in the region. For many countries the first effect was disrupted trade with Russia—as demand contracted and trade finance and payments system arrangements were interrupted. CIS countries, such as Armenia, Azerbaijan, Kazakhstan, Tajikistan, and Ukraine, saw their exports to Russia decline up to 70 percent in the nine months after the crisis. The global crisis also deepened the recession in Western Europe, hurting the export performance of countries in Central and Eastern Europe. Mounting unemployment in Russia and administrative controls to stem capital flight severely curtailed workers' remittances from Russia, whose real value also declined as the ruble depreciated. This was particularly damaging for Russia's smaller neighbors. Between 1997 and 1999 Russian transfers abroad fell from US$771 million to US$493 million. Russian foreign direct investment abroad shrank from US$2.6 billion in 1997 to US$1 billion in 1998.

The crisis made foreign financing scarce and expensive. Net inflows of private debt finance to the region fell by 50 percent between 1998 and 1999 to US$5.8 billion. This was only partly offset by the increase in net official lending, from US$1.3 billion to US$2.2 billion. For many countries privatization prospects were dampened. Despite initial fears, however, net foreign direct investment and portfolio equity flows actually increased in 1998 and 1999 over 1997.

The crisis exposed vulnerabilities in the financial sector of most countries, even those implementing strong adjustment programs before the crisis. As the crisis hit exporters and industrialists across the region, local banks and other lending institutions saw their portfolios deteriorate. In Belarus and Latvia, with a high share of Russian assets in the balance sheets of banks, there was a direct impact on bank portfolios because the market value of those assets collapsed. Across the region, many banks (for example in Ukraine) held large amounts of nonindexed government debt and suffered capital losses as market interest rates rose with the flight of foreign capital. Some banks also had foreign exchange exposures that became more difficult to handle as local currencies depreciated.

The severity of the crisis depended on the extent of economic interdependence with Russia and the policy response to the crisis. In general, the contractions and disruptions quickly translated into less economic activity and more unemployment. In many countries unemployment was already high before the crisis, and social safety nets were incapable of dealing with more unemployment and falling real incomes. As a result, poverty generally worsened. In Moldova, for example, the poverty rate increased from 35 percent of the population in mid-1997 to 46 percent in end-1998, and to 56 percent in mid-1999.

Since mid-1999 the massive real devaluation of the ruble and higher oil prices have fueled a rapid recovery of exports and economic activity in Russia, helped by world demand growth. Oil prices are expected to remain firm in the near term, as are prices for metals and raw materials. However, exporters of food and beverages are likely to face continued deterioration in their terms of trade.

blueprints. Although the specific design of policies, their sequencing, and their speed of implementation are still subject to debate, there was a broad consensus that reforms should include:

- Macroeconomic stabilization
- Price and trade liberalization
- Imposition of hard budget constraints on banks and enterprises
- Enabling environment for private sector development
- Reform of the tax system and restructuring of public expenditure

- Legal and judicial reform
- Reform of public sector institutions.

The question of whether these reform policies matter can be tested against the alternative hypothesis that output levels and annual changes in those levels were determined primarily by initial conditions and external economic shocks, as described earlier.

The extent of economic policy reform has been measured in a liberalization index developed by the World Bank to quantify progress in the transition to a market economy.[4] This index measures reforms needed to make markets the main mechanism for allocating resources, such as eliminating central planning and mandated allocations through government orders and creating conditions to allow private production. The index also covers reforms to ensure the efficient functioning of markets, such as stabilizing the macroeconomic environment, liberalizing the trade regime, and pursuing procompetition policies. The index ranges from zero to one, with zero representing an unreformed, centrally planned economy, and one denoting the standards of a market economy (figure 2.1). In 1998 the index was the highest for countries in Central Europe and the Baltics and the lowest for countries such as Belarus, Turkmenistan, and Uzbekistan, which had yet to embark on a course of reform.

A substantial literature uses cross-country statistical analysis of the transition from 1990 to 1999 to demonstrate that better policies are associated—and significantly so—with higher annual growth of GDP in Central and Eastern Europe and the CIS, even when controlling for the effects of initial conditions and external economic shocks (see annex 2.1 for a summary of the main findings of this literature). The analysis allows for considerable variation in the nature of the relationship between policies and growth. One hypothesis suggests that a minimum critical mass of reforms needs to be in place before economic reforms have the desired effects on performance. Below this threshold, it is possible that additional reforms could have a negative impact on output—that is, a classic J-shaped response of output to policy reform.

In this view, implementing a few limited reforms could disrupt production in state enterprises

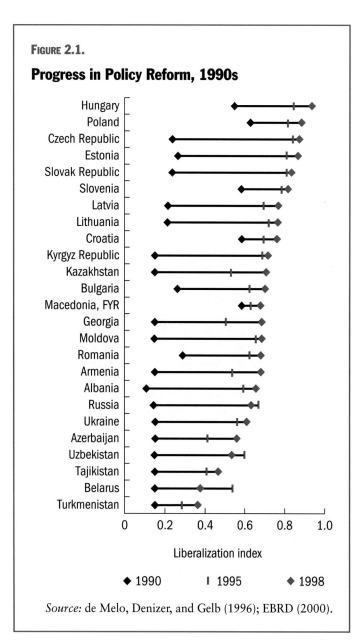

FIGURE 2.1.

Progress in Policy Reform, 1990s

Liberalization index

♦ 1990 | 1995   ♦ 1998

Source: de Melo, Denizer, and Gelb (1996); EBRD (2000).

without generating an attractive climate for restructuring and new investment, resulting in lower output. One empirical test of this hypothesis (de Melo and Gelb 1996) finds that when countries have made only limited progress in reform (defined as a score of less than 0.4 on the liberalization index) additional reforms actually have a negative impact on growth. The response turns positive once a minimum threshold of economic reform has been reached. This suggests that there are important complementarities among elements of a market-oriented reform program that have a decisive impact on the relationship between reforms and growth.

Alternatively, it might take a long time for policy reforms to exert their full impact on output, with the initially adverse consequences in the short-run giving way to beneficial effects later on. The empirical results reported here imply that policy reforms affect output growth over an extended period. Our analysis suggests that this "time lag" in the impact of reforms on performance can be estimated at approximately three years (the hypothesis that the effect is entirely contemporaneous can be strongly rejected; see Selowsky and Martin 1998).

There also are significant differences between the CIS and the other transition economies in the nature of the response of output to policy. A particular difference is on the immediate (contemporaneous) impact of reforms, which is negative in the CIS and positive in Central Europe. This means that liberalization has an up-front "investment cost" in the CIS countries, consistent with greater economic distortions at the start of their transitions. A higher share of negative value activities required vast reallocation of resources after liberalization in the CIS. These countries also faced greater obstacles to achieving that reallocation, such as physical size, distance to external markets, large and inefficient company-town enterprises in isolated regions, and greater political and constitutional turmoil inhibiting investment.

What Initial Conditions Matter and When Do They Matter?

There are reasons to expect that the factors explaining the initial output collapse are not entirely the same as those determining later economic performance. Some developments accompanying the onset of transition, such as the breakdown of payment systems, are likely to have had a stronger impact on the initial period of the transition. Similarly, the effects of some unfavorable initial conditions, such as repressed inflation, are likely to dissipate over time.

In our statistical analysis, the unbundling of initial conditions into structure, distortions, and institutions provides a more nuanced answer to the question of the importance of initial conditions versus policy reforms in explaining the recession and recovery periods of the transition experience (annex 2.2). First, initial conditions are more important factors in explaining the differences across countries during the initial period of output decline (1990–94) than over the full 10 years of transition. The three (aggregate) indicators of initial conditions defined earlier explain 51 percent of the variation in the average rate of growth across countries during 1990–94, but only 41 percent of the variance in average growth during the decade.

Second, our results suggest that different types of initial conditions were more significant in the early and later stages of transition. Initial *distortions* in the economy—including factors such as severe repressed inflation or high black market exchange rates and absence of pretransition policy reforms—are most closely associated with lower performance during the first years of transition. Initial *institutions*—including factors such as absence of "market memory," measured by the number of years under socialism, and general development of national institutions, as determined by the length of prior experience of nationhood—are more strongly associated with variations in subsequent performance.

Third, while initial conditions have a greater impact on the initial collapse of output than on the subsequent recovery, the impact of policies becomes stronger as the transition progresses—although it is still significant in the early stages. Indeed, policy variables are statistically significant in both periods, implying that market-oriented policy reforms not only speed economic recovery and promote growth in the medium-term, but also mitigate the effects of the transition recession in the short term.

What If Policies Themselves Are Endogenous?

Policies, in general, are endogenous. The choice might depend on initial conditions that might influence the possibility of policy consensus behind reform (de Melo and others 1997). They might be influenced by the desire to reclaim nationhood after the dismantling of the Soviet Union. Alternatively, what is feasible at one stage might be partly determined by previous policy decisions. For example, private monopolies that emerged from privatization at an early stage of reform might attempt to block entry or resist a regulatory framework. Or new, small entrepreneurs may try to press for faster reforms in property rights and in the court system.

The literature reports some limited success in finding correlates to policy reform, such as the initial and contemporaneous level of political freedom (Dethier, Ghanem, and Zoli 1999; de Melo and others 1997). Part 3 of this report describes how choices about the structure of the political system can shape the adoption of economic reforms. An important result from the cross-country evidence is that policy reforms remain strongly significant in explaining output performance even when policies are taken as endogenous (that is, when output growth and policies are jointly determined in a simultaneous equation model; see de Melo and others 1997).

Does the Speed of Reform Matter?

The relationship between the speed of reform and economic growth has been the subject of controversy. Some economists argued for advancing reforms in all areas as fast as possible; others criticized such a strategy as imposing unnecessarily high cost. The most interesting part of the debate focuses on the sequencing of policies—on the relative speed of different types of reform. Advocates of moving fast in areas amenable to rapid reform argue that the synergies among different components—for example, privatization together with liberalization of prices and trade—may generate enough gains and winners to maintain the reform momentum. The need to take advantage of windows of opportunity is also cited as important in that decision.

By contrast, advocates of slower reform point out that going ahead with reforms that can be implemented quickly—"stroke of the pen" reforms—without waiting for those that take more time, such as the creation of institutions that support markets, significantly reduces the benefits of these reforms. The loss could be so severe as to generate output losses and also lead to the creation of interest groups opposing those reforms requiring more time. Some of these issues are reviewed on part 3.

The amalgamation of different types of policy reforms into a single aggregate indicator prevents statistical cross-country analysis from directly shedding light on the desirability of progressing rapidly along all dimensions of reform. Some indirect evidence is provided by the finding that output in each year is significantly associated with the level of policy reforms achieved up to that year—that is, with cumulative policy reform. So the quicker a high level of liberalization is reached and sustained the sooner the economy can attain higher growth.[5]

These results are best seen as a broad-brush characterization of the main contours of transition. They do not provide the full story of the transition. Although policies and initial conditions account for more than half the variability of output growth across countries and years, they still leave substantial room for other factors influencing growth.[6] A full explanation of output performance would have to include more country-specific factors—as well as shocks and other omitted factors—and a detailed analysis of individual countries or smaller groups of countries. This is done in the rest of this report.

Annex 2.1. Summary of Cross-Country Empirical Literature on Growth in Transition Economies

Aslund, Anders, Peter Boone, and Simon Johnson. 1996. "How to Stabilize: Lessons from Post-Communist Countries." *Brookings Papers on Economic Activity* 26(1): 217–313.

This paper finds differences in the determinants of output changes during 1989–95 (no significant association with policy reforms) and end-of-period output level (liberalization and inflation significant).

Berg, Andrew, Eduardo Borensztein, Ratna Sahay, and Jeromin Zettelmeyer. 1999. "The Evolution of Output in Transition Economies: Explaining the Differences." IMF Working Paper No. WP/99/73, International Monetary Fund, Washington, D.C.

An extensive exploration of the issues in model specification with annual data for 26 countries from 1991 to 1996 (different period for a few countries). A very general initial model includes:

- Macroeconomic variables (fiscal balance, inflation, and exchange rate regime)
- Structural reforms (Liberalization Index in its three separate components, plus *interactions term* defined by multiplying the Liberalization Index by the share of the private sector in the economy)
- Initial conditions (from de Melo and others 2001, initial GDP per capita and growth, urbanization, natural resource endowment, index of initial repressed inflation or actual initial fiscal imbalance and inflation, share of agriculture, trade dependence, a measure of overindustrialization, and reforms before collapse of central planning)
- Other controls (average OECD growth, terms of trade, and dummies for war or conflict).

In addition to the large number of variables, they include first and second lag of macroeconomic variables and up to third lags of structural reform indexes. The initial conditions are also parameterized by time to allow for their impact to decline or dissipate after a period (but the precise specification and statistical tests are not published with the paper). Both the level of GDP (in logs) and the annual rate of growth are used as endogenous variables.

The initial specification contains too many variables to get significant results about effects of individual variables, but it can be used to test the hypothesis that certain categories of variables are irrelevant. Thus the model rejects strongly the hypothesis that *none* of the macroeconomic policy variables matters and/or that *none* of the structural variables matters for growth.

The initial broad specification is progressively simplified by eliminating variables with low statistical significance to arrive at two final

specifications that include 13–15 policy variables, including lags, plus the controls and initial conditions (the precise number of parameters estimated is not explicitly shown).

Some summary results: most of the variability in growth is associated with differences in policies rather than initial conditions (depending on the time-declining impact of initial conditions); the difference between CIS and Central and Eastern Europe can largely be explained by differences in policies.

Campos, Nauro F., and Fabrizio Coricelli. 2000. "Growth in Transition: What We Know, What We Don't, and What We Should." Centre for Economic Policy Research, London, United Kingdom.

The authors use the contemporaneous Liberalization Index and its components on their regressions; only one component is statistically significant. Inflation is significant (with negative effect on growth) and so is the presence of an International Monetary Fund program. Institutional variables are significant and positive (rule of law and quality of bureaucracy). Initial conditions are measured as the principal components of a set of reasonable-sounding indicators (dependence on Council of Mutual Economic Assistance trade, repressed inflation, and overindustrialization).

de Melo, Martha, Cevdet Denizer, and Alan Gelb. 1996. "From Plan to Market: Patterns of Transition." World Bank, Washington, D.C.

de Melo, Martha, Cevdet Denizer, Alan Gelb, and Stoyan Tenev. 1997. "Circumstance and Choice: The Role of Initial Conditions and Policies in Transition Economies." World Bank, Washington, D.C.

These are two influential papers that introduced the measures of policy reform and initial conditions most widely used in the literature. The first paper introduced the Liberalization Index, defined as a weighted average of policy reforms in three areas: internal markets, external markets, and privatization and private sector entry. The paper's empirical analysis emphasizes "patterns of transition" rather than models of policy response and statistical test of hypotheses.

The second paper focuses on the role of initial conditions, for which the authors calculated a set of 12 indicators widely used in subsequent work (initial income, urbanization, natural resource endowment, location, pretransition reforms, initial repressed inflation, overindustrialization with respect to Chenery's "norms", shares of trade with Council of Mutual Economic Assistance, black market rate for foreign exchange, new versus old states, and years under central planning). The large number of indicators is reduced to a more manageable set of two by the method of principal components. Thus the transformed variables are defined as linear combinations of the initial variables in a way that preserves the maximum of their variability. This is useful for statistical power, but makes it more difficult to determine *what* initial conditions really matter.

The authors estimate a model where growth (in 1992–95) is explained by initial conditions, policy reforms (measured by the aggregate Liberalization Index or its cumulative value), and a war dummy variable. The authors also estimate a simultaneous equations model for growth and the Liberalization Index (with liberalization policies determined by initial conditions plus a war dummy and an index of political freedom), but find that there is negligible simultaneity bias on the growth equation. Both initial conditions and the Liberalization Index are quite significant in the growth equation. The paper also presents the "growth patterns" model discussed below, augmented by the two variables for the initial conditions.

de Melo, Martha, and Alan Gelb. 1996. "A Comparative Analysis of Twenty Transition Economies in Europe and Asia." *Post-Soviet Geography and Economics* 37(5): 265–85.

The authors discuss "patterns of transition" for the 26 European and Central Asian countries plus China and Vietnam. The exogenous variables are the Cumulative Liberalization Index (CLI), plus dummy variables for regional tension and for Central and Eastern Europe. However, the paper postulates a model in which there is *discontinuity* when CLI = 0.4. This is so because the authors define a "nonreform"

and a "reform" pattern of growth, and countries switch from the former to the latter when the CLI reaches 0.4 (that is, changes in CLI at lower or higher levels do not have any effect; only those getting CLI over the threshold have an impact). On the other hand, the two "patterns" are estimated with high degree of generality (with up to 13 parameters). The two resulting patterns are plausible (for example, "reform" has an initial drop in output but it is increasingly positive after the second year), and the hypothesis that they are equal (that is, that policies do not matter) can be strongly rejected.

Fischer, Stanley, Ratna Sahay, and Carlos A. Veight. 1998. "How Far is Eastern Europe from Brussels?" IMF Working Paper No. WP/98/53, International Monetary Fund, Washington, D.C.

The authors find that the Liberalization Index and stabilization variables (inflation and fiscal deficit) are significantly associated with growth. They introduced "reform time" to adjust for different starting points of the transition process in different countries.

Havrylysyhyn, Oleh, and Ron van Rooden. 1999. "Institutions Matter in Transition, but so Do Policies." Paper presented at the Fifth Dubrovnik Conference on Transition, Dubrovnic, June 1999.

The emphasis is on variables defining institutional development: "Index of Economic Freedom" from the Heritage Foundation (1994–97); indicators for democracy, rule of law, and others from the "Nations in Transit" reports from Freedom House; institutional environment from the survey for the World Bank's *World Development Report 1998/99: Knowledge for Development* (1998); and country risk ratings from "Euromoney." They follow de Melo and others (1997) on the treatment of initial conditions (the same variables are aggregated into the same two principal components). A similar aggregation approach is used to summarize the eight institutional variables into one or two principal components. One innovation is to include a simple form of time dependence for initial conditions (impact at t is b_{IC}/t) and instrumental variables (impact on t is t^*b_{IV}).

Hernandez-Cata, Ernesto, 1997. "Growth and Liberalization during the Transition from Plan to Market." *IMF Staff Papers* 44(4): 405–29.

The paper models the reallocation of capital from the old to new sector (as in Berg and others 1999). The paper confirms the significance of liberalization and stabilization, with similar impacts on the CIS and Central and Eastern Europe.

Heybey, Berta, and Peter Murrell. 1999. "The Relationship between Economic Growth and the Speed of Liberalization during Transition." *Journal of Policy Reform* 3(2): 121–37.

The authors find that average growth over the first four years of transition does not depend on the increase in the Liberalization Index over the period, after accounting for possible endogeneity of liberalization policies (the instruments used are the initial level of liberalization, share of industry, and an index of political freedom). The authors conclude that initial conditions are "much more important than policy variables."

Popov, Vladimir. 1998. "Will Russia Achieve Fast Economic Growth?" *Communist Economies and Economic Transformation* 10(4): 421–35.

Popov, Vladimir. 1999. "Shock Therapy versus Gradualism: The End of the Debate." Carleton University, Ottawa.

Castanheira, Micael, and Vladimir Popov. 1999. "Framework Paper on the Political Economy of Growth in Russia and Central and Eastern European Countries." Global Development Network, World Bank, Washington, D.C. Processed.

The authors use only the cross-section variability in the data as they take average rate of growth (over the whole sample or separate subperiods) as a dependent variable. The Liberalization Index is found significant for growth recovery (1994–98), but not for the overall period (1989–98) or the subperiods (1989–96 and 1996–98). Other control variables: war dummy and average inflation. Initial conditions are accounted for by including an Index of Initial Distortions (defense expenditures/GDP −0.03 + deviations in industrial structure and trade

openness from normal level + share of trade with FSU + share of trade with Central and Eastern Europe/3), the initial level of GDP per capita, the decline in government revenues/GDP, and shadow economy/GDP.

Selowsky, Marcelo, and Ricardo Martin. 1998. "Policy Performance and Output Growth in the Transition Economies." *American Economic Review—Papers and Proceedings* 87(2): 350–53.

The paper uses combined cross-section and time series data to test a model, allowing for a delayed impact of reforms on growth, with crude control of initial conditions (Central and Eastern Europe versus the CIS) and other factors (dummy variables for period of war or internal conflict). The Liberalization Index is found to be highly significant and to exhibit significant differences between its initial and long-term impact. There are also differences in the dynamic impact of reform in Central and Eastern Europe and the CIS.

Annex 2.2. Additional Empirical Analysis

As mentioned in the text, the authors undertook additional empirical analysis in preparation for this paper to elucidate the types of initial conditions that made a difference for country performance, as well as possible differences in the role of initial conditions and policies at different stages of the transition.

The analysis of initial conditions was based on the indicators developed by de Melo and others (1997), plus the terms of trade loss estimated by Tarr (1994). The 13 indicators were divided in three groups and then aggregated into three "synthetic" indices—initial structure, initial distortions, and initial institutions. Table A2.1 shows that the three indices "explain" (as indicated by the *R*-squared of the regressions) 51 percent of the variance on average growth across countries during the initial transition recession, and 44 percent during 1995–99.

Table A2.2 presents the results of the regression of the annual rate of growth for all countries on the Liberalization Index and initial conditions, controlling for conflicts (war dummy), allowing for a dynamic impact of policies—as in Selowsky

TABLE A2.1.

Regression of Average Growth on Initial Conditions, 1990–99

Initial conditions	Average growth, 1990–94	Average growth, 1995–99
Structure	–0.30	0.18
Distortions	1.03[a]	0.24
Institutions	0.25	0.82[a]
R-squared	0.51	0.44

a. Significant at 95 percent.
Source: Martin (2000).

TABLE A2.2.

Regression of Annual Output Growth on Policies and Initial Conditions Allowing for Differential Effects Early in Transition, 1990–99

	Endogenous variable: Annual rate of growth 1990–99	
Exogenous variable	Coefficient	t-value
Liberalization (t)	–11.01[a]	–4.08
Liberalization ($t-1$)	8.92[a]	2.60
Liberalization ($t-2$)	3.32	1.60
Liberalization (t), 1995–99[b]	8.26[a]	2.02
Liberalization ($t-1$), 1995–99[b]	–4.03	–0.71
Liberalization ($t-2$), 1995–99[b]	–2.18	–0.60
War	–11.52[a]	–5.45
Initial conditions	0.09	0.38
Initial conditions, 1990–94[c]	1.82[a]	4.50
R-squared (number of observations)	0.60	(200)
Standard error of estimate	6.89	

a. Significant at 95 percent.
b. The coefficient for these variables measured the additional effect of liberalization during 1995–99.
c. The coefficient for this variable measured the additional effect of initial conditions during 1990–94.
Source: Martin (2000).

and Martin (1998)—and for different effects during the early and late 1990s. The table shows that there are differences in the impact of policies and initial conditions in the two subperiods: liberalization policies have a stronger positive impact during 1995–99, while initial conditions have a stronger impact on the earlier period. In both cases the difference is statistically significant, as the hypothesis of equal effect in both periods is rejected at a high level of confidence.

Notes

1. The three aggregate indicators (structure, distortions, and institutions) are a linear combination of the individual components, with weights equal to their respective coefficients in a regression on average growth.

2. The Council of Mutual Economic Assistance is the free-trade area encompassing the Soviet Union and Eastern Europe.

3. Easterly (2000) shows that growth in most developing countries slowed in the past two decades. Median per capita income growth was 0 percent, compared with 2.5 percent in 1960–79. The slowdown is attributed to the deterioration in the external environment, specifically lower growth in OECD countries, particularly Europe and Japan, and higher real interest rates.

4. These indicators, developed by de Melo, Denizer, and Gelb (1996), stop in 1997. More recent work uses transition indicators of the European Bank for Reconstruction and Development, which include 1998 and 1999.

5. The usual caveats about attributing causality to regression coefficients apply. However, the coefficients still provide the best inference available from the combined experience of all transition economies.

6. For example, these two factors would allow "predicting" the rate of GDP growth only with an uncertainty band roughly 11 points wide. More technically, the estimated standard error of the regression with the percentage rate of growth as dependent variable is about 6.89, so that a two-way 90 percent confidence band would have a width of 11.37 points (1.65 times the standard error). This is an extraordinarily large number compared with variations in growth in the OECD countries.

Part 2

Policy and Institutional Challenges Ahead

3

The Quest for Growth

Countries started the transition facing common challenges. The production system was designed for the exigencies of a command economy. Much industrialization was based on cheap energy and subsidized transport. In addition, the coordination and monitoring of central planning meant few links among enterprises, with large state enterprises forming production and delivery chains of vertically integrated, bilateral monopolies or monopsonies under the aegis of branch ministries.

Opening to the world revealed productivity differences across sectors and enterprises, given the energy-intensive structure of production. In April 1992 the Russian Federation's domestic oil price was still only 3 percent of the world price. Shutting down any links in those extensive chains of production and delivery caused adverse output and employment effects to cascade through the economy. Together, changes in relative prices and dislocations of the production system meant that many enterprises subtracted rather than added value at the new prices.

All countries faced this problem at the beginning of transition. To realize the beneficial effects of liberalization, two further policy responses were required. The first was to impose market discipline on inherited enterprises—so that they would face the incentive to restructure and, in so doing, become more productive and able to compete at the new prices. Failure to do so would lead to closure. The second was to encourage the creation of new enterprises, which became possible after liberalization created the legal opportunity for private investment.

It is reasonable to assume that investment in new enterprises would be undertaken only with an expected rate of return at least equal to what could have been realized by investments in an enterprise undergoing restructuring. Since restructured enterprises are, by definition, more productive than old enterprises, this yields a productivity ranking (figure 3.1). The yardstick used here and throughout the report is to rank enterprises by labor productivity, not total factor productivity. (The circumstances under which this is broadly permissible are explored in annex 4.2.) Empirical evidence collected from a broad cross-country survey of enterprises (box 3.1) throughout the region confirms that new enterprises tend to outperform old enterprises along every dimension of performance (figure 3.2).[1]

FIGURE 3.1.

Productivity Distribution of Old, Restructured, and New Enterprises

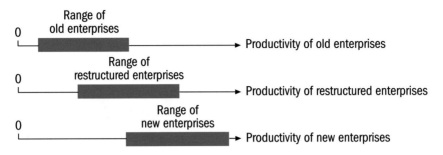

Note: The figure allows for outliers in both directions, as there is no reason why single old enterprises, everything else being equal, might not occasionally produce higher value added per employee than new enterprises, or why new enterprises might not occasionally have disappointing results.

Source: World Bank data.

Aggregate growth in the economy reflects the interplay between old enterprises in need of state support that, by absorbing more resources than they produce, reduce growth, and restructured and new enterprises, which increase it (see Ruehl and Vinogradov 2001). The pattern of growth is initially dominated by the negative contribution of old enterprises, which causes output to decline. Conditions at the beginning of transition—such as repressed inflation,

Box 3.1.

The Business Environment and Enterprise Performance Survey

The World Bank and the European Bank for Reconstruction and Development conducted a large survey of enterprises in 20 transition economies in the early summer of 1999, adding five more transition economies later that year. The survey used face-to-face interviews with enterprise owners or senior managers and was conducted by the same international survey enterprise across all the countries (with the exception of Albania and Latvia, where local survey enterprises were used). The aim of the survey was to investigate how enterprise behavior and performance were related to and affected by the quality of the business environment and the relationship between enterprises and the state. The survey posed detailed questions about the enterprises' business and competitive environment and about the different restructuring actions they had taken in the recent past. (See Hellman and others 2000 and www.worldbank.org/wbi/governance/datasets.htm for a full description of the survey.)

Sampling was random from the population of enterprises in each country, except that minimum quotas were imposed for state-owned and large enterprises. Box table A provides some basic information on the distribution by region, size, origin, sector, and location of the enterprise sample. The survey included some 125 enterprises from each of the 25 countries, with larger samples in Poland and Ukraine (almost 250 enterprises) and in Russia (more than 550 enterprises). The full sample comprises 3,954 enterprises, more than half from the Central and Eastern European region (including the Baltics) and the rest from the countries of the CIS. The sample is dominated by small and medium-size enterprises (SMEs); half of them employed fewer than 50 people, and only 8 percent employed more than 500. More than half the enterprises were newly established private enterprises, 27 percent were privatized, and the remaining 16 percent were state owned. The enterprises are divided fairly evenly between industry (52 percent) and services (48 percent), with 30 percent of enterprises from the manufacturing sector. Almost 50 percent of enterprises are located in large cities or national capitals, with the rest in small towns and rural areas.

(box continues on following page)

Box 3.1 CONTINUED

TABLE A.

Characteristics of the Business Environment and Enterprise Performance Survey Sample, 1999

			Number of enterprises	*Percent*
Region	CIS		1,866	47.2
	Central and Eastern Europe and the Baltics		2,088	52.8
Size	Small (fewer than 50 workers)		1,944	49.2
	Medium (50–500 workers)		1,690	42.8
	Large (more than 500 workers)		318	8.0
Origin	New		2,176	56.5
	Privatized		1,050	27.2
	State-owned		627	16.3
Sector	Industry	Farming	453	11.5
		Mining	33	0.8
		Manufacture	1,191	30.1
		Construction	343	8.7
		Power generation	16	0.4
		Total	*2,036*	*51.5*
	Services	Trading	541	13.7
		Retail	571	14.5
		Transport	232	5.9
		Finance	67	1.7
		Personal services	214	5.4
		Business services	245	6.2
		Communications	15	0.4
		Other	30	0.8
		Total	*1,915*	*48.5*
Location	Capital city		1,220	30.9
	Large city		704	17.8
	Town		1,694	42.8
	Rural		336	8.5

Source: Hellman and others (2000).

Given the sample size and specific quotas, the survey cannot be used to measure the number and share of new enterprises in each country. However, it can provide valuable evidence about how the performance and behavior of new enterprises differ from state-owned and privatized enterprises. It also provides an opportunity to test whether perceptions of the business environment differ systematically across different categories of enterprises. (For a full analysis of the data on small enterprises surveyed, see EBRD 1999).

multiple exchange rates, and the terms of trade losses associated with trade liberalization and the breakup of the Council of Mutual Economic Assistance trading area, which would in turn have been reflected in the inherited capital stock—were important determinants of this decline. With time, restructured and new enterprises acquire the critical mass needed to overcome the negative effects of old enterprises to generate economywide growth. The speed of this depends on policy choices. Differences in conditions at the end of communism—and in exogenous shocks and policy choices in the 1990s—put countries in vastly different circumstances today.

For many countries in the CIS—and for those in Southeastern Europe, such as Bulgaria, FYR Macedonia, Romania, and the Federal Republic of Yugoslavia, which have seen steep declines in incomes since the onset of transition—

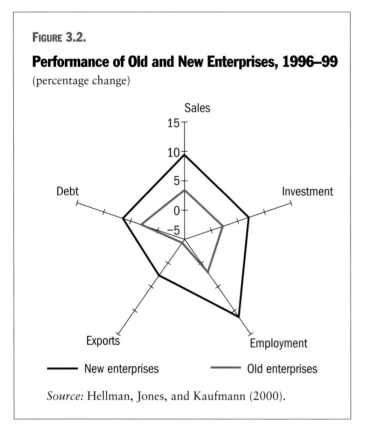

FIGURE 3.2.

Performance of Old and New Enterprises, 1996–99
(percentage change)

Source: Hellman, Jones, and Kaufmann (2000).

public goods and protecting the most vulnerable, is not enough for these countries. The advanced reformers in Central Europe and the Baltics need to consolidate the gains of the first decade of transition and address what could be called "second-generation" issues in the transition toward an effectively functioning market economy. They have to secure control over quasi-fiscal and contingent liabilities. They have to undertake reform in labor and financial markets to allow the benefits of growth to be more widely shared across the population. They also have to restructure social sector expenditures to make them fiscally more affordable without impairing the social safety net. Many of these reforms overlap with those required to join the European Union.

A Tale of Two Approaches

Looking at the assets of old, restructured, and new enterprises reveals that countries restoring sustained growth need to create a policy environment that simultaneously disciplines old enterprises (state enterprises, privatized but unrestructured enterprises, and agricultural collectives) and encourages "new" enterprises (including both greenfield investments and restructured spinoffs from newly privatized enterprises).

Discipline entails hardening budget constraints (a concept owed to Kornai 1986), introducing competition to product markets, monitoring managerial behavior to generate incentives for efficient resource use and prevent such abuse as asset stripping and tunneling (box 3.2), and providing viable exit mechanisms for inefficient enterprises. It thus forces old enterprises to release assets and labor, which then become available for more efficient reallocation to restructured and new enterprises. Old enterprises also divest themselves of social assets—such as housing, health clinics, and kindergartens—which requires shifting the locus of social protection from enterprises to local governments.

Encouragement entails reducing excessive marginal tax rates, simplifying regulatory procedures, establishing secure property rights, and providing basic infrastructure. That allows restructured and new enterprises to absorb labor

restoring sustained growth and rebuilding the state are key priorities.

Without growth it will be impossible to generate income-earning opportunities for households or to generate the resources to provide such basic public goods as a legal and judicial system, secure property rights, and basic infrastructure. Nor will it be possible to maintain investments in education and health that have been adversely affected since the onset of transition, or to put in place a social safety net targeted toward the most vulnerable. Without a functioning state there will be no capacity to provide public goods even if the resources were available.

Growth is also important for the more reform-oriented countries in Central Europe and the Baltics. Per capita incomes in the three wealthiest countries seeking accession to the European Union as a fraction of the European Union average are still only 68 percent for Slovenia, 59 percent for the Czech Republic, and 49 percent for Hungary. However, an exclusive focus on growth, while providing basic

Box 3.2.

The Problem of Tunneling

Tunneling is the legal expropriation of income and assets belonging to minority shareholders (Johnson, La Porta, Lopez-de-Silanes, and Shleifer 2000). Diverting cash flow and asset stripping are forms of tunneling. Managers usually do the tunneling and in purely private enterprises are usually acting at the behest of large or controlling shareholders. In partly state-owned enterprises, managers are usually acting by themselves or at the behest of private shareholders.

Tunneling should be distinguished from theft, which is illegal. However, if expropriation by management occurs in a fully state-owned enterprise, this is almost always illegal. Tunneling should also be distinguished from rent seeking. Rent seeking refers to the efforts of enterprises to obtain advantages through privileges or subsidies granted by the government. Rents are usually extracted from a wide cross-section of society (for example, from all the consumers of a particular product). In contrast, the primary impact of tunneling is on minority shareholders (or the state, if it is a shareholder in the enterprise), although the evidence suggests there are also negative effects on the economy as a whole.

Expropriation of shareholders has been a particular problem in some transition economies, particularly in the CIS. Some forms of tunneling were specific to the early transition, such as finding ways to legally expropriate state assets, though new forms have evolved over the decade. Nevertheless, tunneling is not a phenomenon exclusive to the transition. In the aftermath of the Asian financial crisis of 1997–98, for example, several companies are alleged to have engaged in some form of tunneling.

Why is Tunneling Legal?

Tunneling is legal for two reasons. First, there may be important loopholes in the legal protection of investor rights. Laws governing "related party" transactions are often vague or inadequate. Consider the case where company A is controlled by the managers of company B and the two companies enter into a transaction. If company A supplies inputs at above-market prices (or sells assets at artificially low prices) to company B, someone is effectively tunneling the value out of B and into A through what is known as "transfer pricing." Unless the law specifies clearly that related party transactions require full disclosure and supervision by independent parties (as in the United States), tunneling through transfer pricing is easy and legal.

Second, the courts may be unwilling or unable to apply even precise statutes. There are cases in Western Europe where courts have looked at instances of tunneling and pronounced it legal. For example, in civil law countries, if the courts cannot determine whether someone was harmed, they will often not punish an action that clearly violated a statutory provision (Johnson, La Porta, Lopez-de-Silanes, and Shleifer 2000). Most transition economies have judicial systems based largely on civil law, and judges, in such instances, may be reluctant to interpret the law as preventing tunneling in complex situations.

Tunneling can take a variety of forms. In countries with weak protection of shareholder rights, it is not uncommon for enterprises to consistently transfer small amounts of shareholder value out of companies. Such "seepage" of shareholder value is often considered an ordinary cost of doing business by investors in countries with a weak rule of law. But the evidence indicates that in environments with poor protection of shareholder rights corporate dividends are smaller, the valuation of companies is lower, and financial development is slower than in countries with stronger protection of shareholder rights (Johnson, La Porta, Lopez-de-Silanes, and Shleifer 2000). There is also some evidence that such seepage reduces the growth of and limits investment in capital-intensive sectors.

In periods of economic crisis in a context of weak investor protection, tunneling can increase substantially. If managers foresee their enterprise's demise, they have strong incentives to tunnel enterprise assets. The Russian economic crisis of 1998 reportedly triggered widespread and extreme tunneling (Johnson, Boone, Breach, and Friedman 2000). The costs of such tunneling can be enormous. If investors expect that tunneling has become widespread, the entire capital allocation process in the economy can be disrupted, seriously delaying any economic recovery. Moreover, such expectations can lead to a precipitous drop in the economic value of enterprises due to strongly negative investor sentiment.

Tunneling and Capital Flight

Theoretically, tunneling can remain purely domestic; that is, wealth can be transferred from minority shareholders to managers while remaining inside the country. Empirically, however, evidence suggests that episodes of large-scale tunneling tend to coincide with high levels of capital flight (Johnson, Boone, Breach, and Friedman 2000). There are several reasons for this correlation. The risk that existing laws permitting tunneling could be changed retrospectively creates strong incentives for holding tunneled assets abroad, out of reach of domestic authorities. Moreover, in an environment characterized by poor protection of investor rights, assets tunneled from enterprises are hardly well protected in

(box continues on following page)

Box 3.2 CONTINUED

domestic banks that suffer from the same weaknesses of the broader environment. If managers can tunnel assets freely from their own enterprises, why should they expect domestic bankers to do otherwise?

Despite the links between tunneling and capital flight, tunneling can also be used to prop up related enterprises during temporary periods of poor performance. In such cases tunneling becomes a form of cross-subsidization within a related group of companies. In environments where enterprises might have limited access to short-term credit because, for example, the banking system is weak, "propping" temporarily troubled enterprises through transfers from related companies could ease access to capital in the future. So, despite the negative consequences of tunneling, the function of propping as a backstop in insufficiently developed financial markets could explain why investors are still willing to invest in such an environment (Shleifer and Wolfenson 2000).

Increasing Vulnerability to Economic Crisis

Institutions protecting entrepreneurs against government expropriation are crucial to transition and economic development generally. A lack of protection for the property rights of entrepreneurs hampers growth.

However, to grow in an environment where investors are not fully protected against expropriation by other entrepreneurs—that is, where tunneling is common—is not impossible. The main effects of tunneling are to limit financial development and divert resources toward sectors that are not capital intensive. Nevertheless, weak investor protection and widespread tunneling do increase a country's vulnerability to economic crisis.

Note: Tunneling was first identified analytically by Jensen and Meckling (1976), who focused on the United States, where tunneling is limited. Shleifer and Vishny (1997) survey the literature through 1996.

and assets made inexpensive by the downsizing. By creating a stable and predictable business environment, the policies of encouragement generate incentives for enterprises to invest. As more and more new enterprises enter the market, an increasingly competitive environment develops. At the same time the policy environment must restrain predatory behavior by new enterprises that seek to extract special preferences from the state and, in so doing, erect barriers to competition and further entry.

The more advanced reformers in the CSB, now facing second generation issues, are much farther along in implementing an environment of discipline and encouragement. Discipline has been established, but it needs (as in Poland) to be maintained, because loss-making state enterprises in coal mining, steel, and railways still impose a costly burden on the budget. In these countries new and restructured enterprises still lead growth, but unemployment remains stubbornly high. In addition to maintaining the discipline established during the first decade of reform, the focus of encouragement for job creation in new enterprises needs to be removing bottlenecks in infrastructure and reforming labor and financial markets and the social protection system.

Discipline and Encouragement

As the case of Poland suggests, an important ingredient of market discipline is the hard budget constraint on state enterprises, together with sufficient standards of corporate governance to prevent large-scale asset stripping before privatization. It was understood that no subsidies would go to state enterprises after the beginning of 1990, but it took 18–24 months for the government's commitment to hard budget constraints to be seen as fully credible by enterprise managers. Poland's economic growth—which resumed in 1992, the earliest among the transition economies—was first due largely to better use of existing assets by enterprises spun off from state enterprises. Not until 1995 was there a big boom in domestic investment—and not until 1996, with Poland in its fifth year of growth, was there a take off in foreign direct investment.

At the same time successive governments undertook structural reforms to generate an investment climate favorable for the entry of new enterprises, in particular small and medium-size enterprises (SMEs). Like many other countries with a socialist past, Poland had a high industrial concentration, with the leading enterprise having more than 30 percent in more than 60 percent of the markets (at a three-digit level). The new enterprises signaled that product market competition would press state enterprises to become efficient. During 1990–98 the number of individual- and family-owned enterprises rose from 1.2 million to nearly 2.8 million. Similar figures held for Hungary. In both countries the share of employment and value added of new enterprises, the engines of growth, rose to 50 percent or more.

Protection and Discouragement

The disposition of assets among old, restructured, and new enterprises also provides a useful perspective on such countries as Romania and Russia. They have protected rather than disciplined old enterprises through subsidies—granted through the budget, energy consumption, and the banking sector. In addition, their institutions of public and corporate governance are not strong enough to prevent asset stripping. They discourage or at best only selectively encourage the entry of new enterprises because the state's capacity to provide key public goods is weak and the investment climate poor. Tax rates are high. Licensing and registration procedures are open to abuse. Furthermore, the legal and judicial system is unable to enforce property rights.

Adding to this discouragement, subnational governments engage in anticompetitive practices to protect established enterprises at the expense of new enterprises in their jurisdictions. Examples of protection abound. Transfers to selected enterprises and conglomerates in Russia in 1992 through credit at highly subsidized rates are estimated at 33 percent of GDP, financed through a massive inflation tax on households and enterprises without political connections. Subsidies implicit in soft budgets amounted to another 5 percent of GDP in 1996 and 3.5 percent in 1997.

Romania reverted in 1994 to directed credit, price controls, and budgetary and extrabudgetary transfers—and reopened enterprises earlier declared closed. These attempts to use the economy's old capital stock precipitated a macroeconomic crisis in 1996. Again, such transfers were financed through implicit or explicit taxes on households, new enterprises, and enterprises that restructured enough to survive the market test.

The result was to prevent or postpone closure of the least productive old enterprises and the restructuring of enterprises with good prospects. In addition, the entry of new enterprises that would be viable without state support was restrained. The protect-and-discourage strategy thus creates an environment where resource transfers flow in a direction opposite to that in a discipline-and-encourage environment.

The Associated Fiscal Adjustment...

The two contrasting approaches of discipline and encouragement and protection and discouragement are also broadly mirrored by the associated fiscal adjustment that has taken place. Enterprises used to be a captive source of revenue in transition economies. The state's loss of control over them also meant the loss of fiscal control and the need for political acceptance of a reduced public sector. Government revenues as a share of GDP fell from around 38 percent in 1992 to 31 percent in 1998 in the CIS and from 44 percent to 39 percent in the CSB. Stabilizing inflation, in practice often the first order of business, required that expenditures be reduced too. They fell precipitously from 57 percent of a rapidly declining GDP in 1992 to 37 percent in 1998 in the CIS—and, less sharply, from 45 percent in 1990 of a more modestly reduced GDP to 41 percent in 1998 in the CSB. This situation gave rise to two kinds of adjustment.

First, a substantial amount of spending was moved out of the budgetary arena. Explicit budgetary subsidies to enterprises generally fell across most of the region, but enterprises were still supported in a variety of ways. Implicit subsidies were channeled largely through the energy sector, which would then pass the costs back in the form of arrears to the budget. In addition, bank loans were rolled over and the enforcement of tax and other rules was lax. In Russia, for example, explicit budget subsidies to the enterprise sector declined from 10.2 percent of GDP in 1994 to 5.9 percent in 1998. But total budget subsidies to the enterprise sector, which also include the net increase in tax arrears as well as inflated prices of goods procured by the government and paid for by offsetting tax arrears, rose as a share from 10.9 percent of GDP to 16.3 percent.

Moreover, implicit subsidies extended through bank loans and public utilities were siphoned off along the way, coexisting with wage payment arrears by enterprises, thus not helping workers who would have benefited if soft budget constraints had indeed been an instrument of social protection. Faced with a shrinking tax base and more and more claimants being assisted outside the budget, governments attempted to collect more revenue by raising taxes. This discouraged potential entrants and, with abuses of discretion by government officials, drove them underground.[2] In addition, this pattern of fiscal adjustment, by signaling business as usual, helped protect enterprise managers from restructuring or closure.

A second mode of fiscal adjustment reallocated public expenditures to the social sectors to cushion the impact of transition on the vulnerable. That made it politically possible to discipline old enterprises into shedding labor. In Poland, for example, pensions were critical in preventing the elderly from falling into poverty. Indeed, high social spending was more affordable in the CSB because government revenue was significantly higher than in the CIS countries. That also helped to create a constituency for the discipline necessary to ensure a return to growth.

However, this alone would have been unsustainable without the rapid growth of new enterprises. Their high labor productivity gave them the potential to offer displaced workers a viable outside option rather than a return to subsistence activities, and that created a constituency for encouragement. The CSB still resorted to off-budget activity and created contingent liabilities. But these countries show the overarching role of fiscal policy and the institutions of budget management in supporting a growth-oriented adjustment by redistributing part of the "reform dividend" to those who would otherwise bear its costs.

...And the Role of Labor Markets

As with fiscal policy, two broad patterns of labor market adjustment can be identified. The first, largely associated with the CIS and the countries of Southeastern Europe, involved a decline in employment significantly smaller than the massive collapse of output and labor demand. The adjustment took the form of lower real wages as well as the emergence of arrears and nonpayment of wages. Without vibrant new enterprises, labor moved to low-productivity services and subsistence agriculture. Together with labor hoarding by enterprises, these sectors served as shock absorbers in view of the lack of a functioning social policy.

The second pattern, broadly prevalent in the CSB, saw employment decline with output. Job destruction was concentrated in existing enterprises, while job creation was to be found almost exclusively in new enterprises. Here too there is cross-country variation. For Poland, which exemplifies the discipline-and-encourage approach to transition, enterprise restructuring in key sectors of the economy and concomitant increases in labor productivity meant that output, growing rapidly since 1992, has outpaced job creation to a point where unemployment stood at 17 percent in August 2001. Budget constraints were softer and enterprise restructuring more limited in the Slovak Republic, which grew at an annual average rate of 4.7 percent between 1994 and 2000. The stop-and-go nature of the reform effort resulted in an insufficient creation of jobs in new firms. Employment remained largely unchanged and unemployment reached nearly 19 percent in the second quarter of 2000—the highest rate of unemployment in Central Europe.

In both countries, the aggressive use of social sector expenditures in the form of generous social assistance and unemployment insurance programs cushioned the risk of poverty in the face of high unemployment. But as in many countries in Central Europe and the Baltics, these programs diminished the incentives for workers to look for jobs. This, together with high payroll taxes, has constrained the growth of employment.

Notes

1. "Old" enterprises are defined as enterprises established before 1989 in Central Europe and the Baltics and before 1991 in the CIS. Increments in growth rates are 5 percent, with –5 percent as the

origin and zero the first increment, to capture the negative export growth rate reported by the old enterprises in the sample for 1996–98, a time when overall growth across the region had picked up.

2. Estimates of the unofficial economy as a share of GDP in 1995 are 42 percent in Russia, 49 percent in Ukraine, and more than 60 percent in Azerbaijan and Georgia (Johnson, Kaufmann, and Shleifer 1997).

4

Discipline and Encouragement

What policies and institutions are required to bring about a discipline-and-encouragement environment? While no one policy can be assigned to a single outcome in an interrelated system, it is convenient to think of policies in two groups: those primarily directed at disciplining the old sector and those primarily directed at encouraging the new sector.

Discipline requires imposing hard budget constraints on enterprises and banks. This entails eliminating a wide range of explicit and implicit mechanisms to channel public resources to enterprises and banks, including tax exemptions, fiscal and financial subsidies, budget and tax offsets, directed credits, and contingent liabilities.

However, discipline also refers to measures to prevent the misuse or theft of assets in both private and state-owned enterprises through asset stripping, tunneling, and expropriation of minority shareholders. To prevent such abuses, incentives for managerial behavior need to be aligned with the goal of enhancing efficiency through such reforms as privatization, strengthening the legal framework (particularly the enforcement of property rights), bankruptcy regulation, accounting reform and disclosure, and creditors' and shareholders' rights. Some countries, such as Belarus, Turkmenistan, and Uzbekistan, have managed to maintain discipline over managers in state enterprises without liberalization or hard budget constraints, but this has occurred largely through administrative methods held over from the Soviet-style command economy.

Encouragement starts with liberalizing prices and trade to enable the entry of new enterprises. But it goes much further to encompass policy and structural reforms that promote an attractive investment climate. There are an enormous number of factors that affect the decisions of economic actors to invest. These can be roughly divided into two categories: the quality of public goods and the extent of nonmarket obstacles to competition.

The key public goods that most directly affect the quality of the investment climate are a legal and judicial system capable of enforcing contracts and protecting property rights, a social system that promotes the development and maintenance of human capital, a macroeconomy that ensures stability over time, a banking system that provides effective financial intermediation, and a network of basic infrastructure. Public expenditure must be prioritized to provide the goods that promote investment and growth.

Tearing down the obstacles that discourage investment and competition is just as important. The inheritance of the command economy included stifling administrative barriers to entry, over-regulated labor markets, and tremendous discretion for bureaucrats. New barriers have emerged in the transition. The most prominent of these has been an overly complex and distortionary tax regime that pushes new entrepreneurs into the informal economy. These obstacles create an environment in which corruption and uncertainty undermine investment.

Juxtaposing discipline and encouragement with protection and discouragement highlights two contrasting modes of adjustment. In reality, country outcomes span a range of intermediate possibilities depending on whether liberalization, hard budget constraints, and an enabling business environment were pursued—and in what order and how vigorously. Though it is not possible to categorize transition economies into a spectrum of different modes of adjustment, country examples can be used to exemplify alternative transition paths:

- The policies of discipline and encouragement were pursued most consistently in Estonia, Hungary, and Poland.
- Within the broad category of discipline and encouragement, softer budget constraints—and hence less discipline—prevailed for a long time in the Czech Republic, Lithuania, and the Slovak Republic. Indeed, the resulting lack of industrial restructuring is widely held to have precipitated the Czech crisis in 1996–98. Harder budget constraints and faster restructuring can help reorient these economies toward the path followed by the first group.
- Bulgaria, the Kyrgyz Republic, Moldova, Romania, the Russian Federation, and Ukraine liberalized their economies, but for a long time failed to maintain discipline through hard budget constraints—and they could not contain tunneling and theft through either law or administrative control. The competition for resources between old and new enterprises makes it difficult to provide encouragement if the discipline for old enterprises is relaxed. Russia and Ukraine encouraged new entry

early in the transition. However, the capture of the state by a narrow set of vested interests—old enterprises and well-connected early entrants—discouraged further entry at later stages of transition and created a poor investment climate. This resulted in a pattern of protection and selective encouragement.
- Belarus, Turkmenistan, and Uzbekistan, which neither liberalized nor hardened budget constraints, strongly discouraged new entry. Access to foreign exchange and credit on special terms softened the budget for state enterprises. Reliance on mechanisms inherited from the command economy continued. The survival of a highly centralized structure of political power did limit the extent of asset stripping and other forms of theft that proved so damaging to growth in the previous groups of countries. Yet this element of discipline came at the cost of a highly protective stance that discouraged entry of new enterprises and SMEs.
- For an example of partial liberalization and weak discipline of state enterprises (though with strong restrictions on asset stripping) coupled with an environment strongly supportive of new entry, one must look outside Eastern Europe and the CIS to China (box 4.1).

Why particular countries or groups of countries get on paths of either discipline and encouragement or protection and discouragement can be traced to economic and political conditions they faced at the onset of transition; the structure of political institutions that determined the relative power of winners and losers from reforms; and initial choices regarding the pace, comprehensiveness, and sequencing of reforms. Understanding the forces that shape the environment helps define the key challenge in the political economy of discipline and encouragement; fostering new coalitions of winners and losers is crucial for shifting the incentives of old enterprises and promoting the development of new enterprises and thus for improving the probabilities of reform.

Meeting the challenges of discipline and encouragement is important if growth is to be restored, its quality enhanced, and its benefits

Box 4.1.

Can the CIS Learn from China's Reform Experience?

From 1978 to 1995 GDP per capita in China grew at 8 percent a year and lifted 200 million people out of absolute poverty. Does this experience offer lessons for the countries of the CIS—particularly for such countries as Uzbekistan and Belarus, which have yet to embark substantially on economic reform? Or are conditions so different between China and these countries that China's experience does not offer lessons for these countries?

Since the onset of reforms in 1978, China has been in the midst of two historic transitions: first, from a rural agricultural society to an urban, industrial one and, second, from a command economy to a market-based one. The first transition was driven by reforms in agriculture, a sector that employed 71 percent of the labor force and started a virtuous cycle, not only in agricultural development but also in rural industry. The substantial increase in agricultural productivity fed back into the economy in a number of ways.

First, the increases in productivity freed surplus labor that had been hidden in the commune system to move into rural industry. Second, higher incomes from higher agricultural prices and production provided a market for goods and services produced by rural industry, with product quality upgraded as incomes rose over time.

Third, the high savings rate—more than 30 percent of GDP—together with an implicit public guarantee of savings in the banking system, led Chinese households to hold deposits with the banking system. The ratio of M2 to GDP rose from 25 percent in 1978 to 89 percent in 1994. This allowed the banking system to channel net flows of 5 percent of GDP to borrowers. Some of the flows covered state enterprise losses and helped finance high-productivity investment in new and nonstate enterprises. Seigniorage accruing to the government in the 1990s allowed the budget deficit and substantial needs of loss-making enterprises to be financed through money creation with low inflation, leaving financial workouts and loan recovery to a later phase of reform.

Fourth, township and village enterprises developed rapidly and achieved high productivity growth and, despite unclear property rights, functioned as private enterprises in almost every way. In coastal areas growth depended less on high domestic savings, as the opening of markets was to lead to a massive inflow of foreign direct investment. The explosive growth of enterprises operating under the banner of townships or villages in rural areas was a source of internal competition, while external sector liberalization in coastal areas was a source of external competition for state enterprises.

In general, no other sector in the CIS countries could provide a comparable boost to the economy. In Russia, for example, only 13 percent of the labor force was engaged in agriculture in 1990, compared with 71 percent in China. In principle, the energy sector in Russia, which gained from partial price liberalization on the order of 11 percent of GDP, could have been used to compensate the losers from reform. However, the state's loss of control rights over the sector, which had already occurred during the years of reform socialism, implied that much of the gains went abroad through capital flight, reflecting, among other things, a poor investment climate in the country. This is reflected in the difference in the ratio of fixed investment to GDP, which was 22 percent in Russia compared with around 34 percent in China, a large part of which—perhaps 10 percent of GDP—could be attributed to capital flight and foreign direct investment.

Nor were surpluses available from the household sector. Increasing shortages, caused by the erosion of political control before the breakup of the former Soviet Union and before price liberalization, had led to substantial involuntary savings, resulting in a "monetary overhang"—mostly household claims on the state banking system, estimated at roughly a third of household wealth for the former Soviet Union in 1990. Attempts to sterilize this overhang were unsuccessful, and the savings were extinguished by the burst of inflation following price liberalization at the onset of transition. Not surprising, financial savings were slow to recover from this episode that, together with currency confiscation, led to substitution away from the domestic currency to commodities and foreign exchange. In marked contrast to China, the ratio of M2 to GDP in Russia fell from 68 percent to 17 percent in 1992.

To place the second transition—that from a command to a market economy—in comparative perspective, note that only 19 percent of the Chinese labor force worked in the state sector (and hence were entitled to a range of social benefits), compared with 90 percent in, for example, Russia in 1990. In general, sectors enjoying soft budget constraints were much more important in Russia. In 1985, 93 percent of the labor force was employed in state and municipal enterprises and organizations, including state farms, and a further 6 percent worked in collective farms and consumer cooperatives, leaving only 1 percent in individual and private enterprises. Because of the collapse of demand for industries producing capital goods and defense-related outputs and the difficulty of switching away from trade with the Council of Mutual Economic Assistance to Western markets, a much larger share of the Russian economy was not viable following price and trade liberalization. The costs of propping up rather than restructuring the state sector would have been prohibitive. Thus, a strategy of protecting the state sector through fiscal and financial transfers from the rest of the economy, unlike in China, would not have allowed adequate economic space for new enterprises to emerge as sources of growth.

(box continues on following page)

Box 4.1 CONTINUED

Finally, the government's ability to manage the process was critical. China contained the abuses from partial reform to some extent by exercising tight political control over asset stripping, arbitraging between controlled and market prices for private gain, and corruption. In contrast, the exit from communism, particularly in the countries of the CIS, led to a collapse of state institutions and, in the absence of a framework of property rights, set the stage for widespread tunneling and theft of state assets.

In summary, some aspects of China's experience are relevant and parallel the experience of the most successful transition economies of Central Europe and the Baltics. These include, for example, the strong role played by new and nonstate enterprises in generating growth and the positive role of increasing trade with market economies and foreign direct investment. Yet the large differences in initial conditions between China and the CIS point to the difficulties CIS countries face in trying to follow a similar path. In China, the first transition brought large gains (liberalizing repressed sectors such as agriculture and nonstate industry). Part of these gains was available for transfer to the losers from the second transition from a command to a market economy. Equally important, those losers—those from the unviable sectors—did not account for a big part of the economy. The state's capacity to manage public assets enabled a slower move to market conditions for loss-making state enterprises, before they were subjected to full market discipline in a growing economy. If a country is able to follow such a phased strategy, there is less reason for it to experience a contractionary transition.

However, these conditions were largely absent in the CIS countries where, following price liberalization, loss-making state enterprises accounted for a higher share of the economy and needed to be subjected to hard budget constraints for resources to be liberated and used by the winners (new private enterprises). This led first to a cut in output and activity, then a recovery. In addition to these differences in political and economic conditions, central planning was far more entrenched in Russia than in China. In the 1970s central government agencies in the former Soviet Union physically allocated about 60,000 different commodities throughout the plan. In China the number was about 600, unchanged from 1965. Nor, unlike the former Soviet Union, did China have the problems posed by "giantism" and enormous regional specialization underpinned by high transport intensity and fuel prices far below world levels.

Moreover, the costs of China's approach to transition, arising from soft budget constraints, remain to be fully addressed. The banking system, which was used to support loss-making state enterprises, is saddled with nonperforming loans of 30–40 percent of annual GDP. Restoring the health of the state banking system on account of those loans could lead the stock of domestic government debt to rise from about 20 percent to 75 percent of GDP. Servicing this debt will pose a major fiscal challenge for the government. This mirrors the experience of transition economies such as Bulgaria and Romania, where support for state enterprises resulted in a high proportion of nonperforming loans in the banking sector. Moreover, as in several transition economies, surveys report that asset stripping and excessive wage competition in China's state enterprises are now widespread.

So, despite the different conditions in the CIS and China, what are the lessons for such countries as Belarus and Uzbekistan? In 2000, GDP as a proportion of its 1990 level was 85 percent in Belarus and 94 percent in Uzbekistan, significantly higher than the corresponding numbers in other CIS countries. The initial fall in GDP in Uzbekistan during the transitional recession was more like the shallow dip in Central and Eastern Europe, which may be attributed to low rates of industrialization and urbanization that, together with self-sufficiency in energy, made these countries less vulnerable to the disruption of payments and market links attending the breakup of the former Soviet Union.

The experience of Belarus and Uzbekistan echoes that of China in two ways. First, governments of Belarus and Uzbekistan exercised enough political control over state enterprises to limit the risk of spontaneous privatization and excessive asset stripping. Such control has not always been effective; thus, Uzbekistan has seen sizable capital flight amounting to nearly 20 percent of merchandise exports. Second, governments were able to channel an infusion of resources to priority state enterprises and sectors, such as large-scale chemicals and automobiles in Uzbekistan and agriculture and housing in Belarus, to maintain production. In Uzbekistan this came from redirecting cotton and gold exports, which accounted for 60 percent of export revenues, to other markets at significantly better prices, as well as from newly opened oil deposits that turned the country into a net oil exporter in 1996. The effect of policies that discriminated against agriculture was a transfer of an estimated 4–5 percent of GDP out of the sector during 1996–98. In addition, state banks, used to transfer resources to favored sectors and enterprises, face the prospect of large losses. In Belarus the infusion of resources came from goods-for-energy barter deals with Russia on terms that were highly favorable, both to Belarusian exports and imports (see box 4.3).

But China differs from Belarus and Uzbekistan in one critical way. Little has been done in Belarus and Uzbekistan to create an investment climate conducive to entry of new enterprises. In Belarus, for example, the share of employment accounted for by small enterprises (employing 50 or fewer people) is less than 20 percent, well below the 40 percent threshold needed for a return to sustained growth. It is in this respect, rather than in the infusion of resources to state enterprises, that countries such as Belarus and Uzbekistan would be wise to learn from China's experience and strongly encourage the growth of new enterprises as a basis for wealth creation and economic growth.

widely shared. The challenges are also interrelated. Entrepreneurs have no incentive to bring in new management, develop new products, or seek new markets needed for growth-oriented restructuring if explicit subsidies or implicit support extended through banks and public utilities and protection from competitive pressures keep them afloat. Evidence from business surveys confirms that enterprises facing hard budget constraints and a degree of competition are more likely to undergo managerial turnover and develop new products (Carlin and others 2001).

Industrial enterprises also face major obstacles to downsizing if arrangements to help them divest social assets, such as housing, sanatoriums, and kindergartens, are unavailable. This problem is further compounded by the lack of public resources to finance an adequate system of social protection to replace these divested assets for well-targeted groups. Startups and spinoffs that could fuel innovation and growth do not enter the fray if the tax and regulatory system does not level the playing field between them and incumbent state-owned and privatized but unrestructured enterprises. If the state cannot administer the rule of law, particularly contract enforcement and secure property rights, rent

seeking and widespread theft of erstwhile state assets dominate economic activity. The state cannot afford the social safety net required for restructuring or investments in human capital if, together with enterprises, it is caught in a pervasive web of arrears and unpaid taxes.

The reform agenda required to enable growth to resume calls for effective public and private institutions. Political institutions are critical in mediating the interactions between winners and losers from various reforms. The ability of the state to secure property rights depends on the effectiveness of the legal system. Mechanisms of corporate governance dictate what kind of ownership structure is most likely to bring about efficiency-enhancing enterprise restructuring. Improved budget management is necessary to ensure that the state maintains a responsible fiscal policy. Effective administration of programs of social assistance and insurance are required so that the "reform dividend" generated by growth is used to assist those adversely affected by transition.

But policy choices are critically important as well; the example of East Germany demonstrates how poor policy choices at the start of transition can undermine even the most favorable environment (box 4.2).

Box 4.2.

The German Experience

East Germany opened its border in 1989 and was united with West Germany in the fall of 1990. In many ways the experience of the transition in East Germany has been unique among the former socialist countries. It appeared to start from a privileged position in at least three respects.

First, all economic, political, and social institutions and arrangements of West Germany, as well as its entire legal framework, were adopted without change and without delay. East Germany did not face the difficult challenge of building a new institutional framework from scratch. Given that it is now conventional wisdom to argue that the key deficiency of the transition in many countries has been insufficient attention to building an institutional framework to support a market economy, East Germany appears to have had considerable advantages in its transition.

Second, though critics faulted Western governments early in the transition for not offering enough aid or assistance to the transition economies, East Germany received huge transfer payments financed partially by a new "solidarity tax" leveled on West German incomes. Annual transfers from West to East Germany have been massive, averaging 40–60 percent of East Germany's GDP, totaling about DM 1.2 trillion (US$571 billion) for the 1991–97 period. Current transfers still average DM 140 billion, or more than 4 percent of West Germany's GDP, a year. In comparison, total lending and grants of the World Bank to all transition economies in Europe and Central Asia amounted to DM 43 billion (US$19 billion) in 1991–2000. The transfers to East Germany have financed public expenditure programs, supported private sector investment, and secured transfer payments for social protection that have arisen from the sudden eligibility of East German citizens, including massive retraining and public works programs.

(box continues on following page)

Box 4.2 CONTINUED

Third, unification gave East Germany automatic membership in the European Union (and the World Trade Organization). While the CIS suffered from European antidumping rules and Central Europe's Central Europe Free Trade Agreement members complained of being blocked from the Common Market (while being subjected to cheap imports, especially in the agricultural sector), East Germany benefited from speedy and complete incorporation into a large external market.

In light of these considerable advantages, few would have predicted the difficulties East Germany encountered over the past decade. East Germany's growth performance has lagged behind other transition economies with far fewer advantages (see box figure A). Its initial economic decline was deeper than in its transition economy neighbors. Though East Germany's growth rates were higher than those in other countries in the region for a few years, its subsequent growth has been among the slowest in Europe. The hope that East Germany would quickly catch up with West Germany has not materialized.

FIGURE A.

Comparison of Real GDP, 1989–2000

Index of real GDP (1988 = 100)

Note: The average for the CSB is weighted by population.
Source: World Bank country office data.

How can such poor performance be explained despite the enormous advantages that East Germany enjoyed in comparison with other transition economies? A simple answer is that even a good institutional framework backed by massive subsidies cannot overcome the negative consequences of inappropriate policies. Two early policy choices had particularly damaging consequences. First, the conversion rate of West to East German marks reflected political pressures and not economic realities, vastly overvaluing the East German currency. Second, the attempt to bring East German wages in line with West German wages, while average labor productivity in the East remained at approximately a third of the West, severely damaged East Germany's competitiveness. As a result, a larger segment of the inherited capital stock was scrapped as unproductive and less employment was preserved than would have been warranted with more realistic macroeconomic policy choices in effect.

Erasing the existing capital stock, together with extending West Germany's generous eligibility criteria, increased the need for social transfer payments. Such payments continue to constitute between 55 percent and 65 percent of gross national product. Clearly, the current level of social payments in East Germany would not be sustainable in any economically independent geographic area.

The high degree of subsidization in East Germany, coupled with the relatively high unit labor costs, have coincided with a marked slowdown in the rate of new enterprise growth, as shown in box figure B. The net creation of new enterprises, which had outperformed West Germany in 1991, has persistently declined each year through 1999, falling to a seventh of West Germany's level.

Now East Germany seems to suffer from exactly the same phenomenon as the least successful transition economies in the CIS—anemic growth of new enterprises that have been the main drivers of growth elsewhere in the transition. Indeed, investment data suggests that even German investors are "jumping over" East Germany to invest in the Czech Republic, Hungary, and Poland, where unit wage costs are considerably lower.

(box continues on following page)

Box 4.2 CONTINUED

Though the slow rate of new enterprise growth is mostly attributed to an insufficient institutional framework in the CIS, the East German case demonstrates how poor policy choices at the start of transition can undermine even the most favorable environment.

FIGURE B.

Net New Enterprise Registration in East and West Germany

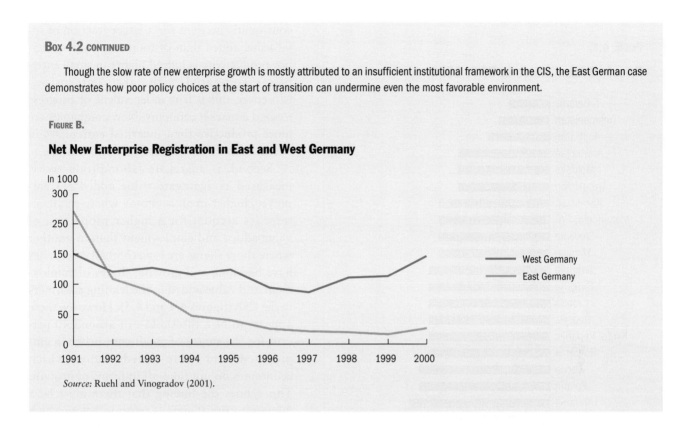

Source: Ruehl and Vinogradov (2001).

New Enterprises Drive the Transition

The success of a discipline-and-encourage strategy is predicated on the ability of new and restructured enterprises to emerge as engines of economic growth. Moving assets from the public to the private sector is thus an important element of transition. In 1999 the share of the private sector in CIS GDP was 20 percent in Belarus; 55 percent in Kazakhstan and Ukraine; 60 percent in Armenia, Georgia, and the Kyrgyz Republic; and 70 percent in the Russian Federation (figure 4.1). These figures compare favorably with Central and Eastern Europe: 55 percent in Macedonia and Slovenia, 60 percent in Bulgaria and Romania, 65 percent in Latvia and Poland, and 80 percent in the Czech Republic and Hungary.

The picture is quite different, however, for new enterprises, which typically need encouragement in the form of a favorable business environment (figures 4.2 and 4.3). Using small enterprises employing fewer than 50 workers as a proxy for new enterprises, their contribution to value added in 1998 was around 55–65 percent of GDP in the Czech Republic, Hungary, and Lithuania, compared with 10–20 percent in Belarus, Kazakhstan, Russia, and Ukraine.[1] Data on small enterprises as providers of employment divide countries into two groups: leading reformers and countries further behind. Small enterprises' share of employment in 1998 was about 50 percent for leading reformers such as the Czech Republic, Hungary, Latvia, Lithuania, and Poland, roughly the same as the European Union. For countries less far along the path to a market economy, such as Belarus, Kazakhstan, Russia, and Ukraine, the share was between 10 and 20 percent.

The share of small enterprises in employment and value added differs widely across the region (see figures 4.2 and 4.3). In many parts of the CIS and Southeastern Europe—where growth is low and income per capita is substantially below pretransition levels—the share of employment in small enterprises hovers around 20 percent. In contrast, the share of small enterprises

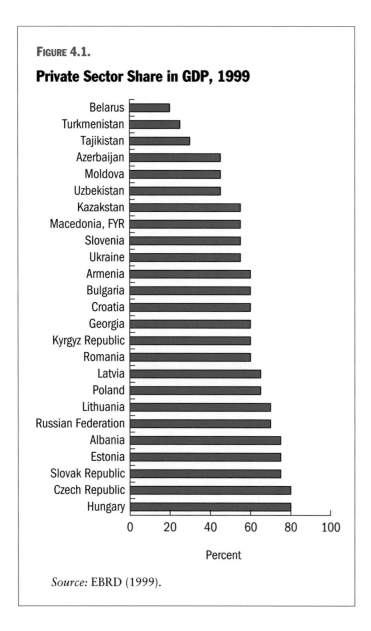

FIGURE 4.1.

Private Sector Share in GDP, 1999

Source: EBRD (1999).

consistently account for a larger fraction of total value added than of total employment. Labor productivity is indeed higher in small enterprises compared with large enterprises. Moreover, this is true independent of progress toward a market economy. New companies are more productive than inherited enterprises in countries as diverse as Hungary and Ukraine.

Second, is aggregate labor productivity, measured as aggregate value added per employee, higher in an economy where small enterprises account for a higher proportion of value added and employment than in another where those shares are lower? Small enterprises have had high and growing shares of employment and value added in the leading reformers in the CSB (figures 4.4 and 4.5). However, there appears to be a threshold—of around 40 percent for the shares of small enterprises in employment and value added—below which economies do not take off in terms of growth. This echoes the finding that there must be a minimum critical mass of reforms, below which the economy does not respond to policies. The shares of new enterprises in employment and value added are high and above the threshold in the leading reformers in the CSB. But both shares remain low and well below the threshold in the slow-growing economies of the CIS. The notion of a threshold is important in the interaction between the old and new sectors of the economy.

Third, can differences in labor productivity between small and large enterprises constitute a source of growth? The higher productivity of small enterprises needs to be complemented by an incentive for labor and capital to move to that sector—for small enterprises to increase aggregate growth. Higher labor productivity in small enterprises implies lower labor intensity per unit of output. This observation and the assumption that small enterprises are less capital-intensive than large enterprises imply that labor and capital have a higher marginal product in small enterprises (annex 4.2). Movements from large to small enterprises are adding value and thus are a source of growth. The large gap in labor productivity in countries such as Kazakhstan and Ukraine shows an unrealized potential for growth in the new sector.

in total employment and value added is more than 50 percent in the CSB, characterized by high and sustained economic growth and either approaching or surpassing pretransition per capita incomes.

The rapid growth of small enterprises in helping bring about a higher contribution to value added and employment among the leading reformers shows that economic policy has directed the process of factor reallocation. That prompts three questions (table 4.1).

First, is labor productivity in small enterprises, measured as value added per employee, higher than in large enterprises in transition economies? In the aggregate, small enterprises

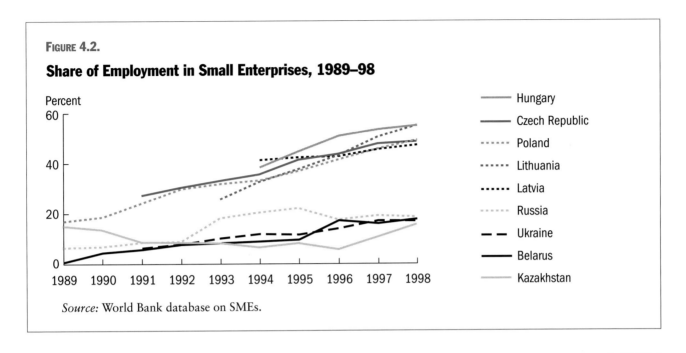

FIGURE 4.2.

Share of Employment in Small Enterprises, 1989–98

Percent

Legend:
— Hungary
— Czech Republic
···· Poland
···· Lithuania
···· Latvia
···· Russia
– – Ukraine
— Belarus
— Kazakhstan

Source: World Bank database on SMEs.

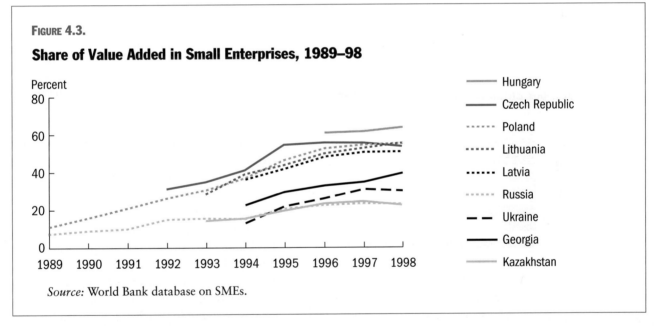

FIGURE 4.3.

Share of Value Added in Small Enterprises, 1989–98

Percent

Legend:
— Hungary
— Czech Republic
···· Poland
···· Lithuania
···· Latvia
···· Russia
– – Ukraine
— Georgia
— Kazakhstan

Source: World Bank database on SMEs.

The difference between the two sets of enterprises—old and new—begins to erode over time for two reasons. Old enterprises either close or restructure, raising labor productivity, and employment growth in new enterprises at some point reduces labor productivity in those enterprises. There is a marked productivity difference between the two sets of enterprises for Russia and Ukraine, but a noticeable narrowing of that difference for the Czech Republic, Hungary, and Lithuania farther along the path to a market economy.

A Small Number of High-Productivity Small Enterprises Is Not Enough

As the transition proceeds, labor shed by downsizing old enterprises either finds its way into new and more productive employment or migrates to unemployment or subsistence activities. Labor hoarding in the old sector may persist for a long time, with new enterprises acting merely as passive receptacles for such transfers. Alternatively, when the investment climate

TABLE 4.1.

SMEs Have Higher Labor Productivity, 1998

(percent)

Countries	SMEs	Share of total employment	Value added (total)	Value added (per employee)
Belarus	37.7	15.9	—	—
Czech Republic	97.0	48.7	53.5	109.9
Georgia	88.6	39.6	39.3	99.2
Hungary	96.1	54.9	63.6	115.8
Kazakhstan	88.6	15.6	22.4	143.6
Latvia	91.2	45.5	50.4	110.9
Lithuania	97.4	55.1	55.3	100.4
Poland	92.1	45.7	54.4	118.9
Russia	56.3	18.6	23.0	123.7
Ukraine	69.2	16.9	30.0	177.5

— Not available.

Note: Average for enterprises of all sizes = 100. Small enterprises are defined as having 50 or fewer employees.

Source: World Bank database on SMEs.

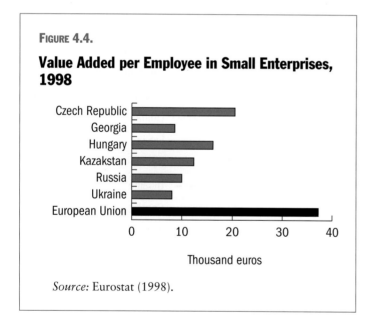

FIGURE 4.4.

Value Added per Employee in Small Enterprises, 1998

Thousand euros

Source: Eurostat (1998).

the old sector and contribute to sustainable growth. Simply having a small number of highly productive small enterprises is not enough. Unless it is combined with rapid growth in the share of employment, the small sector will not develop the critical mass to lead aggregate economic growth (see figures 4.4 and 4.5).

Russia illustrates the inability of the new sector to contribute to sustained growth. The share of value added for small enterprises more than doubled, from 10 percent to 23 percent between 1991 and 1998, in part reflecting a steadily declining GDP. But their share in employment has remained low and largely stagnant. They do not seem to have incentives to increase their employment or to multiply—so they continue to fall well short of the threshold for growth to take off. A large chunk of the labor force remains mired in unrestructured state and private enterprises.

In countries where aggregate employment picked up, it did so after the recovery of aggregate output (figure 4.6). This empirical investigation of new enterprises and their interaction with old enterprises suggests the following:

• A sharp and early decline in aggregate employment precedes the rapid growth of new

is conducive to entry, new enterprises compete with the old sector, rapidly increasing their share in employment and typically attracting the most qualified individuals.

As noted, a threshold of about 40 percent for the shares of small enterprises in employment and value added needs to be crossed for new enterprises to absorb the resources released by

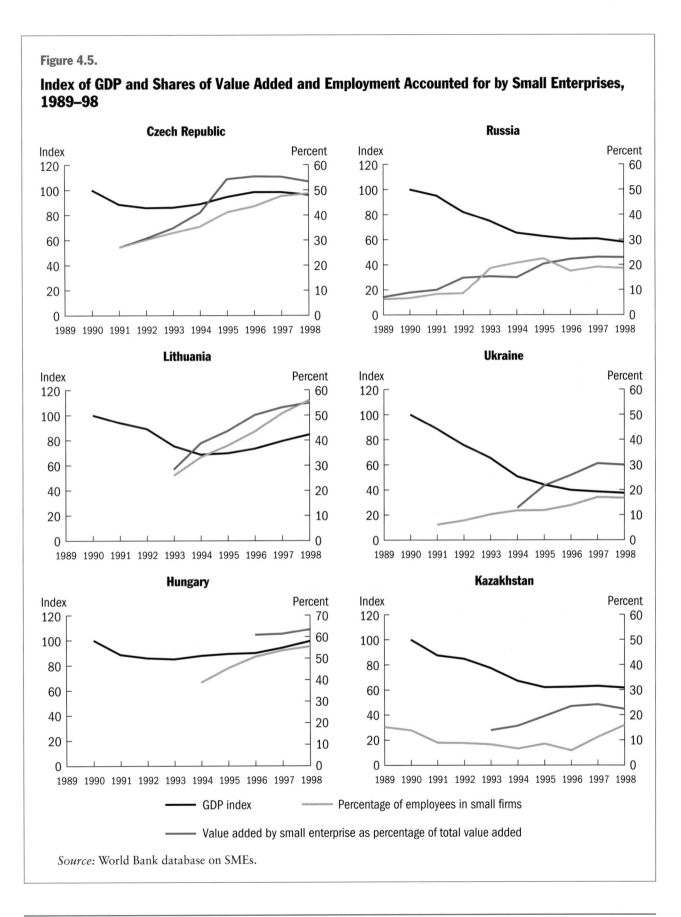

Figure 4.5.

Index of GDP and Shares of Value Added and Employment Accounted for by Small Enterprises, 1989–98

Source: World Bank database on SMEs.

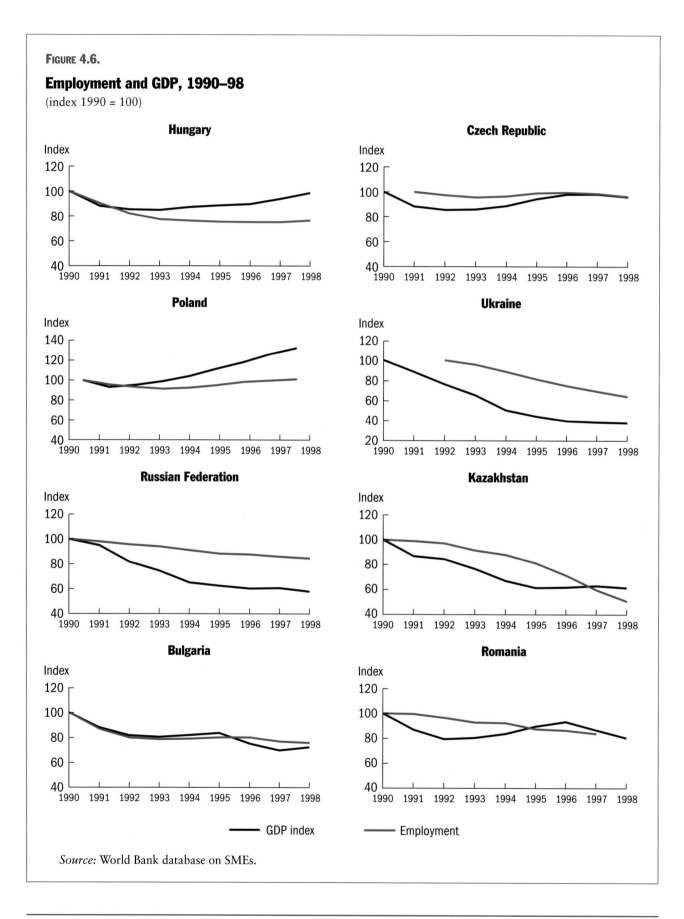

FIGURE 4.6.

Employment and GDP, 1990–98

(index 1990 = 100)

Hungary

Czech Republic

Poland

Ukraine

Russian Federation

Kazakhstan

Bulgaria

Romania

GDP index —— Employment ——

Source: World Bank database on SMEs.

enterprises. With the former as an indicator of the fast dismantling of old industries, the rapid demise of the old sector seems necessary but not sufficient for the growth of new enterprises. A plausible reason would be that the rapid dismantling of the old sector lowers the price of its assets. Cheap resources become easily available to new enterprises, useful when financing is not available and investment not forthcoming. That is why discipline is a crucial element of growth. But it is not enough, for encouragement is also required.

- Countries that reached the trough of the transition recession sooner had faster growth in the new sector. Where sustainable growth returned, the share of small enterprises had reached a critical mass. Where it did not, people remained "unemployed on the job," as in the CIS and countries in Southeastern Europe. Aggregate employment started to fall only late in the process. These observations suggest a sequence where hard budget constraints are imposed and the old sector declines before the new sector can grow.
- While disciplining the old and encouraging the new appear to be complementary, the old sector has generally, though not invariably, proved unable to survive even where budget constraints have been soft and the new sector has not emerged. In such cases, mainly in the CIS, agriculture and low productivity services have served as "shock absorbers" for those forced to leave old industries.

Can We Have It Both Ways, That Is, Protecting Old Inherited Enterprises and Encouraging New Enterprises?

The analysis makes clear that policies encouraging the new private sector while subjecting them to market discipline must get the highest priority. But must discipline and encouragement go together? Or is it possible to encourage the new sector while protecting the state enterprises and privatized enterprises that continue to behave as if they were public? The economic argument seeing discipline and encouragement as complementary goes as follows. Continued resource transfers for nonviable state-owned enterprises, other things being equal, either require the consolidated government to loosen its fiscal stance, raise taxes elsewhere in the economy, or engage in off-budget activity.

- A looser fiscal stance can weaken the credibility of the government's stabilization program and, by increasing market perception of risk, raise domestic interest rates, thus crowding out the new private sector.[2]
- Intensifying taxation of the potentially more efficient emerging private sector can start a vicious cycle that pushes enterprises into the informal sector, thus lowering tax revenue and further increasing tax rates.
- Off-budget activities include issuing loan guarantees, establishing insurance schemes, and providing explicit or implicit cover generally for politically motivated activities that tend to benefit incumbents.

These outcomes end up protecting state enterprises and collective farms and discouraging new enterprises. However, the relationship does not run simply from the costs of propping up unviable enterprises (protection) to discouraging the new private sector. The lack of a vibrant private sector limits the outside options that might attract workers and potential entrepreneurs from old enterprises. It also limits product competition, an essential element of a disciplining environment. Both weaken the incentives for closure and restructuring of nonviable enterprises. These considerations explain why impediments to the efficient exit of enterprises discourage the growth of new enterprises, and why the emergence of a new private sector would accelerate the closure and restructuring of state-owned enterprises.

Further evidence on how protection of the old sector discourages the new sector comes from the following examples. The first is protection through the banking sector. Small enterprises have grown less in such CSB countries as Bulgaria and Romania, where the banking sector was a major conduit for loans to the old state-owned enterprises and farm collectives. In those countries nonperforming loans increased as a share of total banking sector loans during much of the 1990s. Contrast that with the vibrant growth of new enterprises in the Baltics, Hungary, and Poland, where these loans were sharply reduced over time. In 1998 nonperforming loans still represented 34 percent of total loans in Romania, while they were 4 percent in Estonia, 6 percent in Hungary, 11 percent in Poland, and 13 percent in Lithuania. These loans to old enterprises prevented the expansion of bank credit to new, small, and less politically connected enterprises. In addition, they became a major factor in triggering a banking and macroeconomic crisis that called for a sharp stabilization and credit tightening—all reducing the growth of new enterprises.

The second example is protection through special allocation of inputs. In Belarus and Uzbekistan the old industrial sector has remained protected through favorable foreign exchange regimes, directed credit, and high trade protection. Specific large foreign investments have also been favored. As a result new smaller enterprises face the residual of these allocations in the market. What remains in credit and foreign exchange must be purchased at costs several times higher than would have been paid in unified markets. In Uzbekistan small enterprises have to pay three times more for foreign exchange than do large state enterprises to finance their imports. As a result new enterprises have been squelched. In Belarus, the share of small enterprises in the total number of enterprises is a mere 26 percent, substantially lower than other CIS countries. While these special regimes may have helped avoid a sharp output decline in the old industrial sector and aggregate output, they cannot provide the basis for sustained future growth (box 4.3).

Box 4.3.

Belarus

A decade after the beginning of transition, Belarus has emerged as one of the least reformed, but seemingly most resilient, economies in the CIS. GDP in 1999 reached 89 percent of its 1990 level, well above the CIS average of 62 percent (box table A). The country's relatively favorable growth performance stands in stark contrast to its extremely poor record on macroeconomic stabilization and structural reform. Apart from a brief spell of relative stability in 1996 and 1997, inflation ran at triple digits throughout the 1990s, reflecting money-based financing of public sector deficits. The European Bank for Reconstruction and Development ranks Belarus 25th out of 26 transition economies in overall progress in economic reform.

Although Belarus has largely abolished the Soviet command system, a variety of controls over the economy remain. The state has continued to support priority sectors, such as agriculture and housing, with both direct subsidies and soft loans channeled through the banking system. Price controls remain widespread, partly aimed at regulating the prices of certain commodities and partly designed to fight inflation through administrative means. A multiple exchange rate system remained in place until September 2000, operating as a heavy tax on exporters and a subsidy for certain importers. While international trade has been liberalized, some restrictions remain in conjunction with domestic price controls. Privatization of large enterprises has hardly begun, and even many small enterprises remain in state hands.

Given the poor record on macroeconomic stabilization and structural reform, what explains Belarus's relative success in having contained output decline? There are four important considerations. First, Belarus is successful only in relation to the other CIS countries. Compared with transition economies outside the CIS, such as neighbors Lithuania and Poland, Belarus is no more than an average performer.

Second, Belarus has had the benefit of continued cheap energy imports from Russia. In addition to this direct subsidy from Russia, Belarus also tended to accumulate substantial energy arrears to Russia, which were later settled through barter transactions that artificially maintained demand for Belarusian exports—another important form of indirect subsidy from Russia.

Third, by providing subsidies and credit to large enterprises, the state kept industrial output from collapsing in the early stages of transition, as in many other CIS countries. Fourth, by not privatizing large enterprises, the state has retained greater control over productive assets and prevented extreme cases of asset stripping and tunneling.

These considerations suggest that continued state ownership and control of large enterprises, as well as preferential treatment by Russia, have played a key role in maintaining industrial production and bolstering economic growth. Yet the resources that have been used to maintain industrial production have been drained from other sectors of the economy. In particular, the Belarusian system has stifled the growth of new

(box continues on following page)

Box 4.3 continued

enterprises. The multiple exchange rate system and pervasive state controls have shifted private initiative into arbitrage activities and the shadow economy, while investment has remained largely in the state sector. There has been little evidence of restructuring in the state sector, suggesting that the pain of such restructuring has merely been postponed. These factors do not bode well for long-term growth in Belarus.

Table A.

How Belarus Compares with Other Transition Economies

Country	Real GDP in 2000 (1990 = 100)	Average inflation,[a] 1991–2000	EBRD transition indicator rating, 1999[b]	Government revenue to GDP, 1999[c]
CSB average	106	41	3.1	39
Czech Republic	99	13	3.5	41
Hungary	109	20	3.7	42
Lithuania	68	88	3.2	32
Poland	147	26	3.5	43
Romania	83	102	2.8	32
CIS average	62	185	2.3	24
Belarus	89	344	1.6	42
Georgia	30	257	2.9	16
Kazakhstan	65	163	2.7	19
Russian Federation	66	163	2.5	34
Ukraine	43	244	2.5	35
Uzbekistan	97	182	2.0	32

a. Consumer Price Index.
b. Unweighted average of transition indicator ratings across reform categories, which range from 1 (least progress) to 4+ (most progress).
c. General government revenues divided by nominal GDP.
Source: EBRD (2000).

Nevertheless, Belarus's experience suggests important lessons about transition. When compared with the partial and poorly implemented reforms in many CIS countries, Belarus's inaction enabled it to avoid some key mistakes in the early stages of transition. First, while continued state ownership did little to promote more efficient operational or strategic decisionmaking at the enterprise level, it did deter the large-scale asset stripping, tunneling, and tax evasion that has damaged growth in the early stages of transition in some other CIS countries. Nevertheless, the rapid decentralization and even fragmentation of power in other CIS countries at the start of transition might have precluded such a policy option.

Second, the capacity of the Belarusian state to maintain high levels of tax collection (see box table A) highlights the importance of these taxes in smoothing the initial output decline. The strength of fiscal revenues has kept the scope for supporting declining sectors and socially oriented expenditures. Belarus will need to maintain its ability to collect taxes if it chooses to embark on economic reform. Though it may be tempting to explain this fiscal performance as a result of the authoritarian state, such a political regime has not guaranteed similar outcomes in Turkmenistan or Uzbekistan.

The third lesson is that current account revenues matter, especially in transition. Other CIS countries saw their exports to Russia collapse while their energy imports became far more expensive, leading to a massive terms-of-trade shock. While Central European transition economies were redirecting their exports to the European Union, CIS countries had nowhere to go but Russia. Belarus continued to earn export and service revenues by maintaining close economic ties with Russia, thus softening the initial trade shocks.

In summary, although Belarus does not have a viable strategy for sustainable growth, it has—perhaps inadvertently—avoided some mistakes. The ability of the state to prevent the collapse of its capacity and control early in transition appears to have saved the Belarusian economy from the rapid decline felt elsewhere in the region. Yet such an outcome was hardly guaranteed by the lack of economic reform, but rather by dependence on Russia, whose willingness to subsidize, directly and indirectly, Belarus's inaction was a function of the geostrategic importance of the country. Such an option was not necessarily available to other CIS countries.

A key question for the future is whether Belarus will enjoy certain "advantages of backwardness" if it embarks on serious structural reforms. The long delay in privatization could allow Belarus to learn from earlier mistakes of other transition economies. Whether the capacity of state institutions can be simply shifted from maintaining the status quo to implementing forward-looking economic policies in an environment

(box continues on following page)

characterized by the rule of law is uncertain. Surely, if Belarus were to change course now and embark on economic reform, its initial conditions would be far more favorable than those of the other CIS countries in the early 1990s, when demand was collapsing across the old Council of Mutual Economic Assistance. Most of Belarus's trading partners are now growing and this should soften the negative shock of any reform effort.

While these considerations suggest that Belarus may still have the opportunity to develop into a strong economic reformer—once the political will is there—an important question remains. Will economic reforms lead to the same erosion of public institutions observed in other transition economies? Once opportunities for private wealth creation in the private sector arise, skillful civil servants may have greater incentives to extract rents from the private sector or may even switch careers. The key challenge for Belarus, once it starts reforming, will ultimately be the same as for all other transition economies: to establish good governance and strong market-supporting institutions.

The third example is protection through tax and utility arrears. Nonpayments by enterprises to the main utilities in the energy sector remain a major source of subsidization, particularly in Russia and Ukraine, but also in Georgia, the Kyrgyz Republic, and Moldova. This has delayed restructuring of energy-intensive industries and shedding of assets that smaller new enterprises could use. The discretion of negotiating and settling nonpayments complements the natural behavior of these utilities to act as discriminating monopolies. New, more energy-efficient enterprises are charged more to compensate for the revenue losses from the old, less energy-efficient enterprises.

Tax exemptions for large enterprises and agriculture collectives—popular until recently in Ukraine, where these initiatives could be unilaterally introduced by the legislature—generate a highly discretionary tax regime and are an important source of bribes. The same is true for the use of negotiated offsets as a way to pay taxes in Russia, and tax avoidance by large enterprises in Georgia. New small enterprises are usually less powerful in this environment and end up paying higher bribes as a fraction of total profits.

In sum: the softer the budget constraint and thus the stronger the barriers to exit, the lower the contribution of small enterprises to employment (figure 4.7).

Annex 4.1. Assumptions for Small and New Enterprises

This discussion is based on the hypothesis that small enterprises can be taken as approximating new enterprises. For this hypothesis, the margin of error for Central and Southeastern Europe can be deduced from table A4.1. Although it seems safe to assume that most new enterprises are small enterprises, the opposite need not be true.[3] Table A4.1 lists the share of new and small enterprises over total active enterprises in Central European countries for 1995. For example, of all active enterprises in Albania in 1995, 68 percent (from column 2) were created as greenfield. For the same year our assumption would estimate the proportion of small enterprises to be 98.7 percent (from column 3). The difference of 30.3 percent (column 4) is the share of small enterprises that we consider to be new ones but actually are old.

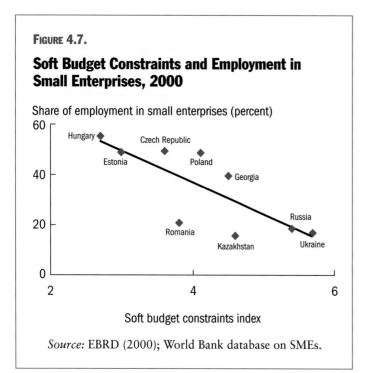

FIGURE 4.7.

Soft Budget Constraints and Employment in Small Enterprises, 2000

Share of employment in small enterprises (percent)

Source: EBRD (2000); World Bank database on SMEs.

TABLE A4.1.

Differences between New Enterprises and Small Enterprises, 1995 and 1998

(percent)

| Country | Enterprises active January 1995 | | | | Projections for 1998 |
	New enterprises	Small enterprises	Small old enterprises	Small old enterprises as percentage of small enterprises	Small old enterprises as percentage of small enterprises
Albania	68.4	98.7	30.3	30.7	18.8
Bulgaria	96.0	98.1	2.1	2.1	1.1
Czech Republic	86.1	98.6	12.5	12.7	7.6
Estonia	81.9	96.4	14.5	15.0	7.8
Hungary	84.5	99.0	14.5	14.6	9.6
Latvia	83.2	95.2	12.0	12.6	6.2
Lithuania	75.4	95.6	20.2	21.1	10.9
Poland	88.6	98.7	10.1	10.2	4.9
Romania	95.8	99.1	3.3	3.3	2.0
Slovak Republic	92.6	98.4	5.8	5.9	3.4
Slovenia	75.7	97.6	21.9	22.4	14.5
Central European countries	88.3	98.6	10.3	10.4	5.7

Source: Eurostat (1998); authors' calculations.

Column 5 shows the ratio of small old enterprises over small enterprises, that is, the probability of picking up a wrong element when sampling from the set of small enterprises. It is therefore a measure of the error implied in assuming that small enterprises equal new enterprises. The size of the error for Albania is large: 30.3 percent means that, within the set of enterprises we assume to be new ones, one out of three is not. But for Bulgaria the error is 2 percent. Although Albania is extreme, many countries show high errors.

Figures for the Czech Republic, Hungary, and Lithuania are a source of concern because this study relies heavily on evidence from the three countries. However, this crude estimate is an upper bound for the actual error. In fact, neither small-scale spinoffs nor new enterprises created as private cooperatives are counted in column 2, although both can be considered new enterprises. The bias is particularly relevant for the countries in the Federal Republic of Yugoslavia, such as Slovenia, where many new enterprises were created as cooperatives.

The error tends to decrease over time. Because the stock of companies in the hands of the state at the beginning of the transition is either liquidated or privatized, the source of the error is extinguished. The last column of table A4.1 shows a projection for 1998 once a mortality rate of 20 percent is assumed for both new and old enterprises. (Most of the data in this report refer to 1998.) The probability of error is estimated to have shrunk considerably for all the countries this paper discusses.

Further evidence can be gathered through the answers to the Business Enterprise Environment and Performance Survey (see box 3.1). The survey results show that 52 percent of new enterprises are controlled by an individual owner (versus 24 percent of old enterprises), and that in two-thirds of the new enterprises the majority ownership is held by no more than three shareholders (true for less than half of old enterprises). Moreover, new enterprises are the ones that rely most on internal funds and family financing and that have more trouble getting bank credit. The higher concentration in ownership and the exclusion from conventional credit channels is important indirect evidence that new enterprises are small.

Annex 4.2. Implications of the Higher Productivity of SMEs

In many transition economies SMEs have higher average value added per employee than the rest of the economy. As a result:

- Factors of production are likely to have an incentive to move to the SME sector, thus, increasing its size as a fraction of the economy.
- An increase in the size of the SME sector is likely to increase the growth rate of the economy.

Because SMEs represent the main source of new enterprises, we refer to the SME sector as "new." The basic argument is that since SMEs are likely to be less capital intensive than larger or old enterprises, a larger value added per

employee means that primary factors of production earn more in that sector. So, by moving into the sector, workers can get better wages, or entrepreneurs can expect a better return for their capital, or both. That is, primary factors in SMEs have more income to distribute among them.

Figure A4.1, based on the aggregate numbers for Russia, illustrates the argument. The two lines show the combination of wages (or marginal product of labor, MPL) and profit rates (or marginal product of capital, MPK) compatible with the observed average product of labor in each sector (normalized so that average value added per worker in the economy and total employment are both equal to 1). The slope of each line reflects the average capital intensity of the sector.[4] The intersection with the vertical axis is the average value added per employee in each sector (as a ratio to the economywide value added per employee).

Assume that the "large enterprise" sector is characterized by point A, where the wage rate is about 60 percent of the average value added per worker in the economy. The production possibilities indicated by the SME line would mean that the new sector can pay wages 50 percent higher at the same profit rate (indicated by a point directly above A), or a much larger profit rate if paying the same wages (points directly at the right of A, on the new line). So there would be strong incentives for both labor and capital to move to the SME sector.

Labor mobility in Russia has probably not been strong enough to equalize wages across sectors. So, on average, MPL for the SME sector is likely to exceed MPL for the large enterprise sector at the current position—particularly considering the effective wage resulting from old enterprises not paying their workers on time or paying in kind, rather than the official wage rate. Because the existing capital stock is likely to be more sector-specific than labor, its returns could be even further from being equalized. Thus, a point like B appears as a reasonable comparison point on the SME sector for a "typical" bundle of labor and capital.

What are the gains to the economy when factors move, say, from A to B? A critical element is the extent to which factors, particularly capital,

FIGURE A4.1.

Factor Price Frontier: SMEs and the Rest of the Economy

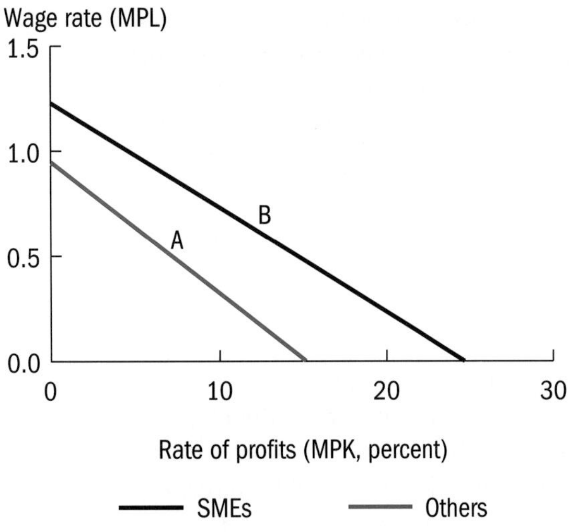

Wage rate (MPL)

Rate of profits (MPK, percent)

—— SMEs   —— Others

Source: Authors.

can be productively reallocated to new uses. For that, we define a "coefficient of shiftability to the SME sector" equal to the ratio of productivity of capital from the old sector to the productivity of new capital.[5] Some types of capital, such as specialized machinery and tools, may not be usable at all (a zero shiftability coefficient). Others, such as liquid assets used as working capital, office equipment, and some real estate, are likely to be fully usable in the emerging sector. In many old enterprises the main obstacle to productive reallocation of capital may be its technological obsolescence—though this also means that it is of low productivity even for the old enterprises.

The figure shows the gain in GDP from reallocating to the SME sector 10 percent of the total labor and capital of the economy, as a function of the "shiftability coefficient" defined above. The polar case of perfect capital shiftability—when capital can move without any loss in productivity—is also of interest because it represents the case of new investment. Figure A4.2 shows the large efficiency gain in allocating those new resources to the emerging sector instead of using them on old enterprises; if 10 percent of labor and capital move to the SME sector, aggregate valued added (GDP) would increase by almost 4 percent (assuming constant returns to scale, as standard on this type of model). The extra value added is the ex post validation of the ex ante potential earning difference, which provides the encouragement for the creation of new enterprises. The large productivity gap in such countries as Kazakhstan and Ukraine may thus be taken as an indicator of how much unrealized growth potential exists in the new sector in these countries.

The other polar case is when only labor can move to the new sector.[6] In this case (showed by the horizontal line in the figure) the gain is simply the difference in marginal productive of labors across the sectors—about 1.2 percent in the "base" case marked by points A and B on the factor price frontier.

Notes

1. The analysis is based on the hypotheses that small enterprises can be taken as a proxy for new enterprises, that spinoffs from the state sector do not mat-

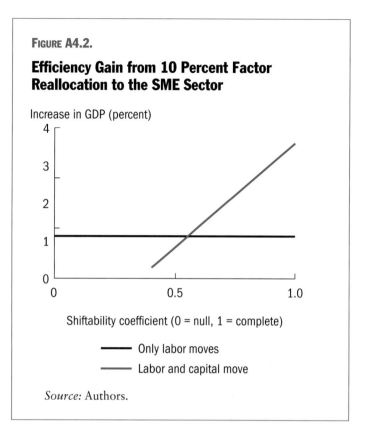

FIGURE A4.2.

Efficiency Gain from 10 Percent Factor Reallocation to the SME Sector

Increase in GDP (percent)

Shiftability coefficient (0 = null, 1 = complete)

— Only labor moves
— Labor and capital move

Source: Authors.

ter because they reflect restructuring, and that the evolution of labor productivity in the manufacturing sector can be taken to approximate the extent of restructuring (see annex 4.1). The corresponding number for Georgia—40 percent—reflects growth of new enterprises plus the destruction of old productive capacity due to armed conflict.

2. In Russia subsidies implicit in soft budgets accounted for two-thirds of net borrowing by the government. As a share of GDP this was 7.5 percent in 1996 and 5.6 percent in 1997. With the government's disinflation policy, this kept real interest rates in the triple digits in 1995 and 1996, coming down to single digits only in 1997.

3. Caves (1998) finds that most newly born enterprises in market economies belong to the first two deciles of the size distribution. A similar result can be expected in transition economies, where starting large enterprises from scratch is more difficult.

4. Thus the SME line's lower slope reflects the assumption that SMEs are on average less capital intensive than large enterprises. For the average capital intensity of the economy we use a capital-output ratio of 6 (EBRD 2000). The SME line is constructed assuming that they used about 8 percent less capital per

worker than the economy average (a capital-output ratio of 5, versus 6.23 for the rest of the economy). If both sectors had lower overall capital intensity, the two lines would rotate out around the w-axis (for each wage they would show a higher profit rate).

5. Thus (1-shiftability coefficient) is the share of productivity "lost" when moving from the old to the new sector. The values on the figure are calculated as follows. Value added per worker in each sector, v_i, can be written as $v_i = r_i {}^* k_i + w_i$ where k_i = capital-labor ratio in sector i, w_i = wage (or marginal product of labor) in sector i, r_i = profit rate (MPK) in sector i, and $i = 0$ (old/large enterprises) or $i = 1$ (new enterprises/SMEs). If α is the "shiftability coefficient"

(0 for fixed factors; 1 for perfect mobility and substitutability across sectors), the percentage gain in aggregate value added from reallocating 1 percent of labor and capital to the new sector is $dV/V = w_1 - w_0 + k_1 (\alpha r_1 - r_0)$. Of course, if the shiftability coefficient, α, is too low—specifically lower than $\alpha^* = r_1/r_0$—it is not worthwhile to reallocate capital, as the loss of output in the old sector would exceed productivity in the new.

6. This is different from the case of $\alpha = 0$ and capital and labor reallocation. Here it is assumed that old capital is left in use in the old sector instead of being reallocated, despite its low (or null) productivity in the new sector.

5

Imposing Discipline

Enterprises that subtract value at the prices prevailing after liberalization contribute negatively to growth. They must be subjected to market discipline through such instruments as hard budget constraints and competition in the markets for their products. Managers' behavior should be monitored using workers' councils or banks while the institutions of corporate governance are strengthened. At the same time, governments need to finance a targeted social safety net for those hurt by the imposition of discipline on inherited enterprises. Both governments and enterprises need to meet their expenditure obligations on time and in cash to prevent payments arrears.

Soft Budget Constraints Can Create Macroeconomic Crises

The loss of fiscal control accompanying the transition has led to a mushrooming of implicit and contingent liabilities. Soft budget constraints are generally more prevalent in the CIS than in the more advanced market reformers of Central and Eastern Europe. An index of soft budget constraints—measured by the proportion of enterprises in the Business Enterprise Environment and Performance Survey (see box 3.1) reporting arrears to the tax authorities and to state-owned energy producers, which are two of the significant sources of implicit subsidy—is highest in the Caucasus and Moldova, followed by the Czech and Slovak Republics and Croatia, followed by the Russian Federation, Ukraine, Romania, the Kyrgyz Republic, and Kazakhstan. By repeatedly allowing enterprises and banks to shift their losses to the budget, governments have injected an enormous moral hazard into the economic environment, with severe consequences for the economy and the credibility of fiscal policy. Some examples:

- The state budget deficit was about 1.3 percent of GDP in the Czech Republic in 1997–98, but the "hidden" deficit out of budget "transformation agencies" and guarantees was almost three times as large. The main reason was the softness of the budget constraint of the enterprise sector—not only for remaining large state-owned enterprises but also for newly privatized enterprises.
- In Croatia and Lithuania part of the very high current account deficit stemmed from the practice of public utilities to borrow abroad with government guarantees. In Bulgaria and Romania an

excessive use of off-balance-sheet items erupted into full-blown macroeconomic crises during 1996–98 when contingent liabilities arising from the growth of bad debts in the banking sector were converted into a fiscal burden requiring explicit financing.

- As a result, all these countries needed "second generation" stabilization efforts in the second half of the 1990s.
- In Russia the failure to impose hard budget constraints through widespread use of arrears and noncash payments led to government borrowing on an unsustainable scale, particularly in light of the global financial crisis in 1998. That eventually led to default on a large part of sovereign debt, an event that had serious repercussions throughout the CIS.

In the poorer CIS countries—Georgia, the Kyrgyz Republic, Moldova, and Tajikistan—none of which entered the transition with external debt, soft budget constraints on public enterprises, the difficulties associated with raising energy prices and disconnecting nonpayers to reduce consumption, and low tax collections have contributed to a rapid buildup of external debt. External shocks, such as the Russia crisis of 1998, have further exacerbated the problem. All four have a long-term solvency constraint and face tight liquidity in the next few years. Preliminary analysis suggests that new financing on highly concessional terms and, in some cases, generous debt relief may be needed to restore them to sustainable debt. The case for international action will be strengthened if the debtor countries implement strong up-front adjustment measures, eliminating tax exemptions and confronting powerful special interests (box 5.1).

Nonpayments Weaken the Incentives for Efficiency and Restructuring

Many governments have chosen to keep unviable enterprises afloat by extending implicit subsidies through the energy companies. In Russia implicit energy subsidies to manufacturing enterprises averaged 4 percent of GDP in 1993–97. They take the form of arrears and noncash settlements (including barter, promissory notes, and tax offsets, where government spending arrears and overdue tax payments are mutually cancelled). In turn, the public utility companies have passed on the costs of the implicit transfers to the general fiscal accounts by running up huge tax arrears and unpaid dues to extrabudgetary funds, so that the burden of subsidies has eventually led to the accumulation of public debt.

In Ukraine it is estimated that regional energy companies alone have provided annual financing to nonpayers on the order of 4 to 5 percent of GDP. Moreover, governments faced with tax and expenditure arrears have complicated the nonpayments problem by encouraging barter and other nonmonetary instruments to conduct mutually offsetting operations.[1] Much of this has continued regardless of government resolutions and legal acts forbidding the absorption of further energy arrears by the budget. Enterprises, their domestic and foreign suppliers (such as Gazprom of Russia), and creditors believed, correctly, that despite the statements, some explicit or implicit government support would be forthcoming. The absorption of gas arrears of public institutions by the Moldovan budget in 2000 was the fifth cycle of contingent liability creation and moral hazard since the country's independence. Payments arrears eventually had to be absorbed by the budget, often through tax offsets, or, for energy-dependent CIS countries, through intergovernmental agreements with Russia or Turkmenistan.

Nonpayments problems have been compounded in countries whose subnational governments have considerable autonomy, such as Russia and Ukraine. Clearance of tax arrears through tax offsets gives subnational governments opportunities to increase their retention of shared taxes at the expense of the center. In Russia subnational governments are more actively engaged than the federal government in clearing tax arrears through offsets and individual tax exemptions and deferrals for inefficient enterprises.

The consequences of the nonpayment syndrome go beyond the budget. The failure to harden budget constraints and the opacity of noncash payments have weakened incentives to use existing assets efficiently and to

Box 5.1.

External Debt and Fiscal Sustainability in the Low-Income CIS Countries

Armenia, Georgia, the Kyrgyz Republic, Moldova, and Tajikistan are among the poorest countries in the world—with per capita incomes in 2000 ranging from US$170 in Tajikistan to US$610 in Georgia. All five have small economies, narrow export bases, and depend heavily on energy imports. Four of the five are landlocked, and several face natural or conflict-related constraints on international trade. All began economic transition a decade ago with almost no debt, but by the end of 2000 their total nominal external debt exceeded US$7.1 billion, or 84 percent of their combined GDP. The net present value of their debt outstanding at the end of 2000 averaged 158 percent of their exports and 358 percent of their central government revenues.

Many factors have contributed to the accumulation of debt. Sharp increases in energy prices and the loss of transfers from the central government of the former Soviet Union after its breakup were massive shocks to these economies. Regional and internal conflicts hindered economic recovery. Policy failures, corruption, and weak governance have played an important role, too.

These countries have not been able to attract much in grant aid from bilateral donors and have relied heavily on the International Monetary Fund and World Bank for financial assistance. In the mid-1990s, the international financial institutions and other international creditors overestimated the implementation capacity of their governments to conduct the complex and socially painful reforms associated with the transition. The terms of some of the financing received were not always suitably concessional. Finally, the 1998 financial crisis in Russia severely disrupted their trade and financial sectors. Four of the five countries (Armenia is the exception) were forced to deeply devalue their currencies, leading to sharp increases in the domestic currency cost of external debt service.

Although the severity of the external debt burden varies among the five countries, the weakness of their external financing and fiscal positions is likely to be a serious constraint to growth and poverty reduction, even in the medium term. Action is needed on two broad fronts if they are to make better progress toward sustained economic growth and poverty reduction with strengthened financial viability.

First, the low-income CIS countries need to improve their policy environments. Fiscal reforms are required to ensure improved efficiency and effectiveness of public expenditures within the tight overall resource constraint. The pace of reform needs to be accelerated in key sectors, such as energy, which have strong links to the fiscal and external debt situation. Major reforms are needed to improve the investment climate, notably the environment for entry by new enterprises, which has proven to be a key success factor in Central and Eastern Europe. Institutional changes to strengthen public and private sector governance will be important in this regard.

Second, they need to work closely with their external partners to secure a volume and blend of financial assistance consistent with their absorptive capacity and policy efforts, as well as their fiscal and debt-carrying capacities. International Monetary Fund and World Bank policy-based credit operations are either ongoing or planned in each of the countries. Other donors need to consider increasing their assistance, notably through grants and other highly concessional funds. The scope for and costs and benefits of external debt rescheduling for these countries also needs to be examined. Donors should provide debt relief promptly and on highly concessional terms where this is demonstrated, as warranted by both financial need and policy efforts.

restructure enterprises. Nonpayments reinforce existing interenterprise relationships. They also weaken competition by segmenting product markets and dealing with a few key suppliers and customers. Furthermore, by reducing transparency in accounting and transactions, they complicate monitoring of enterprise managers. Even healthier enterprises have benefited by colluding with unviable enterprises to divert the implicit subsidies available in the system rather than look for ways to restructure and increase efficiency.

The widespread use of arrears and noncash payments led to the proliferation of vertically integrated conglomerates and provided an impetus

for numerous formal and informal financial-industrial groups, thus impeding competition and new entry. Furthermore, subnational governments have protected incumbent enterprises with which they have built close relationships through nonpayments at the expense of new entrants, inhibiting investments and postponing the resumption of growth.

The experience of the 1990s clearly demonstrates that sustainable growth and low inflation require enterprise restructuring and exit, new entry, and fiscal adjustment. But none of these can be addressed without tackling the nonpayments problem that affects them all. For this, the challenge facing Russia and other CIS countries differs somewhat from the hardening budget constraints that the reforming countries of Central and Eastern Europe faced at the onset of transition. The following actions comprise the main elements of a solution to the nonpayments crisis (Pinto, Drebentsov, and Morozov 2000):

- The government pays its bills in cash and on time and refrains from engaging in mutual offsets to cancel tax and budgetary arrears.
- Energy companies pay their taxes in cash and on time.
- Companies enforce a policy of disconnecting those delinquent on payments, thus imposing a hard budget constraint on those enterprises.
- Social assets traditionally provided by enterprises (such as housing, health clinics, and kindergartens) are divested to local governments.
- Benefits are targeted to the low-income households most affected by an increase in energy prices to international levels.
- Some types of one-company towns in distant regions of the CIS, such as distressed settlements in isolated areas and settlements with a predominantly retired population, get special arrangements.

The substantial real devaluation of 1998 has given Russian enterprises some (temporary) breathing space, making it easier to eliminate the implicit subsidies transmitted through tax and energy payments. Noncash settlements continue to abate as a result of improved enterprise liquidity from the devaluation. Although tax rates continue to be negotiated, almost 100 percent of current taxes are paid in cash.

Budget constraints are hardening though the very channels that once transmitted hidden subsidies: government budget management, taxes, and energy payments. Cash collections from enterprises by regional energy companies have increased significantly, a development attributed to unremitting pressure from such infrastructure monopolies as Gazprom and RAO Unified Energy Systems. Indeed, these monopolies have become potent instruments for hardening budget constraints and insisting on cash payments.

Tax offsets are forbidden for the value-added tax, profits tax, and income tax, and lack of compliance could lead to federal transfers being cut. The result is a chain reaction: the federal budget does not transfer the funds needed for residential electricity and heat, so the local authorities insist that the municipal utility companies foot the bill. The latter in turn insist that the households pay. For enterprises, the main pressure comes from taxes and cash payments for energy. In addition, the restructuring of past arrears is taking place by mutual consent and on condition that current obligations are met in full.

Exit Mechanisms—Implement Now, Revise Later

Turning off the spigot of fiscal and quasi-fiscal support and keeping government agencies current on their obligations is necessary. However, this alone is liable to lead to more accumulation of arrears and, without complementary policies, will not be enough to lead to restructuring or closure. Two such policies are important. First, restructuring and exit will require a transfer of responsibility for housing and other social assets from enterprises to local governments, an area where the roles and responsibilities of local government suffer from lack of clarity and absence of financing. Second, measures of administrative liquidation need to be strengthened.

Almost all countries in the region have bankruptcy laws. In a number of countries there were significant reforms of these laws in 2000. But these formal exit mechanisms have not been particularly effective. The European Bank for Reconstruction and Development's legal indicator survey indicates that there is a gap between the adoption or amendment of bankruptcy legislation and its effective implementation (EBRD 2000). Experience suggests that it is preferable to implement existing insolvency laws and revise them once they have been put into practice.

Competition Is Linked to Innovation and Growth

Encouraging competition in product markets is another important ingredient of discipline. Because socialist economies were highly concentrated, exposing enterprises to internal and external competition is important. Results from the Business Enterprise Environment and Performance Survey (see box 3.1) show that nearly 30 percent of state-owned enterprises face no competitors, compared with 5–9 percent for private enterprises. While more than half of state-owned enterprises have more than three competitors in their main product market, 80 percent or more of privatized and new private enterprises find themselves in that situation (EBRD 1999).

The survey also shows that enterprises facing an intermediate degree of competition (one to three competitors) develop new products, replace managers, or change their organizational structure if they are subject to a hard budget constraint, with their moderate degree of market power providing the reward necessary to innovate. Where monitoring of managerial performance by debtors and external shareholders is weak—as is generally the case in the CIS and Southeastern Europe—competitive product markets can help discipline enterprise managers. The link between competition, innovation, and growth emerges as particularly important. Governments should thus vest the competition policy agency with the authority to enforce competition laws strictly.

Note

1. As an illustration of failing to harden budget constraints by disconnecting nonpayers, the Russian government threatened to block oil producers' access to export pipelines if producers stopped supplying oil to nonpaying domestic refineries.

6

Extending Encouragement

What is needed to encourage the formation, and then growth, of new enterprises? This chapter identifies administrative barriers to entry as one of the most important obstacles. It also looks at aspects of legal and judicial reform that impinge on the security of property rights. This chapter describes what needs to be done to develop a financial sector capable of nurturing new enterprises and monitoring enterprise reform. It also reviews reforms in the tax system and in intergovernmental fiscal relations that support the discipline-and-encourage strategy.

Corruption and Anticompetitive Practices Mar the Investment Climate

The Business Environment and Enterprise Performance Survey (see box 3.1) unbundled factors influencing the investment climate into microeconomic variables (including taxes and regulations), macroeconomic variables (including policy instability, inflation, and exchange rates), and law and order (including functioning of the judiciary, corruption, street crime, disorder, organized crime, and mafia). According to the respondents, taxes and regulations are consistently among the most important impediments to expansion by new enterprises. Within this category, the granting and annual renewal of business licensing—and the opportunities for corruption that this can provide—are seen as serious obstacles. The other obstacles, in order of importance, are inflation, lack of access to finance, corruption and anticompetitive practices, and lack of access to infrastructure services (Hellman, Jones, and Kaufmann 2000).

The situation is reported to be consistently worse in the CIS and Southeastern Europe than in Central Europe and the Baltics. The survey also shows that small enterprises across the region pay, on average, 5.4 percent of their annual revenues in bribes, as opposed to 2.8 percent for large enterprises (World Bank 2000c). The regressiveness of the bribe tax is highest in Armenia, Moldova, Ukraine, and Uzbekistan. The frequency of bribe payments is about double for small enterprises: 37 percent report paying bribes frequently, compared with 16 percent for large enterprises.

New enterprises see corruption and anticompetitive practices as two of the most difficult obstacles across all parts of the region. Business licensing, which falls in the category of taxes and regulations, is seen as particularly troublesome by new enterprises, given the opportunity for arbitrary behavior in interactions between officials and enterprises in granting and renewing licenses. Also troublesome are regulations for customs, foreign trade, foreign currency, foreign exchange, and taxes. Examples of such obstacles abound.

A survey of Russian enterprises by the World Bank in 1996 shows that the average new business applicant had to deal with about 25 different agencies and complete about 70 registration forms. There were 30 kinds of licenses for a business startup. About a third of surveyed enterprises indicated that they were forced to obtain a license that in their opinion was not required.

In Ukraine an International Finance Corporation study showed that small enterprises endure an average of 78 inspections a year, requiring 68 written responses. Dealing with inspections and audits consumes two days a week of the average manager's time and requires cash outlays of about US$2,000.

The administrative problems that new entrants in Armenia (box 6.1) face in registering, locating, and operating their companies are pervasive throughout the region. The solutions lie in simplifying processes to make them transparent and consistent across all government agencies. Similarly, customs procedures need to be reengineered to make them more transparent and

---

Box 6.1.

Reducing the Cost of Entry and Doing Business in Armenia

New enterprises face many problems in Armenia that could be reduced with appropriate measures.

Registration

Company registration is cumbersome, involving half a dozen agencies and includes such antiquated practices as obtaining a company seal. Procedures are described in general terms in the laws, leaving substantial discretion to civil servants. Registration normally takes three to six months.

Policy recommendations are to:

- Develop a centralized registration process with one oversight agency
- Create transparent registration requirements and procedures and make them easily accessible to the public
- Eliminate the outmoded requirement for a company seal.

Permits

Registering ownership rights is a convoluted bureaucratic process, designed more as a data collection system than as a process to register legal rights. Many steps appear irrelevant. Armenia's land cadastre system records ownership based on street addresses or passport numbers, rather than a unique cadastral code established through surveys. Site development is equally difficult, with numerous municipal and state agencies involved in issuing the approvals and clearances required for construction and occupation permits. There is no comprehensive description of the required procedural steps, and the authority of various agencies often overlaps, resulting in frequent delays and contradictory decisions.

Policy recommendations are to:

- Redesign ownership registration by eliminating or streamlining all steps not directly related to registering legal titles
- Assign a unique cadastral code to all real property units and create a consistent register
- Develop clear and transparent rules for site development that are consistent across all government agencies
- Harmonize all requirements of the process throughout the country
- Eliminate duplication of effort by various agencies
- Introduce application forms for all agencies and attach a reliable and clear guide
- Set timetables for each phase.

Source: World Bank data.

to reduce the scope for arbitrary decisionmaking and abuses of power.

Enterprises Lack Confidence in Legal and Judicial Institutions

The state can create a good climate for investment by protecting the security of property and contract rights. Variation in the security of property rights in the region is high (figure 6.1). Fewer than 30 percent of enterprises in such countries as Croatia, Estonia, and Poland lack confidence in the security of property rights, compared with more than 70 percent in Russia and Ukraine.

Institutions contributing to the security of property rights are diverse: property registries; a stable and appropriate body of laws, regulations, and administrative procedures; effective systems to adjudicate administrative and civil disputes; and legal expertise (lawyers, notaries, judges, prosecutors, police, and bailiffs) to ensure that the legal framework is enforced. Data are available on the quality of legal drafting (figure 6.2), which is eventually linked to the stability and appropriateness of the legal framework and to the quality of the judicial system (figure 6.3).

On the basis of the Business Environment and Enterprise Performance Survey, more than 90 percent of enterprises in 13 of the sample countries report that they are not adequately consulted in the drafting process for new laws or policies. More than 80 percent of enterprises in 13 of the sample countries report that they are not adequately informed of changes in rules that affect them before these rules are adopted. The quality of the judiciary is unbundled into fairness (bias, honesty, consistency), cost (financial and time), and likelihood of enforcement (see figure 6.3). There is wide variation in perceptions of the quality of the judiciary. In Hungary, Estonia, and Slovenia only a third of enterprises report that court decisions are unfair, while in Armenia and Lithuania almost 90 percent of enterprises do. In Uzbekistan fewer than half of the enterprises complain about the high cost of litigation, while in Poland more than 90 percent of enterprises do. In Bulgaria and Slovenia only about a quarter of enterprises

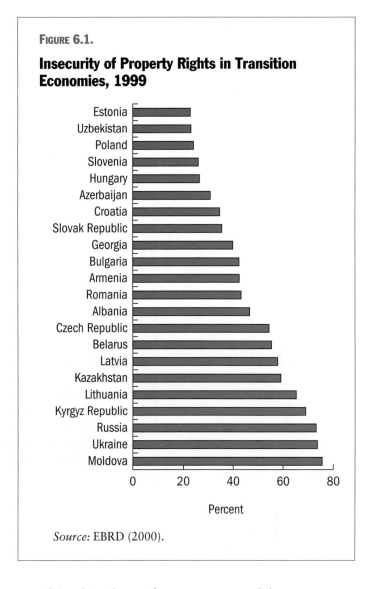

FIGURE 6.1.

Insecurity of Property Rights in Transition Economies, 1999

Source: EBRD (2000).

complain about low enforcement rates, while in Albania almost 90 percent of enterprises do.

Almost two-thirds of the variation in the security of property rights across countries can be attributed to variation in their systems of legal drafting and the effectiveness of their judiciaries. Thus, attention to the process of drafting and enforcing laws may help ensure that laws are suited to achieve economic outcomes—in this case, secure property and contracts.

A study based on a survey of manufacturing enterprises in Poland, Romania, Russia, the Slovak Republic, and Ukraine found that enterprises with the least secure property rights invested nearly 40 percent less than those with the most secure property rights.[1] Moreover reinvestment

Figure 6.2.

Quality of Legal Drafting in Transition Economies, 1999

(percentage of enterprises that complain they are seldom or never consulted about new rules)

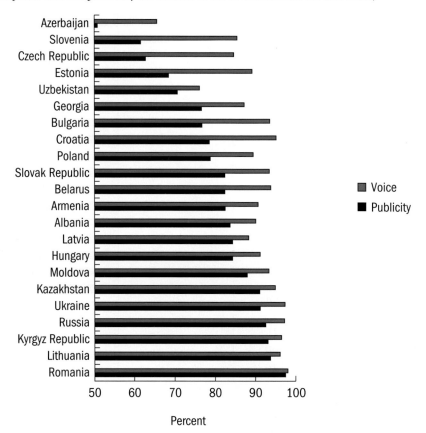

Note: This figure shows partial results from two questions on the Business Environment and Enterprise Performance Survey (see box 3.1). The first question measured enterprises' voice in legal drafting: "In case of important changes in laws or policies affecting my business operation, the government takes into account concerns voiced either by me or by my business association." The second question measured the extent to which the state publicizes new rules (publicity) before their implementation: "The process of developing new rules, regulations, and policies is usually such that businesses are informed in advance of changes that will affect them." For both questions the possible responses were "always, mostly, frequently, sometimes, seldom, or never."

Source: World Bank data.

of profits was a bigger source of investment capital than either bank funds or trade credit in all five countries. In such countries as Russia and Ukraine, which have made less progress in transition than Poland and the Slovak Republic, reforms to secure property rights are more important for promoting the investment climate than reforms in the banking sector. Then, as the transition proceeds and legal and judicial reforms strengthen property rights, a well-functioning financial sector is needed to provide credit to enterprises making new investment and requiring financing beyond their retained earnings.

Financial Deepening Is Slow but Progressing

Although securing property rights appears to be more important than reforming the

FIGURE 6.3.

Quality of Judiciary in Transition Economies

(percentage of enterprises that complain that courts sometimes, seldom, or never exhibit positive qualities when resolving business disputes)

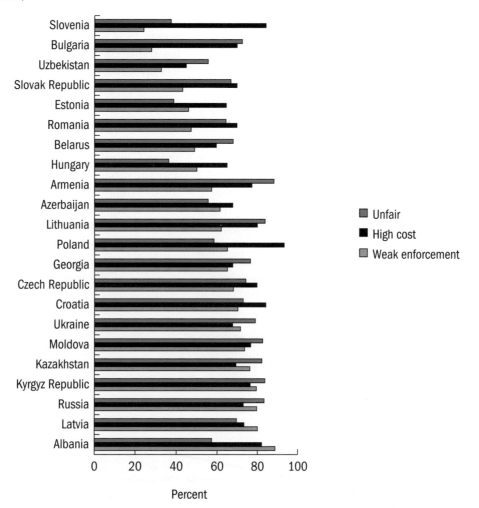

Note: This figure shows partial results from the following question on the Business Environment and Enterprise Performance Survey (see box 3.1): "Now, thinking about our country's legal system, how often do you associate the following descriptions with the court system in resolving business disputes?" The descriptions were: fair and impartial; honest/uncorrupted; quick; affordable; consistent/reliable; able to enforce its decisions. The possible responses were "always, usually, frequently, sometimes, seldom, or never." The "unfair" bar comprises the descriptions of fair and impartial, honest/uncorrupted, or quick. The "high cost" bar comprises the descriptions of quick or affordable. The "weak enforcement" bar comprises the descriptions consistent/reliable and able to enforce decisions.

Source: World Bank data.

banking system in the early stages of transition, financial deepening and development is key to sustaining the growth of the new private sector. While transition economies have come a long way in developing banks and capital markets, their financial sectors remain underdeveloped by international standards. Banking systems in most transition economies remain noticeably small in international perspective, even more so once bank credit to the public sector, often reflecting subsidization of unprofitable activities, is removed and attention is confined to the private sector (figure 6.4).

Similarly, stock market capitalization, a measure of the capacity of securities to provide finance to the real economy, shows that financial development lags behind other countries of the world with similar per capita incomes (figure 6.5). Relative to their peers in the region, Croatia, the Czech Republic, and Hungary boasted the highest stock market capitalization in 1998.[2]

The Banking Sector Is Moving Forward...

Although the financial sector appears underdeveloped from an international perspective, this is not necessarily true for financial intermediation in the banking sector. The ratio of operating costs to total assets reveals that several Central European countries have progressed in recent

years (figure 6.6). In 1997 all Central European countries except Slovenia had operating cost to total asset ratios that were lower than those in countries with comparable incomes elsewhere. While the Baltic countries had not quite matched their peers in the world, their average ratio of operating costs to total assets fell from 7.8 percent in 1996 to 5.6 percent in 1997. The remaining transition economies with data have ratios less favorable than their peers, but they too (except Romania) saw efficiency improve. An alternative measure of efficiency—the difference between the average interest rate on loans to the private sector and the resident deposit rate—also shows Central Europe and the Baltics in a favorable situation, but not Southeastern Europe and the CIS (figure 6.7).

Although domestic credit to the private sector (as a share of GDP) in the transition economies is generally low in comparison with countries of similar per capita incomes (figure 6.4), in many of the most advanced reformers an

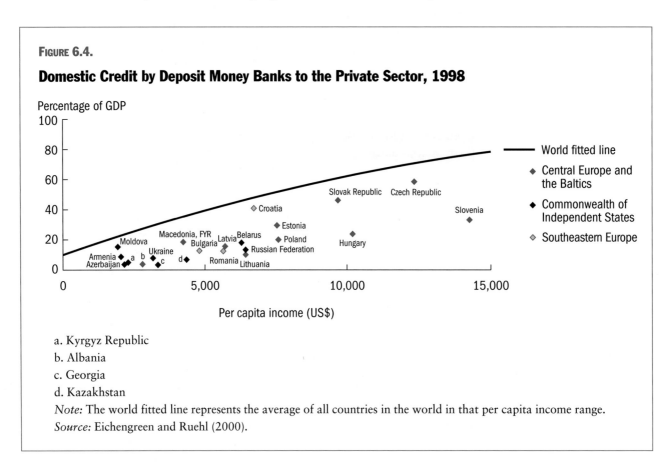

FIGURE 6.4.

Domestic Credit by Deposit Money Banks to the Private Sector, 1998

a. Kyrgyz Republic
b. Albania
c. Georgia
d. Kazakhstan

Note: The world fitted line represents the average of all countries in the world in that per capita income range.
Source: Eichengreen and Ruehl (2000).

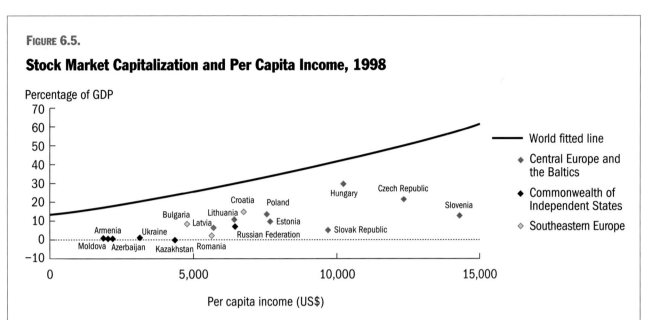

FIGURE 6.5.

Stock Market Capitalization and Per Capita Income, 1998

Note: The world fitted line represents the average of all countries in the world in that per capita income range.
Source: Eichengreen and Ruehl (2000).

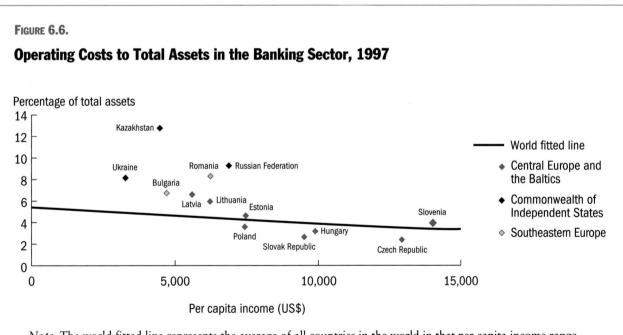

FIGURE 6.6.

Operating Costs to Total Assets in the Banking Sector, 1997

Note: The world fitted line represents the average of all countries in the world in that per capita income range.
Source: Eichengreen and Ruehl (2000).

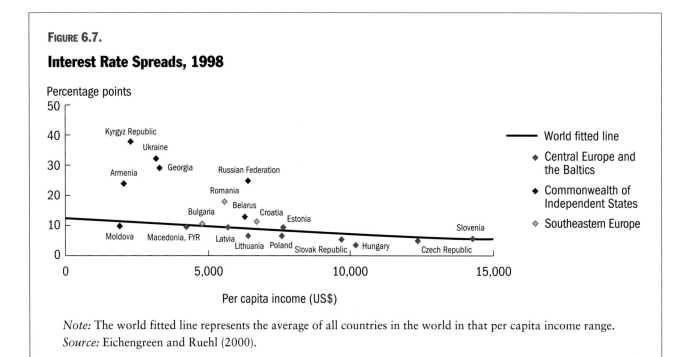

FIGURE 6.7.

Interest Rate Spreads, 1998

Note: The world fitted line represents the average of all countries in the world in that per capita income range.
Source: Eichengreen and Ruehl (2000).

important part of that credit is now flowing to new enterprises. In Estonia, Hungary, and Latvia between two-thirds and three-quarters of total private credit is going to those enterprises.

The Czech Republic and Hungary provide an interesting contrast. The Czech Republic has the highest share of credit to the private sector, about 60 percent of GDP, (see figure 6.4), but only one-tenth of it flows to new enterprises. In Hungary, the credit provided to the private sector is much lower (about 25 percent of GDP), but about three-quarters of it goes to new enterprises. Why? Because in the Czech Republic most banks were still state-owned and largely unreformed, and they continued to lend to their traditional clients: large semi-privatized enterprises. This is consistent with a situation of banks not having been positioned to do their job of screening, together with the limited industrial restructuring and lack of growth in the Czech Republic in recent years.

Hungary, by contrast, sold off almost all its commercial banks to foreign investors early on in the transition. These new private banks applied to their borrowers the hard budget constraints imposed on them by their headquarters and strict supervision by the supervisory agencies in

Hungary. Thus comprehensive financial restructuring and curtailment of loans to the banks' traditional clients have been associated with faster growth of financial intermediation to new private clients. The experience of Hungary suggests that restructuring the financial sector and developing financial intermediation can go hand in hand.

...Can the Discipline-and-Encourage Strategy Quicken the Pace?

Hard budget constraints should apply to banks and enterprises alike. A credible threat of exit is necessary for a competitive banking system. But a bank differs from a nonfinancial enterprise, so a decision on liquidation or restructuring, especially for large banks, must take into account the systemic risk of closure. The efficiency of banks improves if they are privatized to strategic investors. If such investors are not forthcoming, privatization to concentrated owners should be considered, so long as there is a clear separation between investors and borrowers from the bank.

Facilitating the entry of foreign financial intermediaries can accelerate the development of the banking sector and in turn help the growth of start-ups not yet ready to tap capital markets.

Entry by foreign banks and the acquisition of domestic banks by foreign banks are quick ways of importing managerial and supervisory expertise, the latter because supervisory responsibility resides mainly with the home country regulatory authority. While encouraging competition is critical for the long-term health of commercial banks, it should be done without relaxing prudential norms. These norms should cover minimum capital requirements, regulatory capacity, legal recourse, and the independence of supervisory authorities from political interference.

Recent work on the relationship between finance and growth suggests that banks and securities exchanges provide different services, both required in a mature market economy (Levine and Zervos 1998). The financial system in transition economies will most probably remain heavily bank-based for a while. New enterprises need to be nurtured and this phase calls for a bank-based financial sector capable of providing risk assessment and venture capital services. A later phase will call also for an active and liquid securities market that is more suited to funding risky projects and offers fuller risk diversification. This later phase will require even more demanding institutional developments such as a regulatory framework requiring information disclosure and preventing insider trading and other forms of market manipulation.

Privatization Attracts Foreign Direct Investment, and Positive Spillovers Follow

There are significant differences in the levels of foreign direct investment flowing to the transition economies. In the 1991–2000 decade, the CIS received cumulative foreign direct investment per capita of about US$115 compared with US$800 for the CSB. The Czech Republic and Hungary had the highest amounts, almost US$2000, followed by Estonia, Latvia, and Croatia in the US$300 to US$1000 range.

Cash privatization of large enterprises has driven much of these foreign direct investment flows; cumulative foreign direct investment is highly correlated with cumulative privatization revenues (EBRD 2000). However, foreign direct investment has also flown to countries as a response to improved policies and improved overall business environment. Some studies have shown a clear statistical relationship between the growth of foreign direct investment and the indices of economic liberalization discussed in chapter 2 (Selowsky and Martin 1998). The ability to attract foreign direct investment is thus a good proxy for the attractiveness of a country's overall investment climate and is also crucial to promote the entry and growth of SMEs. Actually both are well associated as shown in figure 6.8.

In addition to the positive spillovers of improved technology, better management skills, and access to international production networks, foreign direct investment has proved resilient in volatile international capital markets. Although the Russia crisis of 1998 led to sizable outflows of bond and portfolio equity capital, this was offset by an increase in foreign direct investment in the advanced reformers in Central Europe and the Baltics. Russia and Ukraine, reluctant to attract foreign participation in their privatization programs, had attracted only modest amounts of foreign direct investment but substantial portfolio flows. Much of the latter found its way into financing public sector deficits arising from an overall climate of soft budget constraints. When the government's solvency was questioned in the 1998 crisis, portfolio flows to Russia quickly reversed.

Tax Reform: Broadening the Base and Lowering Rates

The agenda of tax reform in the transition economies is large. Its guiding principle, based on the lessons of theory and experience, is that a tax system raising revenue for the government at least cost to the economy should be stable and broad-based and have low statutory rates. The focus in this section is narrow, restricted to aspects of taxation that bear directly on discipline and encouragement.

The key objective of tax reform is to broaden the base of taxation and reduce statutory rates. This would eliminate tax exemptions enjoyed by favored enterprises, thus hardening budget constraints. It would also reduce the burden of taxation on viable enterprises and encourage the

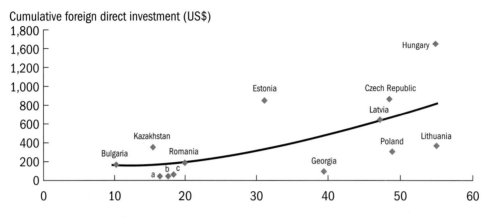

FIGURE 6.8.

Cumulative Foreign Direct Investment Per Capita and Employment in Small Enterprises, 1998

a. Ukraine.

b. Belarus.

c. Russian Federation.

Source: EBRD (2000); World Bank database on SMEs.

informal sector to come within the tax system. The informal sector in 1995 was estimated at 60 percent of GDP in Azerbaijan and Georgia, between 40 and 50 percent in Russia and Ukraine, and between 30 and 40 percent in Bulgaria, Kazakhstan, Latvia, and Moldova. In the Kyrgyz Republic tax exemptions, mostly to foreign joint ventures, have in the past cost the budget the equivalent of 5–7 percent of GDP, while revenue collections remain below 16 percent of GDP. In Russia the potentially large tax base was eroded by exemptions granted by subnational authorities on federal taxes, estimated at 0.8 percent of GDP (World Bank staff estimates).

Taxes on small businesses are widely reported to be a disincentive to creating small enterprises in the region. The turnover threshold for becoming a value-added taxpayer should thus be set high enough to exclude small enterprises, which should be subject to a small-enterprise tax regime, perhaps as simple as a fixed annual fee in lieu of taxes other than wage and social taxes. Larger enterprises might be subject to either a turnover tax at a moderate rate or to a simplified cash flow tax

using simplified accounting. Such an approach would relieve the administrative and reporting burden on the taxpayer and reduce the interaction between the taxpayer and the tax authority.

For agriculture, a property tax needs to be developed as land privatization continues. This could be the primary method of agricultural taxation in the foreseeable future. Paralleling the earlier discussion, a distinction needs to be made between small agricultural units and larger agribusinesses. Smaller agricultural enterprises should be subject to the small business tax (or personal income tax, as appropriate). Larger enterprises should become more fully integrated into the modern income tax and value-added tax systems.

Intergovernmental Fiscal Relations Supporting Discipline and Encouragement

It is important for the incentives facing federal and local governments to be aligned in support of the discipline-and-encourage strategy. Subnational governments should have incentives to identify with small business. To save jobs and to protect existing political structures these governments often protect large (often bankrupt) enterprises in their localities, even though job growth generally increases with the development of small businesses. However, the latter takes time.

To help subnational governments identify with new emerging enterprises, small business taxes and property taxes could be allocated to that level of government. Subnational government officials will then see that the success of small business means more local revenues. Compliance with the property tax will be enhanced if the tax is tied to improvements in public services, such as police protection demanded by local businesses. That in turn increases property values, reinforcing mutual interests.

It is also necessary to ensure that local governments do not face an incentive to treat enterprises differently because they continue to provide social services, such as hospitals, kindergartens, and housing recreation facilities. In many cases municipalities do not have the resources to provide these services. This creates incentives for subnational governments to provide special treatment to unrestructured and sometimes nonviable old enterprises, with the attendant deleterious consequences for the growth of new enterprises.

It is important that an effective strategy be developed and implemented for divesting enterprises of these social services. In some cases this means placing the responsibility of service provision on the municipality. In others it means reassigning responsibilities, or at least financing

the service at a higher level of government. In yet other cases it means a complete redesign of the provision of social services and benefits.

Many countries in the region have shifted social responsibilities to local governments, but have not ensured that local governments have enough resources to manage these responsibilities, either through bigger transfers or greater tax autonomy. In addition, the divestiture of social services is frequently done in a way that leads to confusion over which level of government is responsible for what. Roles and responsibilities of subnational governments have to be clarified. In addition, enough resources must be allocated to the additional responsibilities of absorbing social assets from enterprises. That reduces the incentive for localities to favor old enterprises over new.

Notes

1. The property rights variables used in the analysis combine an index of property rights security comprising extra legal payments for licenses, extra legal payments for services, and payments for protection with a measure of the effectiveness of courts. See Johnson, McMillan, and Woodruff (2000).

2. Several transition economies, notably in Central Europe, appear to perform better when market liquidity is measured by the ratio of turnover (a measure of the liquidity of the securities) to market capitalization. These high turnover ratios, rather than reflecting genuine liquidity of the markets, are driven by high privatization sales captured (the numerator) in conjunction with low levels of capitalization (the denominator).

7

Privatization: Lessons and Agenda for the Future

P rivatization has been key in the transition from plan to market. Rapid privatization early in the transition aimed to get the state out of enterprise management, to create a broad constituency for reforms, and to arrest "spontaneous privatization" from pretransition reform attempts in countries as diverse as Hungary, Poland, the Russian Federation, and Ukraine. Privatization was a way of imposing hard budget constraints and promoting restructuring. It was also a way of creating demand for stronger property rights and institutions of corporate governance, thus contributing to private sector development.

What is the evidence on privatization's effect on restructuring in medium-size and large enterprises over the past decade in transition economies? Djankov and Murrell's (2000) recent review of the literature, covering about 30 studies, concludes that:

- Privatization to concentrated outsider owners (investment funds, foreigners, and blockholders) has benefited restructuring
- Privatization to diffuse owners and to enterprise workers and managers (so-called *insiders*) has not been beneficial; indeed, privatization to workers in the CIS has been worse than state ownership for restructuring.

A reasonable hypothesis for the ineffectiveness of diffuse or insider ownership is the lack of an adequate institutional framework. That framework would include strong mechanisms of corporate governance, including rules to protect minority shareholders; rules against insider deals and conflicts of interest; and adequate accounting, auditing, and disclosure standards. It would also include take-over, insolvency, and collateral legislation, as well as strong creditor surveillance by well-run private banks. Without such institutions those in control of enterprise assets face few restrictions to prevent diversions for private gain.

Other factors may also have contributed to the poor performance of enterprises privatized to insiders or diffuse owners. These owners probably had neither the ability to provide the capital to modernize the enterprise, nor the market experience to cope in a competitive environment, nor the drive and vision to guide the radical restructuring often required to improve enterprise performance.

Furthermore, workers in the CIS, traditionally a weak force in the enterprise, had almost no ownership or management experience. Also, ownership by workers may have done little for restructuring if employment had to be reduced sharply.

Concentrated ownership tends to offer those controlling enterprises the incentive to maximize long-run enterprise profits. Owners can align their interests with minority shareholders and creditors, reducing the likelihood of asset stripping for private gain. But privatization in transition economies shows that concentrated ownership alone is not enough for effective governance.

Concentration of ownership must be deep enough to reduce the divergence between the interests of controlling shareholders and other stakeholders and to lead controlling shareholders to pursue long-run profit maximization. An ownership control of only 20–30 percent may not be high enough to align interests.

The type of concentrated ownership also matters. Enterprises controlled by strategic investors have performed much better than those controlled by investment funds, other stakeholders (holding companies), or other financial institutions. Enterprises controlled by foreign strategic investors have generally been the best performers. This is not entirely unexpected. Such investors, able to provide more resources and skills for restructuring, had an advantage over domestic strategic investors early in the transition.

The selection of strategic investors matters, too. Enterprises sold through transparent tenders or auctions have generally attracted better owners, outperforming enterprises sold directly to politically connected parties, frequently at highly subsidized prices.

So, the ideal strategy is to transfer assets as rapidly as possible to individual investors or concentrated groups of strategic investors through open, fair, and transparent methods. Some countries—such as East Germany, Estonia, and Hungary—adopted this strategy, with satisfactory outcomes. Why did other countries not follow suit?

Privatization to diffuse owners and worker-owners was appealing on equity grounds, and in several countries this was the only way to make private ownership politically acceptable. It was also thought that any inefficiency of diffuse ownership would be only temporary, as secondary markets would consolidate share in the hands of effective owners. In any event, there were few concentrated domestic owners to buy state assets. Selling to foreigners was politically difficult, and such investors were sometimes less available to the CIS countries, given the overall uncertainties about the investment climate and lack of track record. Other factors included country size, geography, political uncertainty, inadequate legal framework, and weak institutional capacity.

Might it not have been preferable to keep the assets in state hands, waiting to identify and then sell the enterprises to reliable strategic investors? Yes, on two conditions. First, the privatization agency needs the autonomy to discharge its functions with transparency and without political interference. Second, there has to be enough institutional capacity to prevent asset stripping by state managers in the interim. In many countries these conditions were not met, resulting in "spontaneous" privatizations by managers when the enterprises were still owned by the state. Take Russia at the end of the Gorbachev era, when the state had lost control over enterprises after the collapse of institutions during the dissolution of the Soviet Union.

The challenge in economies with a large unfinished agenda of privatization is for the state to exercise its control rights to avoid tunneling and theft by enterprise managers during the years it could take to complete privatization and while enterprises remain in state hands. Yes, divestiture to reputable core investors who put their capital at risk is best practice. However, that is difficult to achieve on a large scale in a short period. A major question then is whether intermediate modes of privatization—such as mass privatization through vouchers, or management-employee buyouts—might eventually lead to the same result, even if they temporarily worsen enterprise performance.

Navigating between continued state ownership with eroding control rights and a transfer to ineffective new private owners with an inadequate institutional framework is possibly one of the most difficult challenges confronting policymakers in charge of privatization. There is a substantial risk of asset stripping and losses of economic value in both cases.

How much can tunneling and theft in the intermediate stages be prevented? How fast can reputable concentrated investors become the ultimate owners? Does the outcome depend on the path followed? The present value of the benefits of a specific privatization strategy depends on the answers. For example, do rapid intermediate modalities—such as privatization to diffused owners or insiders—accelerate or retard the eventual takeover of the enterprise by the "right" kind of investor? What are the relative magnitudes of the gains or losses of these intermediate stages of ownership in relation to state ownership? The answers depend on initial conditions and the capacity to reduce tunneling (see box 3.2) and theft and thus enhance the benefits of the strategy.

Traditional Privatization or Rapid Privatization?

If countries choose traditional methods of privatization to effective owners, establishing the necessary legal and institutional framework and giving the privatization agency autonomy and resources are essential. However, if countries choose methods of rapid privatization that lead to diffuse or insider ownership, strengthening and enforcing the regulatory and supervisory framework are crucial to enhance the accountability of corporate boards and managers, to protect the rights of minority shareholders, to promote disclosure, and to ensure that secondary trading is conducted at fair and transparent prices. Building these institutions requires time and resources in both cases.

Where court enforcement of contracts is weak, these provisions should be supplemented by stock market regulation for financial intermediaries, such as investment funds and brokers, which can monitor compliance by other participants in financial markets. This would help set the stage for medium-size and large privatizations in countries that still have a significant reform agenda. It would also improve

the performance of privatized enterprises by assisting a transparent consolidation of widely held shares and new private enterprises. It would also facilitate the development of bank and nonbank intermediation.

The success of the two approaches requires openness to foreign investors. The importance of foreign capital in the first approach is obvious. It makes little sense to exclude foreign investors from a privatization program designed to transfer enterprises directly to effective owners, as foreign investors are often in the best position to provide the resources and skills for restructuring state enterprises. However, foreign investors are equally important in the second approach. They can usually buy large blocks of shares in the secondary market relatively quickly, while also complying with all capital market regulations, thus facilitating the concentration of ownership through fair and transparent secondary trading.

Excluding foreign investors from mass privatization programs using vouchers could force policymakers into difficult choices. For example, the authorities might have to tolerate unfair practices to allow cash-strapped domestic investors to rapidly gain control. The concentration of ownership in many voucher programs, as in the Czech Republic, owed much to poor capital market regulation and weak rule enforcement. But if the authorities had been willing and able to enforce an adequate regulatory framework, they probably would have been forced to accept a longer period of diffuse ownership.[1]

Why Countries Did What They Did

At the end of the 1980s the best-known privatizations were negotiated sales to strategic investors—or privatization by issuing shares—along the lines applied in Great Britain and a few other OECD countries. The circumstances in transition economies demanded different approaches. For example, all transition economies contained thousands of state-owned small business and service units, of a type unknown in the West. Most countries began their privatization by divesting these small enterprises, usually by simple methods based on auctions. Small-enterprise privatization is everywhere regarded as a success. But as the size of the enterprise increased, so did the complexity of privatization solutions.

At the beginning of the 1990s there was a general perception of the advantages of a fairly rapid ownership transfer. If speed was important, what could be done? Quick cash auctions, it was feared, would put most assets in the hands of the old *nomenklatura* or the frontmen for foreigners—with the possibility that the public would turn away from privatization and reform. Speedy privatization was also seen as a response to pretransition attempts at enterprise reform, such as in Russia, that had empowered managers and allowed leasing, cooperatives, and other arrangements often characterized as "spontaneous privatization." Rapid transfer of ownership was seen as a way to stop unfair leakage of assets to managers.

Vouchers were seen as the answer, for they would give purchasing power to the population in a transparent and fair way. Secondary trading, facilitated by investment funds, would allow transparent consolidation of shares. Russia and then Czechoslovakia applied voucher schemes universally, and Armenia, Azerbaijan, Georgia, the Kyrgyz Republic, Lithuania, and Moldova among others used them as the principal method of divestiture. Vouchers were a secondary privatization method in several other countries (see table 7.1).

Russia: From Spontaneous Privatization to Diffuse Ownership

Russia was unique because of the large number of enterprises to be privatized (about 25,000 medium-size to large companies) and the strength of spontaneous privatization by enterprise managers after the dissolution of most branch ministries under Secretary Gorbachev. Auctions had to be conducted across 89 regions over territory covering six time zones. A decentralized and systematic approach had to be developed at the center, with autonomous regional implementation. The intent of the reformers was to award only a

minority of shares to insiders, but it was necessary to settle for 51 percent preferential subscription of share ownership by managers and workers. When coupled with their vouchers, insiders ended up owning on average 66 percent of the shares in privatized enterprises.

Even now, enterprises subject to mass privatization in Russia have done little restructuring. A fair number of them were probably unviable under any form of ownership. Many were producing goods that people did not need or want, and some were using resources not readily shifted to the production of other items. However, it is also true that heavy insider control by managers in an environment of weak or ineffective shareholder oversight caused significant asset stripping. Delays in implementing a legal and governance framework, aggravated by opposition from powerful insiders with a stake in weak corporate governance, led to poorly regulated capital markets and weak enforcement of regulations protecting investors' rights. These factors made the phase of insider control and diffuse ownership very costly, raising questions about what might have happened with slower privatization and a longer period of state control (box 7.1).

The Czech and Slovak Republics: Diverging Paths

The Czech and Slovak republics are an interesting contrast to Hungary and Poland, neighboring countries where vouchers were used on a much smaller scale (World Bank 1999a). The most advanced industrial economy in the former Communist bloc, the former Czechoslovakia remained firmly in the grip of the Communist Party right up to the Velvet Revolution. There was little price liberalization, little tolerance of small private enterprise, and little experimentation with workers' councils in enterprises. The fear of a reversion to communism was perhaps stronger than in any neighboring country.

Economic reformers believed that nothing could be expected from a slow or evolutionary approach. The government apparatus could not be turned into a force for positive change. A fast and massive transfer was needed to create new owners who would support further

TABLE 7.1.

Methods of Privatization of Medium-Sized and Large Enterprises

Country	Direct sales	Vouchers	Management-employee buyout
CSB			
Albania	n.a.	Secondary	Primary
Bosnia and Herzegovina	Secondary	Primary	n.a.
Bulgaria	Primary	Secondary	n.a.
Croatia	n.a.	Secondary	Primary
Czech Republic	Secondary	Primary	n.a.
Estonia	Primary	Secondary	n.a.
Macedonia, FYR	Secondary	n.a.	Primary
Hungary	Primary	n.a.	Secondary
Latvia	Primary	Secondary	n.a.
Lithuania	Secondary	Primary	n.a.
Poland	Primary	n.a.	Secondary
Romania	Secondary	n.a.	Primary
Slovak Republic	Primary	Secondary	n.a.
Slovenia	n.a.	Secondary	Primary
CIS			
Armenia	n.a.	Primary	Secondary
Azerbaijan	Secondary	Primary	n.a.
Belarus	n.a.	Secondary	Primary
Georgia	Secondary	Primary	n.a.
Kazakhstan	Primary	Secondary	n.a.
Kyrgyz Republic	n.a.	Primary	Secondary
Moldova	Secondary	Primary	n.a.
Russia	Secondary	Primary	n.a.
Tajikistan	Primary	Secondary	n.a.
Turkmenistan	Secondary	n.a.	Primary
Ukraine	Secondary	n.a.	Primary
Uzbekistan	Secondary	n.a.	Primary

n.a. Not applicable.
Source: European Bank for Reconstruction and Development data.

market reforms. Vouchers thus became the cornerstone of the reformers' approach. Investment funds were created to consolidate the diffuse ownership of vouchers and to diversify risk. Voucher holders could either bid directly for enterprise shares or buy shares in investment funds, which would then use the vouchers to bid for enterprise shares. The funds were expected both to manage a diversified portfolio of shares (equity mutual funds) and to drive

enterprise restructuring through active governance (venture funds and limited partnerships).

The Czech Republic implemented its mass voucher in two stages or "waves," the first under the former Czechoslovak Federation and the second after the split. The government that ruled the Slovak Republic shortly thereafter decided to abandon the second wave of mass voucher privatization in the belief that the voucher program would not be conducive to sound

Box 7.1.

Historical Counterfactuals: Mass Privatization in Russia

Russia's rapid and massive privatization, which began in the early 1990s, has been the center of significant criticism and debate. The major criticism is that privatization was implemented too quickly and without first putting in place the institutional and legal framework that would have provided the checks and balances needed for proper governance incentives and competition. The results, it is argued, have been significant stripping of assets, concentration of economic power that has prevented further reforms, loss of fiscal revenues, and worsening income inequality.

What would have happened under a slower privatization process—one that waited for strategic investors to emerge, at least for the medium-size and large enterprises, and for key legislative and enforcement capabilities to be in place, particularly in the area of corporate governance? What would have been the costs and benefits of having proceeded more slowly?

At the outset, it is important to distinguish between two different privatization waves that were implemented in Russia since 1992: the mass voucher privatization program and the later loans-for-shares scheme for privatizing a small but highly productive number of very large enterprises. This discussion refers to the voucher program. The second scheme is universally regarded as a poor choice of a privatization strategy.

Russia's mass voucher privatization program was implemented to give managers and workers—"insiders"—the incentive to acquire majority ownership of their enterprises' shares in order to obtain their support for privatization, with managers eventually becoming the most important shareholders. However, because of a weak legal framework for corporate governance plus major political uncertainties in Russia, managers may have had an incentive to maximize their short-term capital gains by selling assets for personal gain (rather than keep the enterprise as a going concern and maximize future profits) and thus decapitalizing the enterprise at the expense of other (smaller) shareholders. This may have had two negative effects: one concerning efficiency, the other, equity. First, there was a bias against keeping enterprises operating as a going concern. Second, regarding equity, wealth was redistributed from the rest of the population to the managers. Asset stripping may have in the end also increased the incentives to send those gains abroad—where they were less likely to be discovered and prompt legal action.

Would a slower approach—keeping enterprises under the control of state and line ministries while legislation and enforcement were improved and strategic investors identified—have led to less asset-stripping and more satisfactory outcomes? Would there have been adequate incentives to develop legislation for decentralized private ownership in the absence of a minimum degree of experience with private property?

In fact, the state did not have full control over its enterprises at the beginning of the 1990s. By 1988 "spontaneous" privatization accelerated as a result of legislation passed in 1987, allowing labor collectives and directors to become independent from the state and in practice receive the rights of owners. The Law on Cooperative Activities of 1988 allowed the formation of cooperatives (headed by the directors) within the enterprises. These cooperatives engaged in the most lucrative activities of the enterprises, while the liabilities remained with the state. As a matter of fact, this situation left enterprises in legal limbo and subject to soft budget constraints. The experience of a wide variety of countries, from Bulgaria to Romania to Ukraine, shows that keeping enterprises in that situation strongly encourages asset stripping as managers and workers remain, in the interim, uncertain about how much they will benefit from the eventual privatization of their enterprise in the future. That uncertainty is a strong incentive for quick asset stripping. This was aggravated by the collapse of state institutions potentially capable of exercising oversight as a result of the nature of the exit from communism in Russia.

The alternative of giving insiders (workers and managers) a smaller share of ownership and thus encouraging the entry of outsiders was considered at that time, but faced strong political resistance from managers and line ministries. But even if it had been feasible, it may not have yielded better results in the particular circumstances of Russia. With weak minority shareholders' rights, the incentives of managers to exploit other shareholders is even higher when the latter hold a larger share of the enterprise, unless they are concentrated and can organize to prevent it. While too much share distribution to insiders may prevent strategic outsiders from coming in, too little may accelerate the incentives for asset stripping by these insiders. In the absence of encouragement for foreign strategic investors and with the collapse of state institutions, the choice between the mass privatization program and a longer period of state ownership, while developing institutions of corporate governance, is an open question.

In summary, these and other historical questions can only be answered over the long run in the context of judging Russia's overall transition experience, both economic and political. In contrast, most policy issues in this area today are more straightforward because of changed initial conditions and do not require a resolution of these questions.

governance. It implemented the second wave through direct sales. But the sales were not conducted through open and transparent methods, and they favored politically connected parties.

The performance of Czech and Slovak enterprises privatized through mass voucher methods was disappointing, for three reasons. First, few investment funds had the resources and the skills to drive enterprise restructuring. Second, little was done to introduce an adequate regulatory framework governing enterprises, investment funds, and capital market activities, particularly to protect minority shareholders' rights. Third, surveillance by creditors was weak because of delays in privatizing the largest banks and weak insolvency and collateral legislation. Indeed, largely unreformed commercial banks, operating in a climate of weak regulation, controlled many of the largest investment funds. The funds also owned bank shares. This cross-ownership weakened the governance structure and softened budget constraints further. All these problems resulted in significant "tunneling"—extraction of assets by enterprise and fund managers (see box 3.2).

In sum, the lack of appropriate accompanying institutional policies and lagging banking sector reform made mass privatization unnecessarily costly in equity, transparency, and microeconomic efficiency. It eventually contributed to a large buildup of contingent fiscal liabilities in the insufficiently reformed, state-dominated commercial banks. By contrast, the best performers tended to be enterprises and sectors sold to strategic investors through transparent methods, including one of the earliest cases of a sale to foreign investors: the Skoda-Volkswagen transaction.

In the Slovak Republic governance of enterprises privatized by direct sales (during the second wave) has not been significantly better than that of those privatized by voucher methods (during the first wave), despite the more concentrated ownership, as judged by the overall poor performance of Slovak enterprises in the second half of the 1990s. The Slovak experience with direct sales provides a sobering lesson and reinforces the conclusion that concentrated ownership is a necessary, but not sufficient condition for effective ownership. A program of direct sales to concentrated owners that follows open and transparent methods is much more likely to produce positive outcomes than a program of direct sales that favors politically connected parties and has the potential for corruption.

Hungary: Bold Moves, Big Gains

In Hungary the rapidly reforming Communist Party led democratization by making a historic compromise with the civil opposition, the majority of which had never been underground. This more pragmatic Communist regime had largely abandoned central planning, allowing a growing share of private ventures and speeding reforms in taxation, banking, foreign trade, and corporate governance during the five years before the political changes.

The new ruling elite in Hungary did not see a return to communism as a threat. The problem lay with the managerial group that governed thousands of more independent, but still formally state-owned, enterprises—and stripped their assets. Transferring ownership titles through mass privatization to the population while leaving governance to these old managers would not be a solution. In addition, Hungary was the most highly indebted country in the region on a per capita basis, and the government was obliged to think about generating cash from privatization. These factors led Hungary to base its privatization on sales to strategic investors and to open the process entirely to foreign investors. The full opening of the privatization program to foreign capital was seen as a bold step that no other government (except Estonia) felt able to take at that time. Foreign capital into Hungarian enterprises and banks brought much needed investment, know-how, and competition—the main reasons for Hungary's good growth in the second half of the 1990s.

By the mid 1990s Hungary had made substantial progress in selling banks to reputable foreign strategic investors and in adopting a strict banking regulation law and a strict bankruptcy law. Hungary had also worked out much of the large stock of bad loans in the banking system. By contrast, this painful task had not even started in the Czech and Slovak republics and would gain momentum only in the late 1990s. Hungary's economic performance in the second half of the 1990s shows that creditor discipline matters as much as good ownership and governance structures in driving economic restructuring and microeconomic efficiency.

Poland: Diversify and Discipline

As early as 1990 Poland planned to privatize a mass of enterprises through vouchers. But politics delayed the scheme, not any calculated assessment by reformers that Poland's promising economic and institutional situation would allow them the latitude to proceed through other privatization options. From the beginning Poland pursued a rich menu of privatization options, including the first five flotations on the Warsaw Stock Exchange and the sale of assets and selected liabilities of some 1,000 medium-sized enterprises through installment sales, a process described as "privatization through liquidation."

Poland's success in privatization and its good growth performance in the second half of the 1990s was also a result of other important complementary reforms. Like Hungary, Poland introduced hard budget constraints in the early stages of the transition, the result of early efforts to restructure and privatize the banks and address the bad loan problem. Poland reinforces the notion that creditor discipline matters as much for enterprise restructuring and performance as effective ownership and corporate governance.

Slovenia: "Internally Privatized" Enterprises Have Contributed Little to Growth

Slovenia inherited the old Yugoslav concept of social capital and social ownership, with the state holding title to few industrial enterprises and banks. Slovenia's privatization (and that of all the parts of former Yugoslavia) reflects this starting point. The Slovene program allocated the majority of shares to state-owned institutional investors (the pension fund and a development fund) and to employees through several subsidized schemes. Few of the former socially owned enterprises ended up in the hands of strategic investors. The evidence suggests that the "internally privatized" enterprises have not flourished, though they seem to be doing slightly better than the socially owned enterprises that were not privatized. Most of the growth in industry and services is explained by new entrants, the recipients of most foreign direct investment.

Other Countries Also Chose Vouchers

Several other CIS countries relied heavily on mass privatization through vouchers. Kazakhstan used

investment funds as vehicles to achieve a consolidation of shares, requiring that all vouchers be placed with funds. Moreover, before privatization, the government established sector holding companies that allowed the state to retain a 39 percent residual share in all enterprises being privatized. A legal framework governing these funds was put together, but was then poorly enforced. The upshot was a dilution of the value of shares held by the initial holders of vouchers. Other variants included state and private enterprise funds in Romania and divestiture by leasing to worker cooperatives in Ukraine.

Were Vouchers a Mistake and Other "What Ifs"

Each country pursued its own strategy; there was no homogenous approach driven by blueprints. This diversity and considerable disappointment raise many questions about the appropriateness of strategies. The most fundamental question has two parts: was mass voucher privatization a mistake? Could that have been foreseen? Would countries that went through mass voucher schemes, with disappointing results, have been better off keeping their enterprises in state hands while trying to accelerate economic reform and creating an institutional and legal framework to attract reputable concentrated investors?

This approach has been successful in China, which has enjoyed sustained high growth rates without, until recently, allowing much in the way of formal transfer of state ownership. There is considerable debate over how China achieved this. Box 4.1 argues that initial conditions in China were different enough to allow growth to be fueled by a massive entry of new enterprises while the state and subnational governments could monitor state enterprises to prevent egregious asset stripping by managers or their allies. But most of the CIS started the transition with a major political transformation in parallel with an economic one. This weakened or eliminated many of the policy and disciplinary mechanisms required to replicate this approach, and the recentralization of political power needed to achieve it would not have been feasible given the political trends.

Answering these broad questions requires a historical counterfactual against which to compare the mass privatization option (see box 7.1). If political centralization or recentralization was not an option, what mechanisms were available to improve governance of state-owned enterprises? Would hardening budget constraints—a key accompanying policy that influences enterprise performance—have been easier under state ownership? Could market and legal institutions supporting property rights evolve in an environment of state ownership? The cases of Belarus (see box 4.3) and Uzbekistan do not support this notion.

Only time will permit a fuller assessment of these fundamental questions. But many useful and practical lessons still emerge from more modest questions. For example, to what extent can the outcomes of privatization be influenced by the complementary policies generally under the control of policymakers? In the former Czechoslovakia, mass voucher privatization would have had a better chance of producing more restructuring and less corruption if the legal framework governing companies, investments funds, and capital market activities had been sharply enhanced and enforced from the very beginning. Earlier efforts at privatizing banks and strengthening creditor rights through improved insolvency and collateral legislation might have aided overall restructuring as well. These reforms would have required intense—but manageable—effort from the Czech and Slovak authorities. Moreover, the efforts probably would have succeeded in attracting larger flows of foreign capital, facilitating secondary trading, and consolidating ownership by strategic investors.

In Kazakhstan the inability to vigorously enforce the legal framework governing investment funds was a major issue. Russia suffered similar weaknesses in the way it implemented privatization. Managers and local officials trying to prevent competition dominated many of the auctions to voucher holders. A weak legal framework to protect minority shareholders inhibited outsider participation in secondary trading, guaranteeing that the managers would continue to control the enterprises.

Summarizing Lessons

This experience suggests the following agenda:

- Privatization should be part of an overall strategy of discipline and encouragement.
- Small enterprises under state ownership (generally enterprises with fewer than 50 employees) should be sold quickly and directly to new owners through an open and competitive auction, without restrictions on who may bid for the shares.
- Medium-size and large enterprises should target sales to strategic outside investors. With a concentrated, controlling interest, they will have a clear stake to best use the enterprises' assets. Although several transaction methods may be used, including negotiated sales, this can be brought about most effectively through competitive "case-by-case" methods, more deliberative than voucher schemes or rapid, small auctions. They use independent financial advisors who both prepare the enterprise for sale and act as sales agents on behalf of the state.
- Investor protection should be enshrined in the legal system and enforced, covering rules to protect minority shareholders; rules against insider dealings and conflicts of interest; creditor surveillance accounting, auditing, and disclosure standards; and takeover, insolvency, and collateral legislation. When court enforcement of contracts is weak, these provisions should be supplemented by a stock market regulation for financial intermediaries, such as investment funds and brokers, who then have an incentive to ensure compliance by other participants in financial markets. This will set the stage for privatization of future medium-size and large enterprises. It will also improve the performance of existing privatized enterprises by assisting transparent consolidation of shares where ownership is diffuse. It will also facilitate bank- and nonbank-based financial intermediation.
- Privatization should be accompanied by increasing competition in the market for the products sold by the enterprise in question

and vigorously enforced by the competition policy authority. This can discipline managers in an environment where corporate governance is weak.

- The cash flow and property rights of the state should be clarified for enterprises in which the state continues to hold an ownership stake.
- Divesting enterprises in sectors characterized by natural monopoly or oligopoly (where average production costs decline continuously as scale increases and the market and society are best served by one or a few enterprises) must proceed with great caution, if at all. Advances in technology have made such sectors increasingly rare. But where they exist—as in local distribution of natural gas—an efficient regulatory regime that protects the public interest is a prerequisite, lest divestiture transform an inefficient public monopoly into a poorly regulated or nonregulated private monopoly.

In Central and Eastern Europe and the Baltics (except the Federal Republic of Yugoslavia), SMEs have been substantially privatized. Voucher privatization or competitive cash auctions are not relevant options. Bulgaria, Croatia, and Romania—with large commercial enterprises still to be privatized—should implement (and, indeed, are implementing) transparent and competitive case-by-case methods to mobilize strategic investors. Progress in the European Union accession will make this more likely to succeed. The Federal Republic of Yugoslavia, now privatizing medium-size enterprises through competitive auctions, will start the privatization of large enterprises through case-by-case methods. A major positive feature of these methods is to restrict the distribution of subsidized shares to insiders to a maximum of 30 percent of shares, thus making the majority of shares available for strategic investors.

In such CIS countries as Armenia, Georgia, the Kyrgyz Republic, Russia, and Ukraine, and where privatization has been important during the past decade, the most critical steps now are to improve the legal framework, assist a transparent consolidation of shares, and develop institutions to help monitor managerial behavior. The remaining privatization agenda must rely on transparent and competitive case-by-case privatization, including the transfer of residual state ownership.

In countries such as Belarus, Turkmenistan, and Uzbekistan, where most medium-size and large enterprises remain in state hands, a major challenge remains. In Belarus and Uzbekistan, as in China, strong central controls have prevented egregious asset stripping in state-owned enterprises. However, there has been little restructuring because these enterprises have been protected through the trade regime and the special allocation of foreign exchange and credit at subsidized prices. Foreign direct investment and entry of new enterprises remain heavily controlled. The challenges in these countries, when they decide to reform, will be to liberalize, encourage new entry, and assemble a legal framework (for private property and contract enforcement) and market institutions to monitor managers. Small enterprises should be quickly privatized through competitive auctions, and medium-size enterprises through case-by-case methods, with a majority share sold to outsiders. Very large enterprises should be privatized only when a clear strategic investor is identified.

Note

1. Capital market regulations in most OECD countries require that a major shareholder or group of connected shareholders acquiring 30 percent of the shares in a company offer to buy out minority shareholders at the assessed market value. Full implementation of this regulation alone would have considerably slowed consolidation of ownership in the Czech Republic in the 1990s. Other regulations restricting insider deals and transactions with connected parties, enhancing disclosure, and ensuring an integrated pricing mechanism would also have slowed the consolidation of ownership. For a review of progress with privatization, see EBRD (2000).

8

Supportive Social Policies

How can social policies support a strategy of discipline and encouragement? By targeting social safety nets to the most vulnerable, such as those affected by the increase in utility prices and by the labor shedding resulting from hard budget constraints on enterprises. By helping local governments take over divested social services previously provided by enterprises, such as housing, kindergartens, and clinics, to permit enterprise restructuring to go ahead. And by reforming expenditures on education and health to allow workers to acquire skills more adapted to new market realities and, more generally, to ensure that the benefits of growth, once it resumes, are widely shared.

The loss of fiscal control accompanying the transition and the need to reduce the fiscal deficit to stabilize inflation reduced government expenditures as a share of GDP everywhere. In Central Europe and the Baltics, which are farthest along in the transition, an important policy priority now is to restructure social sector expenditures to make them fiscally more affordable. In the low-income CIS countries, where the resumption of sustained growth has proved elusive, the priority is to provide a social safety net for the most vulnerable. Meeting those objectives is a challenge. For the advanced reformers of Central Europe and the Baltics the ratio of consolidated public expenditures to GDP is around 45 percent, comparable to those in the high-income countries of Western Europe (World Bank staff estimates). To reduce the tax burden on the private sector while confronting the new costs of complying with European Union directives, these countries will need to improve their efficiency in social service provision and modify pension systems to reduce their fiscal costs.

In the Caucasus and Central Asia public expenditure ranges between 20 and 25 percent of GDP, approaching 30 percent in the Kyrgyz Republic. In these countries public sector revenues were lower than in the rest of the CIS. Several of them, facing unsustainable public debt, need an international workout to reduce debt service and domestic efforts to increase tax revenue to maintain social expenditures.

Reforming Pension Systems

Spending on social insurance programs, which cover pensions and unemployment insurance, accounts for about 10 percent of GDP in the CSB. In Croatia, Poland, the Slovak Republic, and

Slovenia public pension expenditures have climbed to more than 13 percent of GDP—twice the pretransition level and not sustainable. The fiscal burden of pension systems increased in the transition partly because benefits eased the social costs in its early years. Indeed, in most CSB countries the incidence of poverty for households headed by pensioners is much lower than for other socioeconomic groups. However, the aging of the population and the rising payroll taxes needed to finance more generous benefits undermine the financial viability of pension systems and threaten employment creation. The challenge is to make pension systems more sustainable without undermining the socially desirable goal of providing adequate income for retired workers.

Large pay-as-you-go pension systems, with their attendant large unfunded liabilities, burden public finances and savings in the long term. Higher contribution rates by themselves do not solve the problem because they raise labor costs, shift incentives toward informal market employment, and undermine job creation, particularly by new enterprises. In addition, the opportunities for using contractual savings for capital market development are lost. Most countries have begun to reform their pension systems by tightening the link between contributions and benefits, shifting to notionally defined contribution schemes, raising retirement ages, reducing replacement rates, and changing pension-indexation formulas. In addition, several countries in Central and Eastern Europe are taking steps to implement multipillar pension schemes (table 8.1).

A multipillar pension system allows people to diversify risk across countries, regions, and assets. It provides for a portion of the mandatory contributions to the public pension system to fund the individual accounts of each worker. These contributions are managed and invested by private institutions, and pensions are paid according to a defined contribution. The eventual pension system comprises a downsized pay-as-you-go scheme (the first pillar), a benefit from a fully funded scheme (the second), and personal savings (the third).

A key element of these reforms is making explicit at least part of the implicit debt of pension systems, which then has to be financed. (The size of the full implicit debt varies from country to country. In Central and Eastern Europe it ranges from 120 to 250 percent of GDP.) There are three possible sources of financing. The first is to limit first pillar expenditures to create savings in the state pension schemes and reduce future liabilities. The second is to increase payroll taxes and contributions. The third is to use fiscal resources from debt instruments or privatization proceeds. Given the magnitude of the financing needs and the fact that governments may have largely exhausted the first two sources, the resources for paying obligations to current pensioners will have to come from the budget.

The up-front fiscal costs of moving to a multipillar system are large. In reforming countries a second pillar financed by a contribution rate of 6 percent of gross wages, as in Hungary, would require resources equal to around 1.9 percent of GDP annually in the first years. Other countries preparing to establish such a scheme—Bulgaria, Croatia, Estonia, and FYR Macedonia—will also need to plan and budget for these costs in ways consistent with preserving macroeconomic stability. The size of the fiscal costs depends on the design of the second pillar—its size and choice of cohorts—and on the pace that governments move along this path. However, the institutional requirements of introducing multipillar systems are demanding. Financial markets have to be adequately developed, and governments have to regulate and supervise funds.

The CIS typically spends about half what the CSB spends on pensions. But in many cases even that spending is fiscally unsustainable, given poor tax compliance and high ratios of dependents to contributors. Pension systems in the CIS have generally done a much poorer job of keeping the elderly out of poverty. They need to undertake the basic reforms to put their pay-as-you-go systems on sounder financial footing. Some low-income countries—such as Georgia, where resources are constrained and tax compliance especially poor—may need to move to a flat benefit structure to protect the poorest elderly until fiscal conditions permit a move to a more differentiated structure.

Implementation of these reforms will face political opposition and administrative weakness. For example, flat benefits to the most needy may not enjoy broad-based support, as Georgia's recent experience showed. Coverage needs to be

Table 8.1.

Reform Options for Social Protection Programs

| Income level | Social assistance | Social insurance | | Fiscal implications |
		Unemployment	Pensions	
Higher income (Central Europe and the Baltics)	• Means-tested cash benefit assistance program, possibly supplemented by indicator targeting • Deinstitutionalization	Insurance	Multipillar system with minimum poverty-based benefit	Reduced fiscal burden of pay-as-you-go system, but with up-front fiscal cost
Middle to low income (Bulgaria, Romania, the Russian Federation, and Ukraine)	• Categorical cash benefit (universal or targeted by category; means tested only where local institutions are strong) • Lifeline utility tariffs • Deinstitutionalization	Flat benefit or severance	Reformed pay-as-you-go system, with minimum poverty-based benefit	Reduced fiscal burden of pay-as-you-go reallocated toward targeted social assistance
Very low income (Caucuses and low-income Central Asian countries)	• Limited cash benefit, probably based on geographic targeting, community targeting, or indicator targeting • Lifeline utility tariffs • Self-targeting (workfare schemes) • Deinstitutionalization	Flat benefit and severance	Flat benefit	Increase fiscal allocations for all

Source: Authors.

broad enough to ensure that schemes are continued and adequately funded. Making the design and implementation of reforms more difficult are weak actuarial capacity to forecast expenditures and revenues, a lack of auditing of pension funds, and problems in collection. As wages begin to rise, tax collection improves, and institutional capacity develops, countries can move toward a multipillar pension system.

Social Assistance Should Protect Children and the Most Destitute, Adding More as Budgets Allow

With the transition to market, the guaranteed employment, retirement security, and consumer subsidies of the socialist system

diminished considerably. In addition, the real incomes of households fell. Although the Central European countries have spent the bulk of their social protection budgets on pensions, these countries allocated somewhat more resources to social assistance spending to address rising poverty. The CIS generally spent less on social assistance, while indirectly protecting employment by not imposing hard budget constraints on old enterprises and by maintaining subsidies on housing and utilities. The subsidies on utilities have most often been met by forcing the utilities to defer maintenance, or by expecting enterprises to finance them even where housing has been divested. Despite the expansion of social assistance, most programs, including the subsidies on utilities, have not reached great numbers of the poor.

The key objectives for social assistance programs—and probably all that the poorest countries can afford—are to help the most destitute and to ensure that children's mental and physical development is not impaired. In addition to ensuring that young children receive essential preventive health care and can afford to attend school, many countries also face the challenge of offering alternatives to institutions for elderly people unable to live on their own; adults with physical and mental disabilities; and children disadvantaged by poverty, ethnicity, or disability. Some countries are introducing community-based services such as home and day care and special educational programs for children with disabilities, adapting approaches that have been successful in Western Europe and the United States.

In addition, to facilitate the enterprise restructuring critical to sustained growth, countries may wish to offer some protection to those hurt by restructuring. The best way of doing so is to remove barriers to entry of new enterprises. Assistance should be targeted to workers whose skills and experience make them the least likely to be employed by new enterprises.

For low-income countries with limited resources and pervasive poverty, targeting cash benefits—with a possible increase in the resource envelope in some countries in the Caucasus and Central Asia, where spending is low—may have to be improved through geographical targeting, community-based identification, or other indicators. Given the pervasiveness of the informal economy and self-employment, targeting will continue to be imperfect. There may be some scope for self-targeting through some form of public works scheme. There also is considerable scope for improving the targeting of utility and housing subsidies. Rather than offer across-the- board price subsidies, some countries have introduced "lifeline" tariffs for utility services with metered consumption, in which the price subsidy is restricted to the initial block of consumption, called the basic need level. Lifeline tariffs are easier to administer than income-tested schemes and are less distortionary than generalized price subsidies.

Higher-income countries may be able to afford a more generous safety net. Targeting through some forms of means testing may be less prone to error in these economies, to the extent that the tests are more formalized. Unemployment insurance may also be more feasible in these countries, with structural unemployment falling and capacity to implement a true unemployment insurance program growing. But more generous provision of benefits carries the risk of creating a culture of dependency and reducing incentives of workers to find employment—added, of course, to the everpresent problem of becoming a major fiscal burden and a drag on growth.

Severe Cuts Have Compromised the Quality of Education

Some of the fiscal adjustment in the CIS has been at the cost of severe cuts in education, inevitable given the plunge in GDP for all the CIS countries (World Bank 2000b). Public spending on education ranges from less than 2 percent of GDP for Armenia and Georgia to almost 8 percent of GDP for Uzbekistan. The average for OECD countries—with 10 times the GDP per capita—is about 5 percent of GDP. Several countries have maintained reasonable spending on education relative to their GDP. The challenge is to ensure that resources are allocated to best use—across levels, between wage and nonwage expenditures, and across regions within each country. But in the poorest countries of the Caucasus and Central Asia spending cuts have compromised the ability of the education system to prepare students for the emerging market economy (figure 8.1).

The cuts have affected opportunities, access, and coverage (World Bank 2000b). Falling education budgets and protection of employment in the sector are squeezing expenditures on textbooks, school supplies, and school maintenance. In addition, poorer parts of many countries bear a disproportionate share of the adjustment. In Georgia 43 percent of primary and secondary schools in urban areas got textbooks for all children, compared with 27 percent in poorer rural areas. In the Russian Federation richer regions have spent more on education, while poorer regions have struggled to maintain the basic requirements (World Bank 1999b).

By not spending enough to meet the basic needs of the school system, the state effectively shifts educational costs to families. Families contribute to school maintenance and education supplies. In some countries they are asked to supplement the salaries of education personnel through under-the-table payments and various tutoring schemes—if they want their children to pass. At the same time many countries have been slow to implement cost recovery measures for higher education, which tends to favor better-off families.

Poorer countries need to take three sets of measures. The first is to ensure universal basic education, of particular importance to Armenia, Azerbaijan, Georgia, and Tajikistan, where budgetary resources for basic education do not provide universal coverage. The second is to ensure that expansion of tertiary education does not come at the expense of basic secondary education. In some countries higher education enrollments are growing—appropriately reflecting the human capital demands of these emerging economies. This risks absorbing larger shares of education budgets, unless greater cost recovery, lower unit costs, and more encouragement of private financing and delivery of higher education services follow.

The third set of measures is to shift resources from personnel (and energy) into repairing schools and providing adequate educational material. As materials and maintenance expenditures were cut and student enrollments fell, the number of teachers rose sharply. In Russia every region increased its number of teachers, for an overall increase of 25 percent between 1989 and 1996 (World Bank 1999b). In Central Asia increases ranged up to 25 percent (Klugman 1999). Student-teacher ratios are typically low for most of these countries and can be increased without compromising teaching quality or learning outcomes (table 8.2). Countries will need to rationalize and consolidate their school infrastructure, which is often overdimensioned due to falling birth rates and extremely low student-teacher ratios. School consolidation would also enable countries to reduce wage costs. Using OECD standards as a benchmark, up to a third of the teaching labor force can be reduced. That would

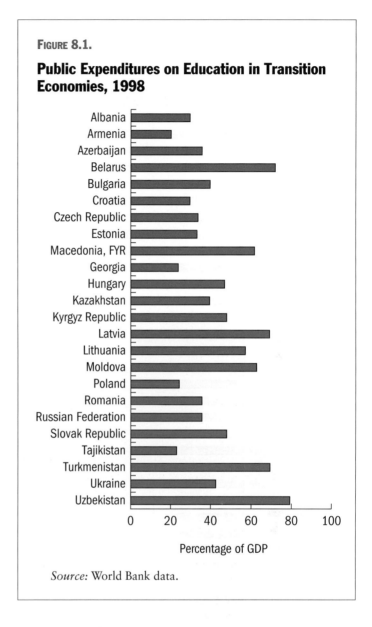

FIGURE 8.1.

Public Expenditures on Education in Transition Economies, 1998

Source: World Bank data.

TABLE 8.2.

Student-Teacher Ratios in Basic Education, 1990 and 1997

(percent)

Countries	1990	1997
Armenia	11.7	8.7
Azerbaijan	10.5	9.9
Belarus	11.8	10.5
Russian Federation	14.0	11.9
Turkmenistan	14.0	13.4

Source: UNICEF–ICDC TransMONEE (1999).

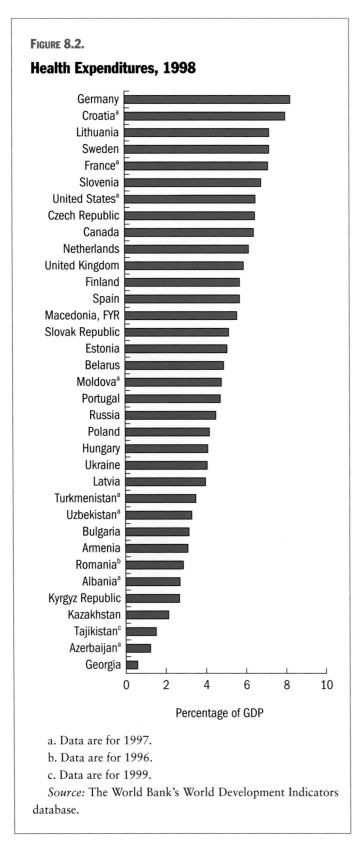

FIGURE 8.2.

Health Expenditures, 1998

Percentage of GDP

a. Data are for 1997.

b. Data are for 1996.

c. Data are for 1999.

Source: The World Bank's World Development Indicators database.

free budgetary resources to better compensate remaining teachers, to repair schools, and to provide instructional materials.

In addition, energy costs for education need to be reduced. In some CIS countries energy expenditures consume between 30 and 50 percent of education expenditures, reflecting the fast rise in energy prices in the past 10 years. In the medium to long run, energy savings will be realized as new schools replace old ones. Short-term measures—insulating school walls, double-glazing windows, and installing meters—can also help reduce energy bills, but these will need up-front investments from the budget.

Containing Costs Will Make Health Care Affordable for Those Who Need It Most

The public health achievements of the socialist era are being undermined. Many countries are not spending enough on public health measures to confront the growing threat of HIV/AIDS and drug-resistant tuberculosis.

Inadequate funding has led to under-the-table payments. Unpaid or underpaid health workers tap patients for side payments, including payments for drugs and other items in short supply. This is financially onerous for poor families who have to sell assets or borrow to finance their health care. In the Kyrgyz Republic a third of all patients seeking inpatient care had to borrow money. Similar figures are reported for Georgia, Tajikistan, and Ukraine.

Often the inability to pay means that patients forgo health care. In Russia data for 1997 suggest that 41 percent of all Russian patients could not afford to purchase required drugs, and 11 percent could not afford any kind of medical treatment (World Bank 2000b). Similarly, 37 percent of pregnant women in Tajikistan did not seek prenatal care because it was unaffordable, and almost a third of births occurred at home, a break from past practices of hospital births. In several countries a privately financed, unregulated system of health care is in a public shell.

In some countries, notably in the Caucasus and Central Asia, public expenditures are inadequate (figure 8.2). However, other countries are spending significant public resources without getting the benefits of quality health care. The challenges facing most transition economies are similar to those facing education: the rationalization of systems with an excess of personnel and

facilities and reallocation of savings on complementary inputs. To reallocate expenditures most effectively, however, governments need to decide what kind of health care system they want, including who provides what and who pays for what.

Part 3

The Political Economy of Discipline and Encouragement

9

The Winners and Losers from Discipline and Encouragement

Why have some governments been able to enact policies to discipline the state sector and encourage new enterprises to create a foundation for sustainable growth? Why have others maintained far less effective strategies of protecting inefficient enterprises and discouraging new entry at considerable social cost? Can these government policy choices be systematically related to particular institutional characteristics of political systems in transition? Part 3 will try to answer these questions.

To develop a better understanding of the political economy of reform in transition economies, we extend the framework developed in part 2 to examine the political dynamics of discipline and encouragement. The economic reforms associated with discipline entail costs for the public in the short term. Imposing discipline on state enterprises requires substantial adjustment to correct decades of inefficient investments and distorted policies. Such adjustment inevitably generates losers in the short term as a result of higher unemployment, higher prices, and lower provision of subsidized social services by enterprises. In contrast, the gains associated with the policies of encouragement accrue primarily over the long term as the institutions needed to promote entry and encourage competition—secure property rights, vigilant contract enforcement, good access to financing—cannot be created overnight.

So, for the public, programs of comprehensive economic reform tend to bring substantial adjustment costs from discipline in the short term for the mere promise of future gains as encouragement promotes greater investment and growth. How can governments assure the public that those future gains will materialize? What guarantees that future governments will not backtrack on reforms before the promised gains materialize? What if the promised gains are directed to groups closely tied to existing elites and not widely distributed across society, as is common in so many highly inegalitarian countries?

The politics of economic reform thus begins with a paradox: people are asked to support policies that impose clear costs in the short term for the promise of long-term gains inherently subject to high risks. To win broad support, the government must convince the public that the government will be able to sustain its commitment to reform to traverse what one author has called the "valley of transition" until the "higher hills" of an efficiently functioning market economy are reached (Przeworski 1991). Recognizing the different time horizons of costs and benefits and the related risks that might lead rational individuals to discount those benefits at the start of reform is central to the political economy of market-oriented transitions. The government must be able to *credibly commit* to short-term losers that they will reap the gains from reforms over the long term.

At the same time, a decade of transition experience has shown that some groups realize substantial gains from the no man's land between the command system and the market economy (Hellman 1998). Uncertainty about property rights before privatization allows insider managers to tunnel assets from nominally state-owned enterprise to newly created spinoffs under managers' personal control. Partially liberalized prices spur arbitrage opportunities between fixed-price and market-price sectors that can generate enormous gains. Incomplete trade liberalization creates highly profitable monopoly rents, especially in economies rich in natural resources. These opportunities to take advantage of the distortions of a partially reformed economy are available only to the select few, namely those with control over nominally state-owned assets and those with close ties to politicians able to award such advantages. As a result, these gains are highly concentrated.

In theory such gains should be short-term, because as transition progresses many of these temporary economic distortions will be eliminated or competition will arise to dissipate the rents. But experience shows that these short-term winners of partial reform can convert a small share of their gains into political influence that can be used to restrict entry, undermine competition, and preserve the very distortions that generate these rents. Such constituencies seek to freeze reform into an equilibrium of liberalization without discipline and selective encouragement, producing a highly unequal pattern of costs and benefits of market-oriented transition over the long term.

Examples of how the short-term winners of partial reform prevent further reforms that would impose discipline and encourage new market entry and competition are well known throughout the region. Enterprise insiders who gained minority stakes in privatized enterprises have opposed improvements in corporate governance and the security of property rights that would

limit insiders' ability to tunnel assets abroad. New banks created in the liberalization of financial markets have fought to keep soft government credits for their enterprise clients, which could be recycled in volatile local bond and foreign exchange markets. Oil and gas exporters who gained from the opening of foreign trade in partially liberalized markets have struggled to build entry barriers to prevent competition from dissipating their rents. The ability of these groups to preserve their extraordinary gains is based on their capacity to influence the political process, and in the most extreme cases, to capture key institutions of the state, highlighting the critical interaction between politics and economics in transition (Hellman, Jones, and Kaufmann 2000; World Bank 2000c).

Who Wins and Who Loses?

The complex dynamics of the political economy of reform can be expressed graphically by tracing the paths of winners and losers with respect to different levels of reform in the discipline and encouragement framework. A typical economy at the start of the transition can be divided into three basic constituencies:

- *State sector workers.* These are workers from state-owned enterprises without the skills to become new entrants in the competitive market. They face significant losses initially because of discipline (unemployment, price increases) and are unlikely to realize any gains from encouragement.
- *Potential new entrants.* These are workers and new entrepreneurs, originally from state-owned enterprises, who have the skills to become new entrants in the competitive market. They face initial losses from discipline as they adjust to the decline in the state sector. However, they are likely to see gains from entry into the market if encouragement is effectively implemented and sustained.
- *Insiders and oligarchs.* These are actors who begin the transition with substantial de facto control rights over state assets and close ties to the political elite inherited from the previous command system. Insiders and oli-

garchs benefit immediately from liberalization and privatization because they can convert their existing control over state assets into substantial gains. Moreover, insiders and oligarchs can reap further gains from rent seeking, arbitrage, and asset stripping if liberalization and privatization are not combined with discipline and encouragement. As discipline is imposed and further reforms encourage competition from new entrants and the rule of law, these initial gains are dissipated unless new barriers to entry can be erected.

Figure 9.1 presents a stylized depiction of the income gains and losses for each of these three groups under different levels of economic reform. The state sector workers face a drop in income as a result of sector downsizing, with little hope of substantial recovery as reform advances. The potential new entrants face a classic J-curve pattern of income, with adjustment costs at low levels of reform as they exit the state sector and gains realized only once enough progress has been made in institutional reforms

to promote and support new entry into the competitive market. The oligarchs and insiders, by contrast, face an inverted U-curve income pattern. Their concentrated gains in the early stages of reform—associated with opportunities for arbitrage, rent seeking, and tunneling—are dissipated as further reforms increase competition and market entry.

For all these constituencies, gains and losses depend on how radical the first move in the reform process is at the start of the transition. The more radical this move, the greater the initial adjustment costs to both state sector workers and potential new entrants. Yet new entrants should begin to see greater gains at an earlier point in the transition if such reforms lead to rapid development of the institutions that encourage entry and competition. For the oligarchs and insiders, radical reforms generate fewer distortions and imbalances for them to extract rents and strip assets. So such reforms reduce the high concentration of initial gains to the oligarchs and insiders.

By contrast, less radical reform programs—liberalization and privatization with weak disci-

---

FIGURE 9.1.

Winners and Losers from Reform

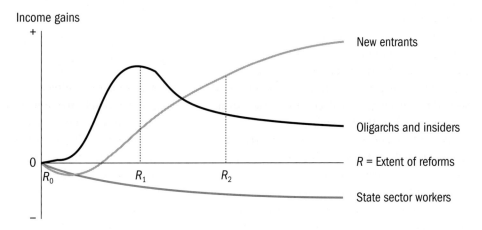

Note: R_0 = no reforms; R_1 = point at which income gains of oligarchs and insiders are maximized; R_2 = level of reforms that allows the winners of reforms beyond R_1 (new entrants) to compensate for or exercise enough political pressure to neutralize the resistance of oligarchs, insiders, and state sector workers.

Source: Authors.

pline and minimal measures to support competition—have the opposite effect. Such partial reform programs at the start of the transition generate lower initial adjustment costs for both state sector workers and potential new entrants, as state sector downsizing is limited and the flow of subsidies continues. Oligarchs and insiders enjoy the highest gains from liberalization and privatization without discipline and encouragement.

Given these patterns of gains and losses, each constituency prefers a different combination of reforms. State sector workers prefer the status quo (R_0) and reject all reforms. Oligarchs and insiders prefer to begin with a partial reform and sustain the reform process through R_1, the point where their gains are maximized and beyond which implementation of policies of discipline and encouragement threatens to undermine gains from rent seeking and tunneling. For new entrants, the process offers sacrifices in the beginning for the promise of gains when the reforms are advanced enough to create an environment conducive to new entry and competition.

For a government to secure the support of the potential new entrants for radical reforms at the start of the transition, the government must be able to make a credible commitment that the reforms will be continued until at least R_2. But the credibility of that commitment will depend on the strength of the oligarchs and insiders, who have an incentive to invest a share of their initial gains in capturing the state to stop the reform process at R_1. Thus at the start of transition, the greater the risk that oligarchs and insiders will capture the state in the future, the less likely that potential new entrants will support a radical reform program at the outset.

Where the risk of capture by oligarchs and insiders is high, potential new entrants and state sector workers have an incentive to reject reforms or to accept partial reform programs that reduce the initial adjustment costs. Yet it is precisely such partial reforms that make state capture by oligarchs and insiders a self-fulfilling prophecy, as these reforms maximize opportunities for rent seeking and theft. This has led to a so-called partial reform paradox in many transition economies: governments that lack credibility and are

highly susceptible to state capture cause potential new entrants at the outset of transition to substantially discount the potential gains from any proposed radical economic reforms, leading them to support partial reforms that offer lower initial costs—even though these partial reforms are more likely to lead eventually to barriers to entry.

The risk of ending up at a low level of reform (R_1) is indeed high. Such partial reforms—liberalization without discipline and with limited encouragement of new entry—are the result of the joint pressure of oligarchs and state workers to prevent further reforms while the gains by new entrants are not high enough to allow them to exercise enough pressure for more comprehensive return. Only a minimum commitment of advancing reforms to at least R_2 will generate enough support—where R_2 is the level of reform that allows the winners of reforms beyond R_1 (new entrants) to compensate for or exercise enough political pressure to neutralize the resistance of oligarchs, insiders, and state workers.

The political problem posed by initial winners from the transition was not foreseen in the early literature on transition. Few recognized that oligarchs and insiders would be able to stall the transition in a state of partial reforms. Yet this has proven to be one of the most serious obstacles to economic reform, particularly in many CIS countries.

The Government Must Be Credible and Able to Constrain Oligarchs and Insiders

Partial reform—liberalization without discipline and selective encouragement—can be a stable equilibrium of reform if government, at the outset of the transition, lacks the credibility to promise that narrow groups with close links to the political elite will not capture the reform process. Public support for radical reforms, therefore, depends on perceptions of government credibility.

By recognizing that different combinations of reforms produce different configurations of winners and losers, the discipline and encouragement framework suggests two political challenges in promoting economic reform:

- Securing up-front support from potential new entrants for comprehensive reforms
- Preventing early winners of liberalization and privatization from trying to sustain a partially reformed equilibrium of rent seeking and theft by undermining further reforms.

To meet these challenges, governments must have the capacity to project credibility to potential new entrants and constrain the oligarchs and insiders.

What influences the capacity of governments in transition economies to make credible commitments that the promised gains from reform will not be expropriated by early winners of reform? Credibility and constraint are rooted in the nature of political institutions, which are shaped by the cultural and historical legacies that guided the exit from communism. Political institutions designed with participation by competing groups to foster political contestability within an agreed set of rules are less likely to be captured by a corrupt political elite or narrow set of interest groups. The rigors of political competition increase the costs to politicians of pleasing narrow constituencies and increase the likelihood that broader interests will be represented in government over time.

In contrast, political systems designed to concentrate power and restrict contestability are at greater risk of being captured by small, powerful interests. In such systems politicians are held accountable to a narrower range of groups, increasing the probability that those with access to political power will expropriate or concentrate the gains from government policymaking. To prevent the early winners from holding the economy in a partially reformed equilibrium, the political system must constrain the power of any narrow group to capture the state. Expanding the range of social groups competing for influence over policymaking increases the costs to politicians of skewing reform in the interests of a single group. So the government's capacity to make a credible commitment to a wide range of groups is much greater in political systems that promote competition and contestability.

These differences in political systems are shaped by a broad range of factors often loosely referred to as "initial conditions," which incorporate historical, cultural, geographical, and other variables that shape the transition path (de Melo and others 1997). But understanding how different political systems shape the configuration and choices of the winners and losers in reform provides important insights into the relationship between democracy and market-oriented reform.

10

Classifying Political Systems
in Transition

To determine the effects of different types of political systems on the capacity of governments to adopt and sustain economic reforms, we first differentiate the range of political systems across the transition economies. One of the most important features of this variation has been the political contestability in the new regimes, that is, the extent to which key decisions of the political process—such as choosing political leaders, adopting laws, and making binding policy decisions—are subject to challenge by freely organized groups in and outside government.

Political contestability can be determined along several different dimensions:

- *Political rights and civil liberties.* The ability to challenge political decisions requires the rights to participate freely in the political process and to express one's views. The extent of such rights can be measured by indicators of political rights and civil liberties.
- *Veto points.* The clearest institutional manifestation of political contestability is the right to veto political decisions. Different types of political systems have different numbers of "veto points," that is, institutional actors who can veto political decisions.
- *Government turnover.* Political contestability can also affect the turnover and tenure of governments. Frequent government turnovers suggest a high degree of political contestability and shape the perceived competitive pressures on incumbent governments. Of course, excessively high government turnover could be a reflection of underlying political instability.
- *War and political violence.* The outbreak of war or political violence, often with ethnic or regional cleavages, indicates extreme contestability over the boundaries and basic organization of the political process.

Developing exact measures of these characteristics for transition economies is difficult given their rapid change. But a combination of indicators allows transition economies to be classified into four "ideal types" based on the extent of political contestability. Freedom House (various years) provides a widely accepted system of annual ratings of political and civil liberties (figure 10.1). On the basis of these ratings, the following country groups can be developed:

FIGURE 10.1.

Classifying Political Systems in Transition Economies, 1990–99

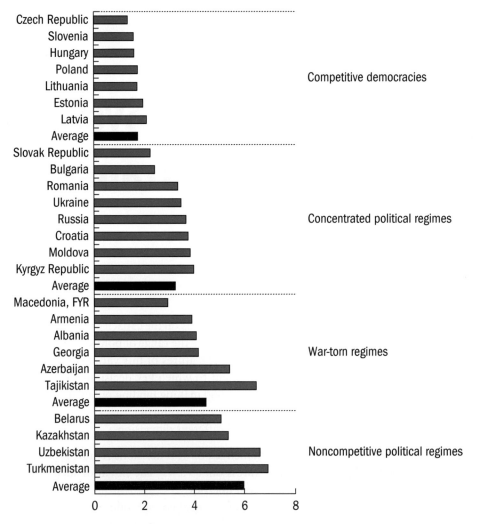

Note: Ratings are based on the average scores for political rights and civil liberties ranging from 1 (free) to 7 (not free) by Freedom House from 1990 to 1999. The thresholds for determining the country groups are: competitive democracies: political rights ≤ 2.0 and civil liberties ≤ 2.5; concentrated political regimes: political rights or civil liberties > 2.5; noncompetitive political regimes: political rights or civil liberties > 5.0.

Source: Freedom House (various years).

- *Competitive democracies* have from the start of transition maintained both a high level of political rights to compete in multiparty democratic elections and an extensive range of civil liberties. They include the Czech Republic,

Estonia, Hungary, Latvia, Lithuania, Poland, and Slovenia.

- *Concentrated political regimes* conduct multiparty elections, but for some period of the transition they have either curtailed full rights to participate in those elections or otherwise limited political competition through constraints on civil liberties. The result has been a concentration of political power, often in the executive branch of government, within the framework of a multiparty electoral system. These countries include Bulgaria, Croatia, the Kyrgyz Republic, FYR Macedonia, Moldova, Romania, the Russian Federation, the Slovak Republic, and Ukraine. The countries span a wide range of political systems. Bulgaria and the Slovak Republic have a high degree of political contestability over the selection of governments, though some of these governments have in turn concentrated political power to limit contestability in policymaking.

- *Noncompetitive political regimes* constrain entry of potential opposition parties into the electoral process and sharply restrict political participation through the exercise of civil liberties. Such systems tend to have few institutionalized limitations to check the executive. These countries include Belarus, Kazakhstan, Turkmenistan, and Uzbekistan.
- In addition to political liberties and civil rights, war and political violence define a fourth group of transition economies, where external conflicts or extreme internal contestability has strained the state at certain periods of the transition.[1] *War-torn political regimes* have engaged in prolonged wars or civil conflicts over the past decade. Such conflicts have generally been rooted in ethnic or territorial divisions. In these countries there is political contestability over the boundaries of the community to be governed or who has the right to select leaders and make binding rules for that community. Such conflicts have placed severe strains on the capacity of the state, resulting in some of the countries in a prolonged loss of political order and control and serious weaknesses in the provision of basic public goods. They include Albania, Armenia, Azerbaijan, Bosnia-Herzegovina, Georgia, and Tajikistan.[2]

Like all ideal types, these four categories are not intended to be absolutes. Several transition economies straddle different categories. Bulgaria and the Slovak Republic lie on the border between competitive and concentrated political regimes. Azerbaijan has characteristics of both war-torn and concentrated political regimes. Moreover, political systems are still evolving, so countries have been shifting over time across different ideal types. Croatia and the Slovak Republic have moved sharply toward a more competitive democratic system following critical elections that ended the lengthy regimes of once powerful political leaders. Romania has shown steady improvements in extending political rights and civil liberties. Such changes suggest that countries are not locked into any particular path of political transition. But because this report summarizes the entire transition path, we rely on measurements averaged across the entire transition period.

Competitive Democracies Have High Political Contestability...

Political contestability is a function of the rights to participate in the political system and the extent to which competing institutional actors have the power to influence political decisionmaking. It is generally measured by the number of political actors whose approval is necessary to adopt binding decisions on the polity. As the number of political parties in a coalition government increases, the number of potential veto points for policy decisions also increases. Similarly, presidential systems in which competing political parties dominate the executive branch and legislature (that is, divided government) should also exhibit higher contestability than those where the president's party also controls the legislature. A simple measure of political contestability based on these veto points has been developed by Roubini and Sachs (1989). The index measures the number of competing political parties in governing coalitions in both parliamentary and presidential systems (data for the transition economies can be found in Frye and Hellman 2001; see also figure 10.2).

Competitive democracies have the highest number of veto points among countries in the

FIGURE 10.2.

Veto Points Index, 1989–99

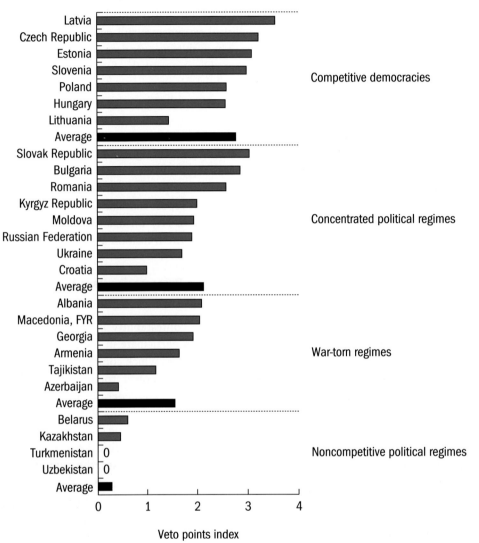

Veto points index

Note: The index for each country is based on the average monthly score from the onset of the transition through mid-1999 on a scale of 0–4, defined as:

0 = One-party government with noncompetitive elections.

1 = One-party majority parliamentary government or united presidential government.

2 = Two-party coalition parliamentary government or divided presidential government.

3 = Three-or-more party coalition parliamentary government.

4 = Minority parliamentary government.

Source: Frye and Hellman (2001).

region. All of them are parliamentary or semipresidential systems governed by multiparty coalitions. Lithuania and Poland could be characterized as semipresidential systems, which combine parliamentary government with a directly elected president. Indeed, one-party majority governments have been rare in most of these countries. Six of the seven competitive democracies have had prolonged periods of coalition governments consisting of three or more political parties. In Estonia, Poland, and Slovenia coalition governments of up to five political parties have not been unusual. While the literature on political economy generally takes a negative view of coalition governments, the most reformist governments in transition economies have tended to be multiparty coalitions (Alesina and Rosenthal 1995; Roubini and Sachs 1989).

Concentrated political regimes generally have fewer veto points on average (see figure 10.2). Five of the eight concentrated political regimes are presidential systems. Bulgaria and the Slovak Republic, on the border between concentrated and competitive political systems, have multiparty coalition governments more similar to a competitive system than a concentrated one. Several of the presidential systems appear to have been ruled by divided governments for much of the transition, mainly because presidents in the Kyrgyz Republic, Russia, and Ukraine did not belong to any political party for extended periods.

Noncompetitive political regimes have the lowest scores on the veto points index. Powerful presidents in Belarus, Kazakhstan, Turkmenistan, and Uzbekistan have essentially created one-party systems with strong restrictions on opposition parties. Similar one-party systems have also been developed in the war-torn political systems, such as Tajikistan, but these countries have generally had much less stable governments as a result of the conflicts.

...and High Government Turnover

Countries with greater political contestability also have, as might be expected, more frequent changes of government (figure 10.3). Indeed, the countries most advanced in economic reform have tended to have the most frequent changes in government, contrary to the conventional view that such turnovers create an uncertain environment that undermines reform. There have been nine governments in Poland, seven in Estonia, and five in Hungary since the start of transition. As a group the competitive democracies have had an average of six government turnovers since the collapse of the Soviet bloc. This contrasts sharply with the other country groups. Concentrated political regimes, except borderline Bulgaria, have tended to have fewer government turnovers, averaging just more than three for the group. In all of the noncompetitive countries, except Belarus, the leader at the time of the dissolution of the Soviet Union has ruled continuously throughout the transition. Political continuity has not positively affected the government's propensity to adopt economic reforms.

Notes

1. This report defines political violence as government turnovers or attempted turnovers through violence.

2. This group includes all countries in the Europe and Central Asia region that have been engaged in prolonged military conflicts, except Croatia and Russia. In Croatia the military conflict did not spark domestic political violence that threatened the incumbent regime of Franjo Tudjman. Russia engaged in a long-term territorial conflict in the breakaway republic of Chechnya and survived a violent attempt to overthrow Boris Yeltsin. However, these two events were unrelated and did not lead to disorder and political fragmentation, as in other countries in the group.

FIGURE 10.3.

Main Political Executive Turnovers, 1989–99

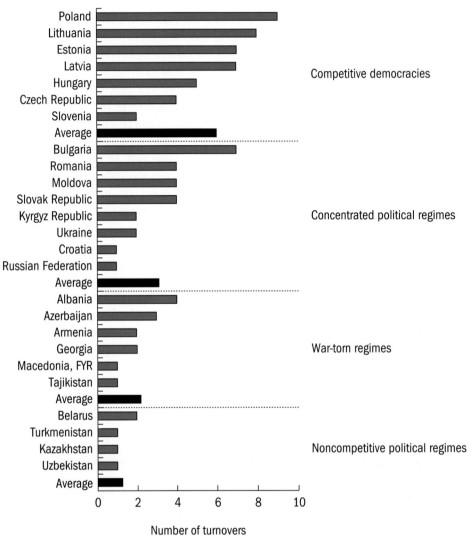

Note: This figure measures the number of times there has been a change of the country's lead executive—president in presidential systems and prime minister in parliamentary or semipresidential systems—since the country gained independence.

Source: Frye and Hellman (2001).

11

Political Systems Influence the Choice of Economic Reforms

The simple classification of political systems in transition economies allows us to examine the relationship among different types of political institutions and the range of outcomes on the spectrum of discipline and encouragement discussed in part 2.

Competitive democracies have proven to be among the most advanced economic reformers in the Europe and Central Asia region, pursuing policies that have promoted SMEs and maintaining hard budget constraints on both new and old enterprises. Concentrated political regimes have been more likely to sustain a pattern of partial reforms that protect old enterprises and create barriers to market entry. Yet in these countries the combination of liberalization and privatization with continued soft budget constraints and a weak rule of law have encouraged even new enterprises to focus their efforts on rent seeking and tunneling instead of productive entrepreneurship.

Noncompetitive political regimes have been most likely to reject key elements of market transition, choosing instead to maintain greater continuity with the structures and practices of the previous command system. Though these regimes protect state enterprises and restrict the activities of new enterprises, lack of any substantial liberalization or privatization has prevented the types of rent seeking and tunneling prominent in the concentrated political regimes, thus avoiding the sharp contractions common among other reform-minded countries. War-torn countries have been characterized by weak state capacity and a zig-zag pattern of economic reform, creating an environment that is not conducive to entry and investment.

To measure the extent of economic reform, we rely on the European Bank for Reconstruction and Development's transition indicators (EBRD 2000), which evaluate annual progress in transition in eight different categories of market-oriented reform on a scale from 1 (little or no reform) to 4.3 (standards typical of advanced industrial economies). Competitive democracies have made the greatest progress in implementing market-oriented reforms, while the noncompetitive regimes have made the least (figure 11.1). Concentrated political regimes and war-torn regimes have made partial progress, advancing in some areas and lagging behind in others.

The direction of the causality underlying these correlations is difficult to untangle completely. Indeed, despite a vast literature examining the relationship between levels of democracy and economic

FIGURE 11.1.

Political Systems and Economic Reform Outcomes, 2000

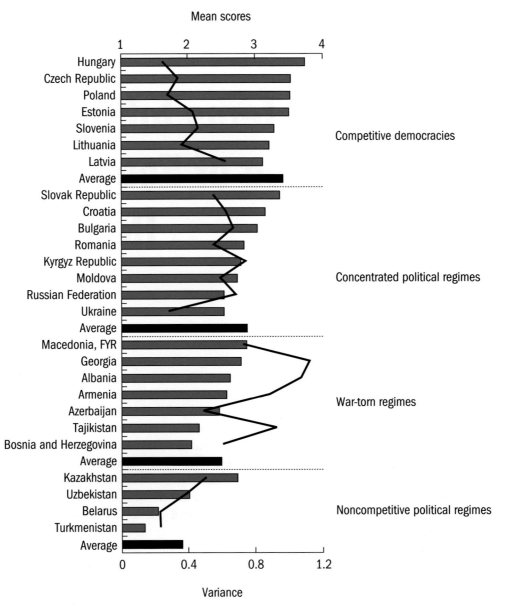

Note: The European Bank for Reconstruction and Development measures annual cumulative progress in transition each year in eight different categories of market-oriented reform on a scale from 1 (little or no reform) to 4.3 (standards typical of advanced industrial economies). Each bar represents the country average across all eight categories. The line represents the variance, which for each country measures the dispersion around the mean across all eight reform categories of the transition indicators.

Source: EBRD (2000).

reform across the world, the results are still largely inconclusive (for a review of this literature, see Haggard and Webb 1993). Though the nature of the political system structures the incentives of politicians to adopt economic policy choices, the reform choices themselves shape the configuration of social groups and the distribution of power that affect the structure and functioning of the political system. For example, economic reforms that enable new entry also strengthen the constituency of SMEs that build support for increasing political competition. Thus, the development of the political system and progress of economic reforms are closely inter-related.

Yet given the sharp break with communism and the disintegration of the Soviet Union, choices about the structure of the political system in transition economies were generally made before decisions about the nature and pace of economic reform. As a result, a stronger case can be made for identifying the direction of causation from political choices to economic choices. Moreover, only a few countries (Belarus, Croatia, and the Slovak Republic) have seen a major change in political regime since the start of transition. This suggests that while the pace and direction of economic reform may have reinforced initial choices about the structure of the political system, economic reforms have yet to decisively shift the course of political transition.

However, after only a decade of transition, these political and economic systems are still in their infancy. As in all countries, one might expect that over the long term, there will be a strong interactions among economic reform, economic performance, and political evolution (Przeworski 1991). Yet in the early stages of transition, political choices appear to be the driving force of change in economic reform.

Political Systems Create Rent-Seeking Opportunities

An important indicator of the opportunities for rent seeking in the transition process comes not just from the overall measure of progress in market-oriented reform, but from different progress across different components of the reform agenda. Imbalances in the reform

process—such as price and trade liberalization with continued restrictions on entry, privatization with soft-budget constraints, and rapid creation of banks without a sufficient regulatory framework for financial markets—create opportunities for rent seeking and theft. One crude indicator of these imbalances comes from comparing the different rates of progress across the eight different components of the European Bank for Reconstruction and Development's transition indicators. Taking the variance (a measure of the dispersion around the mean) of the ratings for each country across these eight reform components gives a rough measure of the imbalances in the reform that give rise to rent seeking (see figure 11.1).

The variances tend to be lowest in the most reformist and least reformist countries. In competitive democracies economic reforms have generally progressed across the board despite differences in the sequencing of reform measures across countries. Similarly, noncompetitive political systems have generally made little or no progress in all of the key areas of economic reform, maintaining substantial continuity with the previous command system. In contrast, the concentrated political regimes and war-torn regimes have tended to advance rapidly in liberalization and privatization with much slower progress in the institutional reforms to support effectively functioning markets, generating much higher variances in their reform scores.

These asymmetries in the reform process create a wide range of arbitrage and rent-seeking opportunities available to a small group, usually with close ties to the government or the existing state-owned sectors. The gap between progress in liberalization and privatization and development of a proper legal and regulatory framework also provides opportunities for theft of both state and private assets through expropriation of minority shareholders.

The pace and symmetry of market-oriented reforms suggest variation across the different political systems in rent seeking and asset stripping. A good proxy measure of such phenomena can be found in recent attempts to develop more systematic, survey-based indices of corruption and state capture. (State capture refers to the efforts of enterprises to influence laws, decrees, regulations, and the like through private payments to public officials.) By capturing state institutions enterprises seek to extract rents from the state through a myriad of preferences, exemptions, and anticompetitive practices. The Business Environment and Enterprise Performance Survey (see box 3.1) provides an index of state capture based on the share of enterprises that reported a direct impact on their business from private influence payments to public officials (figure 11.2; see chapter 3).[1] The extent of state capture can be compared across countries with different types of political regimes.

State Capture Index, 1999

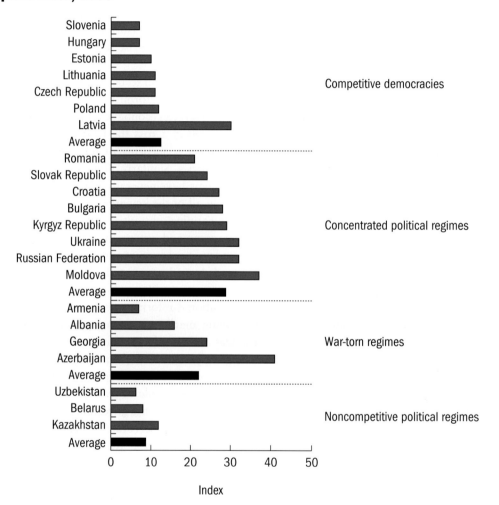

Note: The state capture index is based on the Business Environment and Enterprise Performance Survey. Enterprises were asked to what extent their business was directly affected by private payments to affect the decisions of six institutions: the presidency, legislature, government apparatus, civil courts, criminal courts, and the central bank. The bar for each country represents the share of enterprises that reported a significant impact averaged across the six institutions. As the measurement of this index is subject to a margin of error, any efforts to rank countries would be inappropriate. The data were collected in 1999 and do not reflect the impact of reforms since that time.

Source: Hellman, Jones, and Kaufmann (2000); World Bank (2000c).

There is a stark contrast in the extent and impact of state capture across different political systems. Concentrated political regimes exhibit consistently higher state capture, affecting on average more than twice as many enterprises as in competitive or noncompetitive political systems. Except Latvia, only a small share of enterprises in competitive democracies report a significant impact from state capture. State capture is also low in noncompetitive political regimes, reflecting the weakness of the private sector relative to a highly authoritarian state. War-torn countries have both high and low state capture: low in countries with high domestic instability, such as Albania, Armenia, and Bosnia and high in countries where powerful leaders have begun to consolidate political power, as in Azerbaijan and Georgia. The concentration of political power appears to be an important determinant of the extent of state capture in transition economies (Hellman, Jones, and Kaufmann 2000).

How Do Political Systems Affect Economic Reform?

The data suggest clear links among different types of political systems and alternative paths of economic reform as defined in the discipline and encouragement framework. Of course, the correlation between political regimes and different economic reform paths need not imply causation. There may be other factors, such as historical and cultural legacies, the structure of the economy, and even geographical position that affect both the choice of political regime and the course of economic reform. Such factors are all highly correlated, making it impossible to disentangle empirically the lines of causation. However, the strong similarities in the transition process in countries with similar political systems suggest that political institutions affect choices about economic reform. What are these similarities?

In Competitive Democracies, Inclusion Promotes Support for Comprehensive Reform

In the aftermath of popular revolutions against communist rule, the political institutions in competitive democracies were forged in roundtable negotiations by popular fronts and a wide range of other organized interests from trade unions to religious representatives. Guided partly by the example of Western European democracies, the roundtables produced political institutions that generally tended toward parliamentary systems, promoting party competition and constraining executive authorities.

The inclusive process for creating these political institutions and the broad range of political groups that could compete for power in the new system enhanced the capacity of governments to make credible commitments that the promised gains of economic reform would not be expropriated or otherwise restricted to particular vested interests. This contributed to a wider social consensus on the main directions of reform, despite differences among parties on the sequencing and pace of reforms. It also led to a greater mobilization of organized interest groups in civil society (such as independent labor unions) that would enhance political accountability throughout the transition. So governments mobilized broad public support for comprehensive reform programs early in the transition.

A key factor in building and sustaining this broader consensus on reform has been the historical ties and geographical links of these countries to Western and Northern Europe. The pull of European accession generated strong incentives for a common institutional framework, both for the economy and the polity, creating a focal point for the reform agenda that mitigated possible disputes over alternative institutional designs and regulatory frameworks.

By taking a comprehensive approach early on, such programs generated far fewer opportunities for rent seeking and theft, lowering the returns to such activities in the short term. This weakened the capacity of short-term winners to restrict competition and preserve rent-generating market distortions. Moreover, the regular succession of different coalition governments created genuine competition among groups for political influence. That led to equally fierce competition over rents, quickly dissipating any efforts to concentrate rent flows and preventing theft on a massive scale.

As already suggested, this competition occurred within a broad consensus on the direction and goals of the reform. Even the return to power of communist-successor parties in such countries as the Czech Republic, Hungary, and Poland did not derail reform. Government credibility at the early stages of transition enabled a first move on the reform path that limited the rents from arbitrage opportunities in distorted markets. It quickly created new constituencies with an incentive to push for further reform. It also signaled to investors the government's commitment to more long-term structural reforms. Some groups gained immediate advantages from liberalization and privatization. But they could not convert the gains into enough political influence to erect barriers to competition and entry that would have preserved limited opportunities for rent seeking and theft along the way.

From their first moves in the reform process, new governments tended to focus on promoting new constituencies of winners, removing entry barriers, and quickly tackling severe macroeconomic instability. They also supported the losers from the dislocations of the reform by maintaining adequate social protection (Orenstein 2001). Early efforts by enterprise insiders to spontaneously privatize enterprises sparked a substantial political backlash in the Hungarian and Polish electoral arenas (and much later in the Czech elections), curbing the practice with varying effectiveness. As a result the concentration of economic power in the early stages of transition in these competitive democracies was far less than in other parts of the region (evident in the data on inequality). As reforms progressed to promote entry and improve the enabling environment, they strengthened the constituencies with a stake in moving the reform agenda forward in the difficult areas of structural and institutional change.

What enabled this virtuous circle? One key factor was the much higher state capacity than anywhere else in the region. The fairly peaceful exit from communism did not destroy key state institutions. Facilitating more effective implementation of reforms, the legacy of public administration provided important preconditions for promoting new entry, such as greater security of property and contract rights and better public infrastructure.

In Concentrated Political Regimes, Oligarchs and Insiders Capture the State

In concentrated political regimes the collapse of communism was more a result of the contest among competing elites than a broad social movement. The new political regimes were not forged though roundtable negotiations among potential competitors, rather, the regimes were designed by incumbent leaders to consolidate their power. These new regimes tended to be presidential systems with power concentrated in the executive branch. Political parties were weak and did not represent a broad range of social interests. Moreover, the old *nomenklatura* remained strong, especially in the economy.

Though comprehensive reforms were proposed in some concentrated political regimes in the early stages of transition (Russia in 1991), they were rarely adopted in full, and the ones adopted were poorly implemented. The regimes lacked the credibility to build and sustain broad popular support for such reforms. Instead, they tended to fall back on partial liberalization and privatization. The soft budgets and remaining barriers to entry generated tremendous opportunities for rent seeking and theft, especially in economies rich in natural resources.

Such exits from communism also led to much sharper deteriorations of state capacity than among the competitive democracies of Central Europe. In former Soviet states, secessions were consciously intended to weaken federal control by radically decentralizing authority over public bureaucracies, sparking a wave of asset stripping. In Bulgaria and Romania, for example, the collapse of incumbent regimes caused greater uncertainty than in the negotiated transitions of Central Europe, eroding state control. Furthermore, the deterioration of public administration profoundly reduced the state's capacity to raise revenue, implement proposed economic reforms, and build broader consensus around reform goals.

The partial reforms merely increased and concentrated rents and the opportunities for tunneling and theft. Comprehensive price liberalizations were often followed by a stream of executive orders and decrees (with exceptions for some sectors and goods). Licensing and other regulatory barriers preserved trading monopolies. Explicit controls on foreign competition were set.

The winners from these partial reforms reaped spectacular gains. Those with control rights over valuable assets and political access to rent-seeking opportunities could easily privatize those assets in an environment of poorly defined property rights, nonexistent corporate governance, and an inadequate regulatory framework. As long as the stock of rents was not depleted, these winners had a strong incentive to preserve their advantages, using their considerable resources to block reforms that threatened those advantages.

Countervailing pressures from competing groups were weak, and without genuinely broad-based social movements, no clear goals were articulated at the start of transition. Nor was there much social mobilization from the collapse of communism. As a result, these countries embarked on transition without building a broad social consensus on the goals of reform and without a means of organizing the public behind these goals. Effective political parties never materialized to mobilize social support, and residual support for the Communist Party remained high. That set the stage for much greater political polarization over economic reform, and that polarization in many cases became a pretext for further centralization of political power and limits on political competition (EBRD 1999).

Lacking strong social support and a solid political base, incumbent politicians in concentrated democracies sought alliances with powerful incumbent enterprises for funding and support. This naturally made the state highly subject to capture. The early winners from the mass of arbitrage opportunities had a strong interest in using their political influence to preserve rent-generating distortions that intensified the winners' economic power. Direct barriers to entry solidified their gains, weakening new constituencies that might counterbalance these powerful incumbents.

The social costs of state capture have been high in these countries. But the direct costs to politicians of poor policy choices were low thanks to

limited institutional restraints to promote accountability and weak intermediate organizations to channel the dissatisfaction of losers. Many concentrated democracies languished in an equilibrium trap of partial economic reforms in which the concentration of both political and economic power preserved market distortions generating highly concentrated gains to narrow vested interests at considerable social cost.

In Noncompetitive Political Systems, Leaders Savor Status Quo and Economic Stability

In noncompetitive political regimes leaders from the Soviet era generally pursued economic stability, while securing their dominance of the post-Soviet political system. Concerned about rival sources of power in both the economy and the polity, they largely rejected market-oriented reforms. They feared the opening to global market forces and the rise of oligarchs in partially reformed economies. Instead, they preferred to maintain continuity with key elements of the previous command system to maintain the state's (and the leaders') predominant role and to avoid any destabilizing adjustment costs associated with reform.

In these cases economic reform was driven not by the winners or losers of reform, but by authoritarian political leaders trying to maintain political control and ensure some economic stability. Limited economic reform went hand in hand with limited political reform, as incumbent leaders severely restricted political opposition.

The political imperative to maintain state power and the lack of economic reform avoided the disintegration of state capacity that plagued many other transition economies. So although the state in these countries does not provide the institutional foundation for the market economy, it still provides public goods—but at levels similar to the communist era. This suggests that if a new government introduced comprehensive economic reforms it would have stronger capacity to implement them and would begin with a less daunting decline in living standards.

Despite these possible advantages, incumbent political leaders face little pressure to pursue reforms. By maintaining dominant state ownership in the economy and considerable discretionary capacity to intervene in economic affairs, these leaders ensure their positions remain powerful. Overt restrictions on political competition reduce even further the risk of challenges to incumbents' power.

In these systems few viable constituencies have the capacity to push for economic reforms. The economic elites tend to be closely allied with (or co-opted by) incumbent political leaders. There is no critical mass of new actors with an interest in reforms. Trade unions, business associations, and other civil groups that might represent broader social interests are circumscribed or tied to the state. In addition, the lack of reform isolates these countries from the global economy, leading to autarky that undermines what external constituencies might do in promoting reform.

The extent of economic reform is thus highly dependent on the political leader's preferences. Although many authoritarian leaders in other regions adopted comprehensive economic reforms, this has not yet happened in any of the transition economies. Why? Authoritarian leaders in the region have tended to inherit their power and support from the surviving structures of the former communist system. This has created a strong link between authoritarian political power and command administrative methods in the economic sphere in transition economies.

In War-Torn Regimes, Violence and Lack of Credibility Prevent Reform

In war-torn political systems, efforts to promote comprehensive reforms at the early stages of transition were thwarted by contestability over who had the rights to make binding decisions for the community and over the definition of the community. Societies with deep-rooted ethnic divisions face a high risk that governments dominated by one group will seek to expropriate wealth and resources from rivals, while encoding advantages for themselves into the developing institutional structure.

Facing such threats, minority ethnic groups in several countries in the region have violently challenged the legitimacy of the state. Croats in Bosnia-Herzegovina, Armenians in the Azerbaijani enclave

of Nagorno-Karabakh, Albanians in the Kosovo region of Yugoslavia, Abkhaz and Meshketians in Georgia, fundamentalist Muslims in Tajikistan—all are cases of minority groups seeking to pre-empt through violent means the creation of a state dominated by the ethnic majority. Governments in such environments could not make credible commitments about the distribution of future gains from reforms or about not expropriating wealth.

During periods of peace and relative stability, governments in these countries have tried to adopt comprehensive reform programs, but they continue to be undermined by severe credibility problems. War and instability radically shorten time horizons, so ethnic groups are not prepared to accept short-term sacrifices for the promise of long-term gains.

Prolonged conflict also sharply reduces output, living standards, and the resources of the state. Physical and human capital deteriorate. Poverty increases. Even the capacity of the state to provide the most basic public goods falls apart.

War also can concentrate economic power in the hands of smugglers, arms traders, and paramilitary groups, who use their power in peacetime to secure their positions in the economy. These "winners" use the instability of war to centralize control over state assets and distribution networks, particularly energy. They also tend to maintain close relationships with political leaders, who depend on them to fund and supply the war. Given the weakness of countervailing interests, constraining the power of such groups during peacetime is difficult. Manipulating privatization to enhance their control over assets, the winners use their influence to preserve exemptions and other preferences that undermine competition and to weaken the development of the rule of law.

This combination of political instability, a weak state, and powerful economic groups rooted in illicit and opaque trade has undermined reform in most war-torn regimes.

Note

1. Hellman, Jones, and Kaufmann (2000) present evidence from the Business Environment and Enterprise Performance Survey to show that enterprises that engage in state capture get substantial rents.

12

Confronting the Political Challenge

After a decade of transition, the political challenges of pressing ahead with the remaining reform agenda differ substantially in each of the four groups of countries. To build a foundation of public support for economic reform, governments should focus on smoothing the curves of winners and losers in the short term (see figure 9.1). That entails lowering the short-term adjustment costs for the potential new entrants and the high concentration of gains for the short-term winners such as oligarchs and insiders. Also needed are political changes to enhance the government's credibility and capacity to constrain the power of constituencies seeking to sustain partial reforms regardless of the social costs.

To smooth the short-term loser's curve, governments need to mitigate the adjustment costs associated with comprehensive economic reforms by preserving a social safety net that cushions the dislocations of the downsizing state sector. Such support is also an important way for the government to signal its commitment to defending broad public interests in reform, which will enhance government credibility.

To smooth the short-term winners' curve, governments need to reduce the incentives that lead oligarchs and insiders to block reform midstream through taxation or other redistributive schemes. But where the state is highly susceptible to capture by these groups, the likelihood of implementing such schemes is small. So reducing the concentration of gains to oligarchs and insiders must be based on changes in the structure of political power. Mobilizing collective action by a broader range of social groups that will gain from further reforms could pressure politicians to reduce state capture. Reforming the political system—to increase participation and enhance political competition—can break the link between highly concentrated economic power and political power.

Increasing transparency and accountability in government increases the costs to politicians of skewing economic reform in the interest of narrow constituencies. Of course, the oligarchs and insiders will oppose such political reforms, recognizing the threat to their advantaged positions. Consequently, successful political reforms in states captured by such groups are likely only after significant changes in the underlying correlation of power in the system.

Not all the transition economies battle these same problems. A decade of variation in reform paths and political developments has left countries with very different political challenges.

For Concentrated Political Regimes, Mobilizing Potential Winners

Breaking the political economy equilibrium underlying state capture and partial reforms is the most important and difficult challenge in advancing the transition in countries with concentrated political regimes. The vested interests underlying soft budget constraints, barriers to entry, opaque regulatory frameworks, and land reform have accumulated considerable economic and political power, raising more barriers to political entry for the losers of such policies. State capture at all levels of the political system and the lack of accountability for politicians and public officials make it difficult for even the most committed reformers to overcome the powerful vested interests against reform. In addition, weak state capacity has limited the state's autonomy to tackle these groups effectively.

Reforms have proven most difficult politically where the rents have been most concentrated, particularly in energy and finance. In nearly all the concentrated democracies with substantial natural resources, energy lobbies have been among the most formidable opponents of reforms. Their political power, often exceeding that of major political parties, cannot be underestimated.

The political leverage of the power and energy sectors comes not just from their resources, but through the vast network of nonpayments. As studies of the virtual economy suggest, dominant power and energy monopolies are the key sources of value in the complex web of nonpayments because the monopolies continue to provide oil, gas, and electricity to loss-making enterprises, often in exchange for overvalued barter goods (Gaddy and Ickes 1999). Being the main conduits of the state's soft-budget constraint gives them considerable political influence over the state.

Many other groups could be considered winners from the distortions of partial reforms. Natural resource extraction and export enterprises have gained from distorted domestic prices,

subsidized inputs, and monopoly production and distribution rights. Commercial banks have taken advantage of macroeconomic volatility, inefficient financial markets, and lax regulatory structures to reap gains from arbitrage. Politicians and bureaucrats have used their discretionary powers to intervene in the economy to extract bribes and other advantages from enterprises and households. Enterprise insiders have manipulated unclear property rights and weak corporate governance to divert enterprise assets and cash flow into offshore companies and other subsidiaries under their direct ownership. These practices have been largely at the expense of unprotected small shareholders.

The winners from these market distortions and inefficiencies have powerful incentives to preserve them and the associated rent flows, regardless of the social costs. Large exporters lobby for entry barriers. Commercial banks oppose stabilization programs and proposals to enhance the central bank's regulatory powers. Insider-owners undermine efforts to clarify corporate governance and to introduce greater transparency into the distribution of property rights. Public officials resist deregulation and efforts to limit discretionary interventions. Although the gains from such distortions tend to be highly concentrated, the losses are dispersed among consumers, savers, minority shareholders, start-up companies, small and medium-size businesses, and foreign investors.

This pattern of dispersed losses and concentrated gains holds the key to designing politically feasible strategies of economic reform. In many concentrated democracies, reformers often attempt to overcome political obstacles by augmenting executive power to counter the power of vested interests. Yet given the state capture in these countries, such efforts tend to fail. At various times the presidents of both Russia and Ukraine were granted extraordinary decree-making powers to push through economic reforms that did not break the stalemate on further reforms. Instead, concentrated gains and widely dispersed losses suggest the mobilization of the losers in the existing low-level equilibrium through greater political inclusion. How such a strategy should be designed depends on factors specific to each country. But some general approaches have worked in other transition economies.

Mobilize the electorate. Electoral appeals to mobilize the losers of partial reform have built support for macroeconomic stabilization and for banking reform. Given the wide and generally regressive impact of high inflation, political parties in several transition economies have mobilized enough electoral support for macroeconomic stabilization to overcome the opposition of powerful commercial banks and other actors that gained from macroeconomic volatility. In addition, banking crises in the Czech Republic and Hungary sparked electoral appeals to disgruntled savers, helping to break the stalemate over banking privatization and regulatory reform.

Mobilize excluded enterprises. Another important strategy for weakening the opposition of narrow vested interests to reforms is mobilizing collective action among enterprises excluded from these concentrated gains. SMEs, new enterprises, and second tier enterprises suffer most from existing weaknesses in the enabling environment, from discretionary taxation and regulation and from anticompetitive barriers. However, they lack vehicles of collective action and influence with the government. In Central Europe business associations have strengthened the voice of this tier of the economy, constraining public officials and checking influential enterprises and financial-industrial groups. In the concentrated democracies, such associations have remained weak, and political parties have not sought strategic alliances with such actors as an alternative basis for support and funding.

The Business Environment and Enterprise Performance Survey (see box 3.1) showed vast differences across transition economies in how many enterprises were members of business associations and how they used these associations to seek remedies to problems with the government. In Hungary more than 75 percent of the enterprises surveyed reported membership in a trade association, and 60 percent said they would rely on such associations first in handling problems with the government. But in Russia fewer than 20 percent of the enterprises reported membership in business associations, and less than 10 percent relied on them for resolving problems with the government (World Bank 2000c).

The unofficial sector is a large and potentially influential constituency that has not been effectively mobilized in the concentrated democracies. Enterprises in the unofficial economy generally suffer most from the weakness in the enabling environment, especially in the opportunity costs associated with limitations on their capacity to expand operations. Tax reforms that lower marginal rates can promote entry from the unofficial to the official economy. This would promote growth and possibly crystallize an important political constituency to remove obstacles in the business environment that work only to the advantage of a narrow group of powerful enterprises. Given the size of the informal sector in many of these countries, the potential political consequences of mobilization could seriously shift the balance of power away from incumbent vested interests to a much broader collection of economic actors. However, there are few examples of rapid shifts from the informal to the formal sector, or of the political mobilization of such economic actors.

One way to promote new enterprises and those in the unofficial sector is to align the incentives of local governments to increase entry. Tax-sharing schemes between central and local governments can be modified so that property taxes on small business are assigned exclusively to local governments, encouraging them to reform the enabling environment.

Ensure—and use—a free media. The emergence of a free press and broadcast media can overcome the coordination dilemmas associated with reforms that generate concentrated winners but highly dispersed losers in many sectors. The media can promote collective action among these dispersed losers of partial reforms and increase the political pressure on those who gain from the general equilibrium underlying these economies. The challenge for reformers in concentrated democracies is to use the media to make clear the links between the rents from partial reforms and the direct costs to society.

But the problem in many of the concentrated political regimes is that ownership of the media is closely intertwined with powerful financial-industrial groups. In other concentrated political regimes the media remains largely under the control of the state. This naturally limits what the media can do in breaking the partial reform trap.

Make obvious what is hidden. Tax arrears and nonpayments need to be linked in the public mind with delayed public sector wages and pensions and poor provision of social services. The complex web of hidden subsidies to powerful business needs to be exposed, making clear that such subsidies tend to benefit incumbent managers (often through offshore accounts) rather than workers. Barter and arrears in the energy sector need to be linked to domestic power and fuel shortages and outages that plague many of these countries.

Converting hidden and discretionary subsidies to enterprises into budgetary subsidies to support worker training, severance schemes, and better local services in communities affected by downsizing is vital for discipline and encouragement.

The potential for mobilizing these dispersed losers is particularly high in countries whose social sectors need resources, but whose high-profile conglomerates in key sectors enjoy a range of explicit tax and duty exemptions and maintain high tax arrears. This is particularly true in some of the small, fairly open economies, such as Georgia or Moldova, where trade flows are a major source of the tax base and powerful interests in control of those flows are the main tax evaders. Explaining to the public the costs of evasion should be an important element of any strategy to mobilize support for further reforms. Having made clear who benefits from partial reforms—and how those benefits come directly at the expense of large but dispersed domestic constituencies—reformers can begin to build political coalitions to marshal the potential winners from further reforms.

Allow political competition and economic competition to reinforce each other. Enhancing political contestability by mobilizing civil society,

strengthening political parties and other organizations representing the collective interests of alternative constituencies, and developing institutional restraints will expand political access beyond vested interests and increase the costs to politicians of maintaining partial reforms. But breaking the equilibrium of partial reforms is a challenge that can be addressed only through simultaneous economic and political reforms. Though exogenous shocks often create windows for decisive action by committed reformers, their capacity to spur profound changes in the structure of political and economic power simultaneously is highly constrained, and their agenda highly overloaded.

Our analysis suggests that promoting entry and competition on the margin, whenever and wherever possible, creates the necessary preconditions for a gradual move out of the partial reform trap. As more enterprises enter the market economy, the competition for rents should also promote competition for political influence, which weakens the capacity of powerful enterprises and sectors to capture the state and oppose reforms that might undermine their advantages. Promoting entry and competition on the margin will not accomplish radical changes in the short run, but it may be the most effective means of creating demand for reforms in the long run.

For War-Torn Political Systems, Restoring Stability and Reducing Uncertainty

Though the magnitude of the challenges faced by these countries in light of the extreme degradation of state capacity and concomitant sharp decline in living standards may be among the most serious in the region, the precondition for success is clear: without resolving the underlying divisions behind political fragmentation and violence, further reforms are unlikely to be successful.

Once some measure of stability is restored and uncertainty reduced, these countries need to rebuild basic state capacity and restore public goods for the functioning of the market. Attention has to go to strengthening the state's capacity to collect tax revenue to meet the considerable fiscal challenge. Rapid liberalization in the immediate aftermath of conflict is critical to eliminating the rents associated with controls on prices and distribution networks that fuel the winners of the wartime economy. In addition, comprehensive structural reforms, focused on privatization and demonopolization, are needed to prevent these wartime winners from solidifying their position through state capture in the postwar economy.

Given deteriorated state capacity in most of these countries, direct assistance and participation by bilateral and multilateral donors will be critical in generating the resources, providing the necessary technical assistance, and buttressing the political commitment for these fundamental tasks of state building.

For Noncompetitive Political Systems, Taking Advantage of State Capacity

A change in political regime could create opportunities for implementing a comprehensive reform strategy. Regime change is often accompanied by a resurgence of political competition, a strengthening of political parties, and a rejuvenation of civil society that can pressure new political leaders to pursue policy innovation and improve economic performance. As suggested earlier, these regimes can take advantage of higher levels of state capacity to implement reforms. This suggests that there might be some advantages of tardiness (in the spirit of Alexander Gershenkron's famous phrase) that would enable these countries to shift from a minimal reform equilibrium to a more comprehensive set of reforms without the same deterioration of state capacity that marked countries that began the transition with partial reforms.

For Competitive Democracies, Using Momentum to Build Coalitions for Reform

As advanced democracies around the world have amply demonstrated, multiparty competition can pose periodic risks to macroeconomic stability often aligned with the electoral cycle, or what is referred to as the political-business cycle (Alesina, Roubini, and Cohen

1997). Incumbent parties can win support by expanding fiscal expenditures before key elections, possibly requiring sharp contractions after the elections. Some competitive democracies (Hungary and Poland) have faced or are now grappling with high budget deficits, with possibly destabilizing consequences.

Some competitive democracies have combined budget deficits with high current account deficits. The rapid inflow of foreign capital has risks and benefits. Banking systems in many of these countries are not sufficiently developed and regulated to handle these inflows. A key challenge is to prevent a mismatch between demand for private sector borrowing and the capacity of the domestic banking system to make credit allocation decisions, monitor borrowers, and enforce discipline on delinquent borrowers. The risk of political interference in banking systems remains and must be strenuously avoided. Preserving and enhancing the independence of regulatory and supervisory bodies in the financial system is crucial to preventing recurrent crises.

Success should not breed complacency in meeting the remaining challenges of structural reform, particularly in the public sector and in politically sensitive areas of the economy. Maintaining the main pillars of the social safety net as a cushion in the beginning of reform was important in the success of these countries. However, it has also left them with highly overstaffed bureaucracies and high public sector wages, dampening their growth potential.

Strong political resistance to downsizing and wage cuts can be expected from public sector workers. Local governments will oppose any policies that reduce government control over the provision of health services and education. Resistance from these constituencies will be difficult to overcome, just as in many advanced industrial democracies. Countering this opposition means developing mechanisms to mobilize politically the new and rapidly expanding private sector, especially SMEs, whose interests are directly affected by the discretionary power of public sector bureaucracies.

Beyond the public sector, many of the competitive democracies still need to restructure politically sensitive sectors, such as agriculture, coal, mining, railways, shipbuilding, and steel. The dynamics of political coalition-building that foster a broader consensus on the course of economic reforms also tend to give these sectors considerable power to demand subsidies, protectionist measures, and other advantages as a condition for their political support. The agricultural lobby, in particular, is a powerful obstacle to reform.

As the reform agenda loses urgency over time, government capacity to take on powerful lobbies will diminish. But the lack of reforms in these important sectors holds back growth in the new private sector, weakening the overall performance of these economies. One continuing source of pressure for reform in some of these sectors is European Union accession. Again, it is important to mobilize domestic constituencies—especially the vibrant new sector, which bears the brunt of the costs of postponed reforms—to build a coalition with the strength to overcome the opposition to further reforms.

Conclusion

The key challenge of the political economy of reform is to create the conditions that will generate incentives for new market entry and shift the emphasis of enterprises from rent extraction to entrepreneurship and productive investment. Though initial conditions cannot be changed, measures to compensate for the structural peculiarities of different economies can be suggested. Though the "first move" of the reform process cannot be undone, coalitions of winners and losers can be fostered to weaken the grip of vested interests and deconcentrate monopoly power. Though the concentration of economic power tends to be supported by a concentration of political power, reforming political institutions can alter the incentives of public officials to limit or even reverse these imbalances. Such changes are crucial for shifting the incentives of old enterprises and promoting the proper development of new ones.

Initial conditions and political institutions affect the likelihood that some countries will follow particular reform paths. But these structural factors can never predetermine outcomes in such complex and multifaceted processes as transition. A decade of transition shows the critical role of political leadership in shaping reform. A thorough political economy analysis of winners and losers from reform can set the parameters for understanding the likely pressure points in any system and provide guidance for crafting feasible reform strategies. But it cannot predict the quality or strength of the leadership of the reform process that will motivate the pace and direction of reforms.

Political economy analysis has an inherent status quo bias (Fernandez and Rodrik 1991). But experience from around the world shows that talented political leaders can maneuver countries out of so-called reform traps and shift equilibrium paths. Critical elections can break long-term stalemates on reform. New leaders can mobilize alternative coalitions and spark collective action that tips the balance of power between the potential winners and losers from further economic reforms. Clever reformers can devise win-win strategies that co-opt their opponents to build support for reform. We cannot predict the "quality of reform-mongering," to use Albert Hirschman's phrase (1963, p. 225), either within or across countries. However, it is the essential ingredient in understanding the politics of economic reform.

Selected Bibliographic Guide to the Political Economy of Transition

The simultaneous political and economic transitions in Eastern Europe and the former Soviet Union have spawned an enormous literature across a wide variety of disciplines. Though numerous references are provided in the text, the list below highlights some key contributions. Many of the writings have informed the arguments in this paper.

The Socialist System: Reform and Collapse

Åslund, Anders. 1991. *Gorbachev's Struggle for Economic Reform*, 2nd ed. Ithaca, NY: Cornell University Press.

Easterly, William, and Stanley Fischer. 1995. "The Soviet Economic Decline." *World Bank Economic Review* 9(3): 341–71.

Ericson, Richard. 1991. "The Classical Soviet-Type Economy: Nature of the System and Implications for Reform." *Journal of Economic Perspectives* 5(4): 11–27.

Fischer, Stanley, and Alan Gelb. 1991. "The Process of Socialist Economic Transformation." *Journal of Economic Perspectives* 5(4): 91–105.

Garton Ash, Timothy. 1983. *The Polish Revolution: Solidarity 1980–82*. London: Jonathan Cape.

_____. 1990. *We the People: The Revolution of '89 Witnessed in Warsaw, Budapest, Berlin & Prague*. Cambridge, MA: Granta Books.

IMF (International Monetary Fund), World Bank, OECD (Organisation for Economic Co-operation and Development), and EBRD (European Bank for Reconstruction and Development). 1991. *A Study of the Soviet Economy*. vol. 3. Washington, D.C.

Kornai, János. 1992. *The Socialist System: The Political Economy of Communism*. Princeton, NJ: Princeton University Press.

Murrell, Peter, and Mancur Olson. 1991. "The Devolution of Centrally Planned Economies." *Journal of Comparative Economics* 15(2): 239–65.

Comparative Economic Performance

The Nature and Causes of the Transitional Recession

Blanchard, Olivier, and Michael Kremer. 1997. "Disorganization." *Quarterly Journal of Economics* 112(4): 1091–127.

Calvo, Guillermo, and Fabrizio Coricelli. 1993. "Output Collapse in Eastern Europe: The Role of Credit." *International Monetary Fund Staff Papers* 40(1): 32–52.

Ericson, Richard E. 1999. "The Structural Barrier to Transition Hidden in Input-Output Tables of Centrally Planned Economies." *Economic Systems* 23(3): 199–224.

Gomulka, Stanislaw. 1998. "Output: Causes of the Decline and Recovery." Working Papers Series No. 8, Center for Social and Economic Research, Central European University, Warsaw, Poland.

Kornai, János. 1993. "Transformational Recession: A General Phenomenon Examined through the Example of Hungary's Development." *Economie Appliquée* 46(2): 181–227.

Rodrick, Dani. 1992. "Making Sense of the Soviet Trade Shock in Eastern Europe: A Framework and Some Estimates." In Mario Blejer, Guillermo A. Calvo, Fabrizio Coricelli, and Alan H. Gelb, eds., *Eastern Europe in Transition: From Recession to Growth?* World Bank Discussion Paper No. 196, World Bank, Washington, D.C.

Roland, Gerard, and Thierry Verdier. 1999. "Transition and the Output Fall." *Economics of Transition* 7(1): 1–28.

Explaining Variation in Economic Reform Outcomes

Bokros, Lajos. 2000. "Visegrad Twins' Diverging Path to Relative Prosperity. Comparing the Transition Experience of the Czech Republic and Hungary." Conference at the Czech National Bank, Prague. September.

de Melo, Martha, and Alan Gelb. 1996. "A Comparative Analysis of Twenty Transition Economies in Europe and Asia." *Post-Soviet Geography and Economics* 37(5): 265–85.

de Melo, Martha, Cevdet Denizer, and Alan Gelb. 1996. "From Plan to Market: Patterns of Transition." *World Bank Economic Review* 10(3): 397–424.

de Melo, Martha, Cevdet Denizer, Alan Gelb, and Stoyan Tenev. 2001. "Circumstances and Choice: The Role of Initial Conditions and Policies in Transition Economies." *World Bank Economic Review* 15(1): 1–31.

EBRD (European Bank for Reconstruction and Development). Various years. *Transition Report*. London.

IMF (International Monetary Fund). 2000. *World Economic Outlook 2000: Focus on Transition Economies*. Washington, D.C.

World Bank. 1996. *World Development Report 1996: From Plan to Market*. Washington, D.C.

Key Topics on Economic Reform

General

Åslund, Anders. 1995. *How Russia Became a Market Economy*. Washington, D.C.: Brookings Institution.

Blanchard, Olivier. 1997. *The Economics of Transition in Eastern Europe*. Oxford, England: Clarendon Press.

Blanchard, Olivier, Rudiger Dornbusch, Paul Krugman, Richard Layard, and Lawrence Summers. 1991. *Reform in Eastern Europe*. Cambridge, MA: MIT Press.

Clague, Christopher, and Gordon C. Rausser, eds. 1992. *The Emergence of Market Economies in Eastern Europe*. Cambridge, MA: Blackwell Publishers.

Coricelli, Fabrizio. 1998. *Macroeconomic Policies and the Development of Markets in Transition Economies*. Budapest: Central European University Press.

Dabrowski, Marek, Stanislaw Gomulka, and Jacek Rostowski. 2000. "Whence Reform? A Critique of the Stiglitz Perspective." Centre for Social and Economic Research, Warsaw. Processed.

Klaus, Vaclav. 1997. *Renaissance: The Rebirth of Liberty in the Heart of Europe*. Washington, D.C.: Cato Institute.

Kornai, János. 1990. *The Road to a Free Economy. Shifting from a Socialist System: The Example of Hungary*. New York: W. W. Norton.

_____. Forthcoming. "Ten Years After 'The Road to a Free Economy,' The Author Self-Evaluation." In Boris Pleskovic and Nicholas Stern, eds., *Annual World Bank Conference on Development Economics*. Washington, D.C.: World Bank.

McMillan, John, and Barry Naughton. 1992. "How to Reform a Planned Economy: Lessons from China." *Oxford Review of Economic Policy* 8(1): 130–43.

Poznanski, Kazimierz Z., ed. 1993. *Stabilization and Privatization in Poland*. Boston, MA: Kluwer Academic Publishers.

Qian, Yuan, Gerard Roland, and Chenggang Xu. 1999. "Why is China Different From Eastern Europe: Perspectives from Organization Theory." *European Economic Review* 43(4–6): 1085–94.

Sachs, Jeffrey. 1996. "The Transition at Mid Decade." *American Economic Review Papers and Proceedings* 86(2): 128–33.

Stiglitz, Joseph E. 1999. "Whither Reform? Ten Years of the Transition." Keynote address, World Bank Annual Bank Conference on Development Economics, Washington, D.C.

Speed and Sequencing of Reforms

Aghion, Philippe, and Oliver Blanchard. 1994. "On the Speed of Transition in Central Europe." In Stanley Fischer and J. Rotemberg, eds., *National Bureau of Economic Research Macroeconomic Annual 1994*. Cambridge, MA: MIT Press.

Åslund, Anders, Peter Boone, and Simon Johnson. 1996. "How to Stabilize: Lessons From Post-Communist Countries." *Brookings Papers on Economic Activity* 26(1): 217–313.

Dewatripont, Mathias, and Gerard Roland. 1992a. "Economic Reform and Dynamic Political Constraints." *Review of Economic Studies* 59(4): 703–30.

_____. 1992b. "The Virtues of Gradualism and Legitimacy in the Transition to a Market Economy." *Economic Journal* 102(411): 291–300.

_____. 1995. "The Design of Reform Packages under Uncertainty." *American Economic Review* 85(5): 1207–23.

Fischer, Stanley, Ratna Sahay, and Carlos A. Vegh. 1996a. "Stabilization and Growth in Transition Economies: The Early Experience." *Journal of Economic Perspectives* 10(2): 45–66.

_____. 1996b. "Economies in Transition: The Beginnings of Growth." *American Economic Review* 86(2): 229–33.

Kornai, János. 1990. *The Road to a Free Economy. Shifting from a Socialist System: The Example of Hungary*. New York, NY: Norton.

Lipton, David, and Jeffrey D. Sachs. 1990. "Creating a Market in Eastern Europe: The Case of Poland." *Brookings Papers on Economic Activity* 20(1): 75–147.

McKinnon, Ronald. 1992. *The Order of Economic Liberalization: Financial Control in the Transition to a Market Economy*. Baltimore, MD: John Hopkins University Press.

Murphy, Kevin M., Andrei Shleifer, and Robert W. Vishny. 1992. "The Transition to a Market Economy: Pitfalls of Partial Reform." *Quarterly Journal of Economics* 107(3): 889–906.

Murrell, Peter. 1992a. "Conservative Political Philosophy and the Strategy of Economic Transition." *East European Politics and Societies* 6(1): 3–16.

_____. 1992b. "Evolutionary and Radical Approaches to Economic Reform." *Economics of Planning* 25(1): 79–95.

Sachs, Jeffrey. 1993. *Poland's Jump to the Market Economy.* Cambridge, MA: MIT Press.

_____. 1994. "Life in the Economic Emergency Room." In John Williamson, ed., *The Political Economy of Policy Reform.* Washington, D.C.: Institute for International Economics.

Privatization and Corporate Governance

Aghion, Philippe, and Olivier Blanchard. 1998. "On Privatization Methods in Eastern Europe and their Implications." *Economics of Transition* 6(1): 87–99.

Amsden, Alice, Jacek Kochanowicz, and Lance Taylor. 1994. *The Market Meets Its Match: Restructuring the Economies of Eastern Europe.* Cambridge, MA: Harvard University Press.

Balcerowicz, Leszek, Cheryl Gray, and Iraj Hoshi, eds. 1998. *Enterprise Exit Processes in Transition Economies.* Budapest: Central European University Press.

Black, Bernard S., Reinier Kraakman, and Anna Tarassova. 2000. "Russian Privatization and Corporate Governance." *Stanford Law Review* 52(6): 1731–808.

Blasi, Joseph R., Maya Kroumova, and Douglas Kruse. 1997. *Kremlin Capitalism: The Privatization of The Russian Economy.* Ithaca, NY: Cornell University Press.

Boycko, Maxim, Andrei Shleifer, and Robert Vishny. 1995. *Privatizing Russia.* Cambridge, MA: MIT Press.

_____. 1996. "A Theory of Privatization." *Economic Journal* 106(435): 309–19.

Djankov, Simeon. 1999. "The Restructuring of Insider Dominated Firms." *Economics of Transition* 7(2): 467–79.

Earle, John S., Roman Frydman, and Andrzej Rapaczynski, eds. 1993. *Privatization in the Transition to a Market Economy.* Budapest: Central European University Press.

Frydman, Roman, Cheryl W. Gray, and Andrzej Rapacszynski, eds. 1996. *Corporate Governance in Central Europe and Russia,* vols. 1–2. Budapest: Central European University Press.

Frydman, Roman, and others. 1993a. *The Privatization Process in Central Europe.* Budapest: Central European University Press.

_____. 1993b. *The Privatization Process in Russia, Ukraine, and the Baltic States.* Budapest: Central European University Press.

Lipton, David, and Jeffrey D. Sachs. 1990. "Privatization in Eastern Europe: The Case of Poland." *Brookings Papers on Economic Activity* 20(2): 293–341.

Nellis, John. 1999. "Time to Rethink Privatization in Transition Economies?" *Finance and Development* 36(2): 16–9.

Roland. Gerard. 1994. "On the Speed and Sequencing of Privatization and Restructuring." *Economic Journal* 104(426): 1158–68.

Roland, Gerard, and Thierry Verdier. 1994. "Privatization in Eastern Europe: Irreversibility and Critical Mass Effects." *Journal of Public Economics* 54(2): 161–83.

Stark, David, and Laszlo Bruszt. 1998. *Postsocialist Pathways: Transforming Politics and Property in East Central Europe.* Cambridge, MA: Cambridge University Press.

Empirical Assessments of Privatization

Blasi, Joseph, and Andrei Shleifer. 1996. "Corporate Governance in Russia: An Initial Look." In Roman Frydman, Cheryl W. Gray, and Andrzej Rapacszynski, eds.,

Coporate Governance in Central Europe and Russia, vol. 2. Budapest: Central European University Press.

Brown, David, and John Earle. 2000. "Privatization and Enterprise Restructuring in Russia: New Evidence from Panel Data on Industrial Enterprises." Working Paper, Russian-European Centre For Economic Policy, Moscow.

Djankov, Simeon, and Peter Murrell. 2000. *The Determinants of Enterprise Restructuring in Transition: An Assessment of the Evidence*. Washington, D.C.: World Bank.

Earle, John, and Saul Estrin. 1998. "Privatization, Competition, and Budget Constraints: Disciplining Enterprises in Russia." Working Paper No. 128, Stockholm Institute of Transition Economics, Stockholm.

Frydman, Roman, Cheryl W. Gray, Marek Hessel, and Andrzej Rapaczynski. 1997. "Private Ownership and Corporate Performance: Evidence from Transition Economies." EBRD Working Paper No. 26, European Bank for Reconstruction and Development, London.

_____. 1999. "When Does Privatization Work? The Impact of Private Ownership on Corporate Performance in the Transition Economies." *Quarterly Journal of Economics* 114(4): 1153–92.

Lieberman, Ira W., Stilpon S. Nestor, and Raj M. Desai, eds. 1997. *Between State and Market: Mass Privatization in Transition Economies*. Washington D.C.: The World Bank and the OECD (Organisation for Economic Co-operation and Development).

Megginson, William E., and Jeffry M. Netter. 2001. "From State to Market: A Survey of Empirical Studies on Privatization." *Journal of Economic Literature* 39(2): 321–89.

Barter, Arrears, and Noncash Payments

Commander, Simon, and Christian Mumssen. 1998. "Understanding Barter in Russia,"

EBRD Working Paper No. 37, European Bank for Reconstruction and Development, London.

Gaddy, Clifford, and Barry Ickes. 1999. *Russia's Virtual Economy*. Washington, D.C.: Brookings Institution.

Ivanova, Nadezhda, and Charles Wyplosz. 1999. "Arrears: The Tide that is Drowning Russia." Working Paper, Russian-European Centre for Economic Policy, Moscow.

Johnson, Simon, Daniel Kaufmann, John McMillan, and Christopher Woodruff. 2000. "Why Do Firms Hide? Bribes and Unofficial Activity After Communism." *Journal of Public Economics* 76(3): 495–520.

McKinnon. Ronald I. 1991. *The Order of Economic Liberalization: Financial Control in the Transition to a Market Economy*. Baltimore, MD: John Hopkins University Press.

Tanzi, Vito, ed. 1992. *Fiscal Policies in Economies in Transition*. Washington, D.C.: International Monetary Fund.

Woodruff, David. 1999. *Money Unmade: Barter and the Fate of Russian Capitalism*. Ithaca, NY: Cornell University Press.

Social Safety Nets and Reform

Commander, Simon, and Fabrizio Coricelli, eds. 1995. *Unemployment, Restructuring, and the Labor Market in East Europe and Russia*. Washington, D.C.: World Bank.

Cook, Linda, Mitchell Orenstein, and Marilyn Rueschemeyer, eds. 1999. *Left Parties and Social Policy in Postcommunist Europe*. Boulder, CO: Westview Press.

Graham, Carol. 1995. "The Politics of Safety Nets." In Larry Diamond and Marc F. Plattner, eds., *Economic Reform and Democracy*. Baltimore, MD: Johns Hopkins University Press.

Kornai, János. 1997. "Reform and the Welfare Sector in the Post-Socialist Countries: A

Normative Approach." In Joan Nelson, Charles Tilly, and Lee Walker, eds., *Transforming Post-Communist Political Economies*. Washington, D.C.: National Academy Press.

Kramer, Mark. 1997. "Social Protection Policies and Safety Nets in East-Central Europe: Dilemmas of the Post-Communist Transformation." In Ethan Kapstein and Michael Mandelbaum, eds., *Sustaining the Transition: The Social Safety Net in Postcommunist Europe*. New York, NY: Council on Foreign Relations.

Milanovic, Branko. 1998. *Income, Inequality, and Poverty during the Transition from Planned to Market Economy*. Washington, D.C.: World Bank.

World Bank. 2000. *Making Transition Work for Everyone: Poverty and Inequality in Europe and Central Asia*. Washington, D.C.

Accession to the European Union

Begg, Iain. 1999. "EU Investment Grants Review." World Bank Technical Paper No. 435, World Bank, Washington, D.C.

Drulák, Petr, ed. 2001. *National and European Identities in EU Enlargement: Views from Central and Eastern Europe*. Prague: Institute of International Relations.

European Commission and the World Bank. 1998. *European Union Accession: The Challenges for Public Liability Management in Central Europe*. Washington, D.C.

_____. 2000. *European Union Accession: Opportunities and Risks in Central European Finances*. Washington, D.C.

Funck, Bernard, and Lodovico Pizzati, eds. 2001. *Labor, Employment, and Social Policies in the EU Enlargement Process*. Washington, D.C.: World Bank.

Garibaldi, Pietro, Mattia Makovec, and Gabriella Stoyanova. 2001. "From Transition to EU Accession: The Bulgarian Labor Market during the 1990s." World Bank

Technical Paper No. 494, World Bank, Washington, D.C.

Kaminski, Bartlomiej. 1999a. "Hungary: Foreign Trade Issues in the Context of Accession to the EU." World Bank Technical Paper No. 441, World Bank, Washington, D.C.

_____. 1999b. "The Role of Foreign Direct Investment and Trade Policies in Poland's Accession to the European Union." World Bank Technical Paper No. 442, World Bank, Washington, D.C.

Nabli, Mustapha. 1999. "Financial Integration, Vulnerabilities to Crisis, and EU Accession in Five Central European Countries." World Bank Technical Paper No. 439, World Bank, Washington, D.C.

Nunberg, Barbara. 2000. "Ready for Europe: Public Administration Reform and European Union Accession in Central and Eastern Europe." World Bank Technical Paper No. 466, World Bank, Washington, D.C.

Petkova, Ivanka, Elitsa Markova, Irena Mladenova, and Ruslan Stefanova, eds. 2000. *Regional Cooperation in Central and Eastern Europe*. Sofia: Economic Policy Institute.

Tang, Helena, ed. 2000. *Winners and Losers of EU Integration: Policy Issues for Central and Eastern Europe*. Washington, D.C.: Bertelsmann Foundation and the World Bank.

Ulgenerk, Esen, and Leila Zlaoui. 2000. "From Transition to Accession: Developing Stable and Competitive Financial Markets in Bulgaria." World Bank Technical Paper No. 473, World Bank, Washington, D.C.

World Bank. 1997. "Poland—Reform and Growth on the Road to the EU." Country study, Washington, D.C.

_____. 1998. "Slovak Republic—A Strategy for Growth and European Integration." Country study, Washington, D.C.

_____. 1999a. "Slovenia—Economic Transformation and EU Accession." Country study, Washington, D.C.

_____. 1999b. "Hungary—On the Road to the European Union." Country study, Washington, D.C.

_____. 1999c. "Estonia—Implementing the EU Accession Agenda." Country study, Washington, D.C.

_____. 1999d. "Czech Republic—Toward EU Accession." Country study, Washington, D.C.

_____. 2000. "Progress Toward the Unification of Europe." Paper for the *World Free of Poverty* series, Washington, D.C.

_____. 2001. "Bulgaria—The Dual Challenge of Transition and Accession." Washington, D.C.

The Politics of Economic Reform in Transition Economies

Balcerowicz, Leszek. 1994. "Understanding Postcommunist Transitions." *Journal of Democracy* 5(4): 75–89.

_____. 1995. *Socialism, Capitalism, Transformation.* Budapest: Central European University Press.

Bunce, Valerie. 1999. "The Political Economy of Post Communism." *Slavic Review* 58(4): 756–93.

Ekiert, Grzegorz, and Jan Kubik. 1998. "Contentious Politics in New Democracies: Hungary, the former East Germany, Poland, and Slovakia." *World Politics* 50(4): 547–81.

Elster, Jon, Claus Offe, Ulrich K. Preuss, Frank Boeuher, Ulrike Goetting, and Friedbert W. Rueb. 1998. *Institutional Design in Postcommunist Societies: Rebuilding the Ship at Sea.* Cambridge, MA: Cambridge University Press.

Fish, M. Stephen. 1998. "The Determinants of Economic Reform in the Post-Communist World." *East European Politics and Societies* 12(1): 31–78.

Greskovits, Bela. 1998. *The Political Economy of Protest and Patience: East European and Latin American Transformations*

Compared. Budapest: Central European University Press.

Hellman, Joel S. 1998. "Winners Take All: The Politics of Partial Reform in Postcommunist Transitions." *World Politics* 50(2): 203–34.

Offe, Claus. 1991. "Capitalism by Democratic Design? Democratic Theory Facing the Triple Transition in East Central Europe." *Social Research* 58(4): 893–902.

Przeworski, Adam. 1991. *Democracy and the Market: Political and Economic Reforms in Eastern Europe and Latin America.* Cambridge, MA: Cambridge University Press.

Roland, Gerard. 2000. *Transition and Economics: Politics, Markets, and Firms.* Cambridge, MA: MIT Press.

Shleifer, Andrei, and Daniel Treisman. 2000. *Without A Map: Political Tactics and Economic Reform in Russia.* Cambridge, MA: MIT Press.

Corruption, State Capture, and the Rule of Law

Frye, Timothy. 1997. "Contracting in the Shadow of the State: Private Arbitration Commissions in Russia." In Jeffrey D. Sachs and Katharina Pistor, eds., *The Rule of Law and Economic Reform in Russia.* New York, NY: Westview Press.

Frye, Timothy, and Andrei Shleifer. 1997. "The Invisible Hand and the Grabbing Hand." *The American Economic Review* 87(2): 354–8.

Hay, Jonathan R. and Andrei Shleifer. 1998. "Private Enforcement of Public Laws: A Theory of Legal Reform." *American Economic Review* 88(2): 398–403.

Hendley, Kathryn, Peter Murrell, and Randi Ryterman. 2000. "Law, Relationships, and Private Enforcement: Transactional Strategies of Russian Enterprises." *Europe-Asia Studies* 52(4): 627–56.

Hellman, Joel S., Geraint Jones, and Daniel Kaufmann. 2000. "Seize the State, Seize the Day: State Capture, Corruption, and

Influence in Transition." Policy Research Working Paper No. 2444, World Bank, Washington, D.C.

Johnson, Simon, Daniel Kaufman, and Andrei Shleifer. 1997. "The Unofficial Economy in Transition." *Brookings Papers on Economic Activity* 27(2): 159–239.

Johnson, Simon, Daniel Kaufmann, and Pablo Zoido-Lobaton. 1998. "Government in Transition: Regulatory Discretion and the Unofficial Economy." *American Economic Review* 88(2): 387–92.

Johnson, Simon, John McMillan, and C. Woodruff. 2000. "Entrepreneurs and the Ordering of Institutional Reform—Poland, Slovakia, Romania, Russia, and Ukraine Compared." *Economics of Transition* 8(1): 1–36.

La Porta, Rafael, Andrei Shleifer, Robert W. Vishny, and Florencio Lopez-de-Silanes. 1998. "Law and Finance." *Journal of Political Economy* 106(6): 1113–55.

Sachs, Jeffrey D., and Katharina Pistor, eds. 1997. *The Rule of Law and Economic Reform in Russia.* Boulder, CO: Westview Press.

Shleifer, Andrei, and Robert Vishny. 1998. *The Grabbing Hand: Government Pathologies and Their Cures.* Cambridge, MA: Harvard University Press.

Volkov, Vladimir. 1999. "Violent Entrepreneurship in Post-Communist Russia." *Europe-Asia Studies* 51(5): 741–54.

World Bank. 2000. *Anticorruption in Transition: A Contribution to the Policy Debate.* Washington, D.C.

Classifying Political Regimes in Transition

Kitschelt, Herbert, Zdenka Mansfeldova, Radoslaw Markowski, and Gabor Toka. 1999. *Post-Communist Party Systems: Competition, Representation, and Inter-*
Party Cooperation. Cambridge, MA: Cambridge University Press.

Linz, Juan J., and Alfred C. Stepan. 1996. *Problems of Democratic Transition and Consolidation: Southern Europe, South America, and Post-Communist Europe, Part IV.* Baltimore, MD: Johns Hopkins University Press.

Roeder, Philip G. 1994. "Varieties of Post-Soviet Authoritarian Regimes." *Post-Soviet Affairs* 10(1): 61–101.

Governance

Elster, Jon, Claus Offe, and Ulrich K. Preuss. 1998. *Institutional Design in Post-Communist Societies.* New York, NY: Cambridge University Press.

Offe, Claus. 1991. "Capitalism by Democratic Design? Democratic Theory Facing the Triple Transition in East Central Europe." *Social Research* 58(4): 865–92.

Przeworski, Adam, and others. 1995. *Sustainable Democracy.* Cambridge, MA: Cambridge University Press.

Nationalism, Ethnic Conflict, and Secession

Fearon, James D., and David D. Laitin. 1996. "Explaining Interethnic Cooperation." *American Political Science Review* 90(4): 715–35.

Laitin, David D. 1998. *Identity in Formation.* Ithaca, NY: Cornell University Press.

Offe, Claus. 1997. "Ethnic Politics in East European Transitions." *Varieties of Transitions: The East European and East German Experience.* Cambridge, MA: MIT Press.

Vujacic, Veljko. 1996. "Historical Legacies, Nationalist Mobilization, and Political Outcomes in Russia and Serbia: A Weberian View." *Theory and Society* 25(6): 763–801.

References

The word "processed" describes informally reproduced works that may not be commonly available through library systems.

Alesina, Alberto, and Howard Rosenthal. 1995. *Partisan Politics, Divided Government, and the Economy.* New York, NY: Cambridge University Press.

Alesina, Alberto, Nouriel Roubini, and Gerald Cohen. 1997. *Political Cycles and the Macroeconomy.* Cambridge, MA: MIT Press.

Aslund, Anders. 2001. "The Myth of Output Collapse after Communism." Carnegie Endowment Working Paper No. 18, Carnegie Endowment for International Peace, Washington, D.C.

Aslund, Anders, Peter Boone, and Simon Johnson. 1996. "How to Stabilize: Lessons from Post-Communist Countries." *Brookings Papers on Economic Activity* 26(1): 217–311.

Balcerowicz, Leszek. 1995. *Socialism, Capitalism, Transformation.* Budapest: Central European University Press.

Berg, Andrew, Eduardo Borensztein, Ratna Sahay, and Jeromin Zettelmeyer. 1999. "The Evolution of Output in Transition Economies: Explaining the Differences." *IMF Working Paper* No. WP/99/73, International Monetary Fund, Washington, D.C.

Campos, Nauro F., and Fabrizio Coricelli. 2000. "Growth in Transition: What We Know, What We Don't, and What We Should." *Centre for Economic Policy Research,* London.

Carlin, Wendy, Steven Fries, Mark Schaffer, and Paul Seabright. 2001. "Competition and Enterprise Performance in Transition Economies: Evidence from a Cross-Country Survey." *EBRD Working Paper* No. 63, European Bank for Reconstruction and Development, London.

Castanheira, Micael, and Vladimir Popov. 1999. "Framework Paper on the Political Economy of Growth in Russia and

Central and Eastern European Countries." Paper for the Global Development Network conference, World Bank, Washington, D.C. November.

Caves, R. 1998. "Industrial Organization and New Findings on the Turnover and Mobility of Firms." *Journal of Economic Literature* 36(4): 1947–82.

de Melo, Martha, and Alan Gelb. 1996. "A Comparative Analysis of Twenty Transition Economies in Europe and Asia" *Post-Soviet Geography and Economics* 37(5): 265–85.

de Melo, Martha, Cevdet Denizer, and Alan Gelb. 1996. "From Plan to Market: Patterns of Transition." World Bank, Washington, D.C.

de Melo, Martha, Cevdet Denizer, Alan Gelb, and Stoyan Tenev. 1997. "Circumstances and Choice: The Role of Initial Conditions and Policies in Transition Economies." Policy Research Working Paper No. 1866, World Bank, Washington, D.C.

Dethier, Jean-Jacques, Hafez Ghanem, and Edda Zoli. 1999. "Does Democracy Facilitate the Economic Transition?" World Bank, Washington, D.C. Processed.

Djankov, Simeon, and Peter Murrell. 2000. *The Determinants of Enterprise Restructuring in Transition: An Assessment of the Evidence.* Washington, D.C.: World Bank.

Easterly, William. 2000. "It's Been a Rough Ride, Toto, but I think We're Back in Kansas." World Bank, Washington, D.C. Processed.

Eichengreen, Barry, and Christof Ruehl. 2000. "Financial Sector Developments in Transition Economies." University of California at Berkeley. Processed.

EBRD (European Bank for Reconstruction and Development). 1999. *Transition Report 1999.* London.

_____. 2000. *Transition Report 2000.* London.

Eurostat. 1998. *New Enterprises in CEC in 1997.* Studies and Research, theme 4.

Available at http://www.europa.eu.int/comm/eurostat.

Fernandez, Raquel, and Dani Rodrik. 1991. "Resistance to Reform: Status Quo Bias in the Presence of Individual-Specific Uncertainty." *American Economic Review* 81(5): 1146–55.

Fischer, Stanley, and Alan Gelb. 1991. "The Process of Socialist Economic Transformation." *Journal of Economic Perpectives* 5(4): 91–106.

Fischer, Stanley, Ratna Sahay, and Carlos A. Veight. 1998. "How Far is Eastern Europe from Brussels?" IMF Working Paper No. WP/98/53, International Monetary Fund, Washington, D.C.

Frye, Timothy, and Joel Hellman. 2001. "Political Data-Base of Post-Communist Countries." World Bank, Washington, D.C. Processed.

Freedom House. Various years. *Freedom in the World: The Annual Survey of Political Rights and Civil Liberties.* New York. Available at www.freedomhouse.org.

Gaddy, Clifford, and Barry Ickes. 1999. *Russia's Virtual Economy.* Washington, D.C.: Brookings Institution.

Haggard, Stephan, and Steven Webb. 1993. "What Do We Know about the Political Economy of Economic Policy Reform?" *World Bank Policy Research Observer* 8(2): 143–67.

Havrylysyhyn, Oleh, and Ron van Rooden. 1999. "Institutions Matter in Transition, but So Do Policies." Fifth Dubrovnik Conference on Transition, Dubrovnic. June.

Hellman, Joel. 1998. "Winners Take All: The Politics of Partial Reform." *World Politics* 50(2): 203.

Hellman, Joel S., Geraint Jones, and Daniel Kaufmann. 2000. "Seize the State, Seize the Day: An Empirical Analysis of State Capture and Corruption in Transition Economies." Policy Research Working Paper No. 2444, World Bank, Washington D.C.

Hellman, Joel S., Geraint Jones, Daniel Kaufmann, and Mark Schankerman. 2000. "Measuring Governance Corruption and State Capture: How Firms and Bureaucrats Shape the Business Environment in Transition Economies." Policy Research Working Paper No. 2312, World Bank, Washington D.C.

Hernandez-Cata, Ernesto. 1997. "Growth and Liberalization during the Transition from Plan to Market." *IMF Staff Papers* 44(4): 405–29.

Heybey, Berta, and Peter Murrell. 1999. "The Relationship between Economic Growth and the Speed of Liberalization during Transition." *Journal of Policy Reform* 3(2): 121–37.

Hirschman, Albert O. 1963. *Journeys Towards Progress.* New York, NY: The Twentieth Century Fund.

IMF (International Monetary Fund), World Bank, OECD (Organisation for Economic Co-operation and Development), and EBRD (European Bank for Reconstruction and Development). 1991. *A Study of the Soviet Economy*, vol. 3. Washington, D.C.

Jensen, Michael C., and William H. Meckling. 1976. "Theory of the Firm: Managerial Behavior, Agency Costs, and Ownership Structure." *Journal of Financial Economics* 3(4): 305–60.

Johnson, Simon, and Andrei Shleifer. 2001. "Privatization and Corporate Governance." Paper prepared for the 12th Annual East Asian Seminar on Economics, June 28–30, National Bureau of Economic Research, Cambridge, MA.

Johnson, Simon, Daniel Kaufmann, and Andrei Shleifer. 1997. "The Unofficial Economy in Transition." *Brookings Papers on Economic Activity* 27(2): 159–239.

Johnson, Simon, John McMillan, and Christopher Woodruff. 2000. "Entrepreneurs and the Ordering of Institutional Reform—Poland, Slovakia, Romania, Russia, and Ukraine Compared." *Economics of Transition* 8(1): 1–36.

Johnson, Simon, Peter Boone, Alasdair Breach, and Eric Friedman. 2000. "Corporate Governance in the Asian Financial Crisis." *Journal of Financial Economics* 58(1–2): 141–86.

Johnson, Simon, Rafael La Porta, Florencio Lopez-de-Silanes, and Andrei Shleifer. 2000. "Tunneling." Harvard Institute of Economic Research Discussion Paper No. 1887, Harvard Institute of Economic Research, Cambridge, MA.

Klugman, Jeni. 1999. "Financing and Governance of Education in Central Asia." *MOCT–MOST: Economic Policy in Transitional Economies* 9(4): 423–42.

Kornai, János. 1986. "The Soft Budget Constraint." *Kyklos* 39(1): 3–30.

Levine, Ross, and Sara Zervos. 1998. "Stock Market, Banks, and Economic Growth." *American Economic Review* 88(3): 537–58.

Maddison, Angus. 1982. *Phases of Capitalist Development.* Oxford, U.K.: Oxford University Press.

Martin, Ricardo. 2000. "Revisiting Regression Analysis: Initial Conditions, Policies, and Growth." Background paper, World Bank, Washington D.C.

Orenstein, Mitchell. 2001. *Out of the Red: Building Capitalism and Democracy in Post-Communist Europe.* Ann Arbor, MI: University of Michigan Press.

Pinto, Brian, Vladimir Drebentsov, and Alexander Morozov. 2000. "Give Macroeconomic Stability and Growth in Russia a Chance: Harden Budgets by Eliminating Non-Payments." *Economics of Transition* 8(2): 297–324.

Popov, Vladimir. 1998. "Will Russia Achieve Fast Economic Growth?" *Communist Economies and Economic Transformation* 10(4): 421–35.

_____. 1999. "Shock Therapy versus Gradualism: The End of the Debate." Carleton University, Ottawa. Processed.

Przeworski, Adam. 1991. *Democracy and the Market: Political and Economic Reforms in Eastern Europe and Latin America.* New York, NY: Cambridge University Press.

Roubini, Nouriel, and Jeffrey Sachs. 1989. "Political and Economic Determinants of Budget Deficits in the Industrial Democracies." *European Economic Review* 33(5): 903–33.

Ruehl, Christof, and Viatcheslav Vinogradov. 2001. "A Simple Model of the Transition from Central Planning." Center for Economic Research and Graduate Education of Charles University and the Economic Institute of the Academy of Sciences of the Czech Republic, Prague. Processed.

Selowsky, Marcelo, and Ricardo Martin. 1998. "Policy Performance and Output Growth in the Transition Economies." *American Economic Review–Papers and Proceedings* 87(2): 350–53.

Shleifer, Andrei, and Robert Vishny. 1997. "A Survey of Corporate Governance." *Journal of Finance.* 52(2): 737–83.

Shleifer, Andrei, and D. Wolfenson. 2000. "Investor Protection and Equity Markets." Harvard University and University of Michigan. Processed.

Tarr, David. 1994. "The Terms of Trade Effects of Moving to World Prices on Countries of the FSU." *Journal of Comparative Economics* 18(1): 1–24.

UNICEF–ICDC (United Nations Children's Fund–International Child Development Centre). 1999. "TransMONEE." Database.

World Bank. 1998. *World Development Report 1998/99: Knowledge for Development.* Washington, D.C.

_____. 1999a. *Czech Republic: Capital Market Review.* Washington, D.C.

_____. 1999b. "Russia: Regional Education Study." Human Development Sector Unit, Europe and Central Asia Region, Washington, D.C.

_____. 2000a. *Poverty Reduction and the World Bank: Progress in Fiscal 1999.* Washington, D.C.

_____. 2000b. *Making Transition Work for Everyone: Poverty and Inequality in Europe and Central Asia.* Washington D.C.

_____. 2000c. Anticorruption in Transition: A Contribution to the Policy Debate. Washington, D.C.

_____. 2001. *World Development Indicators, 2001.* Washington, D.C.